A note about this combined book

Welcome to *The Non-Designer's Design & Type Books, Deluxe Edition.*

This is a collection of two complete books: *The Non-Designer's Design Book, Third Edition* and *The Non-Designer's Type Book, Second Edition.*

The Non-Designer's Design Book has been in print since 1994, and I've been amazed as I've watched its progress. The four simple principles embodied in it have been responsible—I've been told—for changing lives, saving marriages, getting jobs, changing careers, developing businesses, and discovering hidden talents and passions. As well as making things look better. Wow. I've seen the principles described on blogs, explained on the web sites of print shops, written about in magazines, included in other books—often without credit to me. But that's okay. As Chaucer said, "Go, little book."

This is the first edition of the book that is in color. The cost and trouble of color printing has been spectacularly reduced, and rare is the home or office that doesn't have a color printer. So I've added a chapter about the color wheel, a magical tool that simplifies color choices, and redesigned all of the examples with color. I hope you find it helpful.

The second half of *The Non-Designer's Design Book* is about designing with type; specifically, how to choose several typefaces that work together. I include the type information because if a printed piece doesn't have type on it, it's not graphic design. Typography is the foundation of all graphic design.

So the type information segues into the next book, *The Non-Designer's Type Book*, which is filled with practical, usable information about how to create professional-level typography. I am astounded at the high-level pieces I see, such as full-page ads in slick magazines or commercials on television, that have an ignorant use of type. Where did those highly paid designers study where they didn't learn how to make a real apostrophe? I find myself hollering at the ads, "Hang those quotation marks! Stop hitting two Returns between paragraphs! Why are you still putting two spaces after periods?"

Sorry.

But there's just no excuse anymore. And now that we live in a world where every-one has become more visually aware, every one of us must rise to the occasion. Using the design and typographic principles outlined in these two books, your work will not only look better, but it will, in the very process, communicate more clearly. And clear communication can make the whole world happier.

With a smile, Robin

The Non-Designer's Design & Type Books, Deluxe Edition
ROBIN WILLIAMS

NOTE: This edition is a collection of these two books:
The Non-Designer's Design Book, Third Edition, ISBN 10: 0-321-53404-2, ISBN 13: 978-0-321-53404-0
The Non-Designer's Type Book, Second Edition, ISBN 10: 0-321-30336-9, ISBN 13: 978-0-321-30336-3

The Non-Designer's Design Book, Third Edition, is the first book in this combined volume. The index for *The Non-Designer's Design Book* immediately follows the text and begins on page 212.

The Non-Designer's Type Book, Second Edition, follows *The Non-Designer's Design Book,* beginning after page 216 at the gray thumbtab. Note that this book's pages are numbered separately, and its index begins on page 231 at the very back of the book.

Peachpit Press
1249 Eighth Street
Berkeley, California 94710
510.524.2178
510.524.2221 FAX

Interior design:	Robin Williams
Production:	Robin Williams
Editor:	Nancy Davis
Cover design and production:	John Tollett
Prepress:	David Van Ness

Peachpit Press is a division of Pearson Education.
Find us on the web at www.Peachpit.com.
To report errors, please send a note to errata@peachpit.com.

ISBN 13: 978-0-321-53405-7
ISBN 10: 0-321-53405-0

10 9 8 7 6 5 4 3 2

Printed and bound in the United States of America

The Non-Designer's Design Book

THIRD EDITION

design
and
typographic
principles
for the
visual
novice

Robin Williams

Peachpit Press
Berkeley
California

The Non-Designer's Design Book
third edition
ROBIN WILLIAMS

©2008 by Robin Williams

Peachpit Press
1249 Eighth Street
Berkeley, California 94710
510.524.2178
510.524.2221 FAX

Editor:	Nancy Davis
Interior design:	Robin Williams
Production:	Robin Williams
Cover design and production:	John Tollett

Peachpit Press is a division of Pearson Education.

Find us on the web at www.Peachpit.com.

To report errors, please send a note to errata@peachpit.com.

The quote by Jan White on page 187 is from the out-of-print book *How to Spec Type*, by Alex White. Reprinted courtesy of Roundtable Press, Inc. Copyright 1987 by Roundtable Press, Inc.

The portions of "Ladle Rat Rotten Hut" and other stories, such as "Guilty Looks Enter Tree Beers," "Center Alley," and "Violate Huskings" are from a long out-of-print book by Howard L. Chace called *Anguish Languish*. It is our understanding that these delightful stories are now in the public domain. They are easily found on the Internet.

To Carmen Sheldon,
my comrade in Design,
my friend in Life.
with great love,
R.

*M*ore matter is being printed and published today than ever before, and every publisher of an advertisement, pamphlet, or book expects his material to be read. Publishers and, even more so, readers want what is important to be clearly laid out. They will not read anything that is troublesome to read, but are pleased with what looks clear and well arranged, for it will make their task of understanding easier. For this reason, the important part must stand out and the unimportant must be subdued . . . .

The technique of modern typography must also adapt itself to the speed of our times. Today, we cannot spend as much time on a letter heading or other piece of jobbing as was possible even in the nineties.

Jan Tschichold 1935

The **function** of Readability is often ta-ken too literally and over-emphasized at the Cost of INDIVIDUALITY.

Paul Rand 1914 • 1996

typefaces
Miss Fajardose
Garamond Premier Pro Regular *and Italic*
Type Embellishments One

typefaces
flyswim
Schablone Rough
Helvetica Regular
Schablone Isabellidough Positive

Contents

Design Principles

Designing With Type

Extras

So, Does it Make Sense? 197

Answers to Quizzes 201

Typefaces in this Book 205

Appendix 210

Index 212

It stinks.

Herb Lubalin

 **But,** is it appropriate?
Edward Gottschall

Is this book for you?

This book is written for all the people who need to design pages, but have no background or formal training in design. I don't mean just those who are designing fancy packaging or lengthy brochures—I mean the assistants whose bosses now tell them to design the newsletters, church volunteers who are providing information to their congregations, small business owners who are creating their own advertising, students who understand that a better-looking paper often means a better grade, professionals who realize that an attractive presentation garners greater respect, teachers who have learned that students respond more positively to information that is well laid out, statisticians who see that numbers and stats can be arranged in a way that invites reading rather than sleeping, and on and on.

This book assumes you don't have the time or interest to study design and typography, but would like to know how to make your pages look better. Well, the premise of this book is age-old: knowledge is power. Most people can look at a poorly designed page and state that they don't like it, but they don't know what to do to fix it. In this book I will point out four basic concepts that are used in virtually every well-designed job. These concepts are clear and concrete. If you don't know what's wrong with it, how can you fix it? Once you recognize the concepts, you will notice whether or not they have been applied to your pages. *Once you can name the problem, you can find the solution.*

This book is not intended to take the place of four years of design school. I do not pretend you will automatically become a brilliant designer after you read this little book. But I do guarantee you will never again look at a page in the same way. I guarantee if you follow these basic principles, your work will look more professional, organized, unified, and interesting. And you will feel empowered.

With a smile,

Robin

The Joshua Tree Epiphany

This short chapter explains the **four basic principles** in general, each of which will be explained in detail in the following chapters. But first I want to tell you a little story that made me realize the importance of being able to name things, since *naming* these principles is the key to having power over them.

Many years ago I received a tree identification book for Christmas. I was at my parents' home, and after all the gifts had been opened I decided to go out and identify the trees in the neighborhood. Before I went out, I read through part of the book. The first tree in the book was the Joshua tree because it only took two clues to identify it. Now, the Joshua tree is a really weird-looking tree and I looked at that picture and said to myself, "Oh, we don't have that kind of tree in Northern California. That is a weird-looking tree. I would know if I saw that tree, and I've never seen one before."

So I took my book and went outside. My parents lived in a cul-de-sac of six homes. Four of those homes had Joshua trees in the front yards. I had lived in that house for thirteen years, and I had never seen a Joshua tree. I took a walk around the block, and there must have been a sale at the nursery when everyone was landscaping their new homes—at least 80 percent of the homes had Joshua trees in the front yards. *And I had never seen one before!* Once I was conscious of the tree—once I could name it—I saw it everywhere. Which is exactly my point: Once you can name something, you're conscious of it. You have power over it. You own it. You're in control.

So now you're going to learn the names of several design principles. And you are going to be in control of your pages.

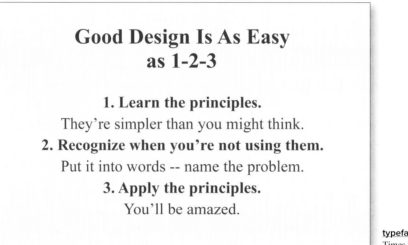

**Good Design Is As Easy
as 1-2-3**

1. Learn the principles.
They're simpler than you might think.
2. Recognize when you're not using them.
Put it into words -- name the problem.
3. Apply the principles.
You'll be amazed.

typefaces
Times New Roman Regular
and Bold

Good design
is as easy as . . .

1 Learn the principles.
They're simpler than you might think.

2 Recognize when you're not using them.
Put it into words — name the problem.

3 Apply the principles.
You'll be amazed.

typefaces
Univers 75 Black
Univers 65 Bold
Cochin Italic
Potrzebie (numbers)

The four basic principles

The following is a brief overview of the basic principles of design that appear in every well-designed piece of work. Although I discuss each one of these principles separately, keep in mind they are really interconnected. Rarely will you apply only one principle.

Contrast

The idea behind contrast is to avoid elements on the page that are merely *similar.* If the elements (type, color, size, line thickness, shape, space, etc.) are not the *same,* then make them **very different.** Contrast is often the most important visual attraction on a page—it's what makes a reader look at the page in the first place.

Repetition

Repeat visual elements of the design throughout the piece. You can repeat colors, shapes, textures, spatial relation- ships, line thicknesses, fonts, sizes, graphic concepts, etc. This develops the organization and strengthens the unity.

Alignment

Nothing should be placed on the page arbitrarily. Every element should have some visual connection with another element on the page. This creates a clean, sophisticated, fresh look.

Proximity

Items relating to each other should be grouped close together. When several items are in close proximity to each other, they become one visual unit rather than several separate units. This helps organize information, reduces clutter, and gives the reader a clear structure.

Umm . . .

When gathering these four principles from the vast maze of design theory, I thought there must be some appropriate and memorable acronym within these conceptual ideas that would help people remember them. Well, uh, there is a memorable—but rather inappropriate—acronym. Sorry.

Good
communication
is as

stimulating

as black coffee . . .

and just
as hard
to sleep after.

ANNE MORROW LINDBERGH

typefaces
Mona Lisa Solid
Escalido Gothico

Proximity

Very often in the work of new designers, the words and phrases and graphics are strung out all over the place, filling corners and taking up lots of room so there won't be any empty space. There seems to be a fear of empty space. When pieces of a design are scattered all over, the page appears unorganized and the information may not be instantly accessible to the reader.

Robin's Principle of Proximity states that you **group related items together,** move them physically close to each other so the related items are seen as one cohesive group rather than a bunch of unrelated bits.

Items or groups of information that are *not* related to each other should *not* be in close proximity (nearness) to the other elements, which gives the reader an instant visual clue to the organization and content of the page.

A very simple example illustrates this concept. In the list below, on the left side, what do you assume about all those flowers? Probably that they have something in common, right? In the list below-right, what do you assume? It appears that the last four flowers are somehow different from the others. You understand this *instantly.* And you understand it without even being conscious of it. You *know* the last four flowers are somehow different *because they are physically separated from the rest of the list.* That's the concept of proximity—on a page (as in life), **physical closeness implies a relationship.**

My Flowers
Marigold
Pansy
Rue
Woodbine
Daisy
Cowslip
Carnation
Primrose
Violets
Pink

My Flowers
Marigold
Pansy
Rue
Woodbine
Daisy
Cowslip

Carnation
Primrose
Violets
Pink

typefaces
Spring Regular
Formata Light

Take a look at this typical business card layout, below. How many separate elements do you see in that small space? That is, how many times does your eye stop to look at something?

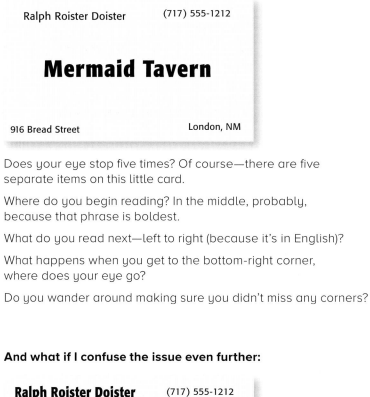

Does your eye stop five times? Of course—there are five separate items on this little card.

Where do you begin reading? In the middle, probably, because that phrase is boldest.

What do you read next—Left to right (because it's in English)?

What happens when you get to the bottom-right corner, where does your eye go?

Do you wander around making sure you didn't miss any corners?

And what if I confuse the issue even further:

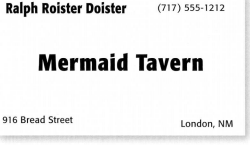

Now that there are two bold phrases, where do you begin? Do you start in the upper left? Do you start in the center?

After you read those two items, where do you go? Perhaps you bounce back and forth between the words in bold, nervously trying to also catch the words in the corners.

Do you know when you're finished?

Does your friend follow the same pattern you did?

When several items are in close proximity to each other, they become *one* visual unit rather than several *separate* units. As in life, **the proximity, or the closeness, implies a relationship.**

By grouping similar elements into one unit, several things instantly happen: The page becomes more organized. You understand where to begin reading the message, and you know when you are finished. And the "white space" (the space around the letters) automatically becomes more organized as well.

A problem with the previous card is that not one of the items on the card seems related to any other item. It is not clear where you should begin reading the card, and it is not clear when you are finished.

If I do one thing to this business card—**if I group related elements together, into closer proximity**—see what happens:

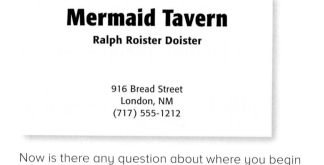

Mermaid Tavern
Ralph Roister Doister

916 Bread Street
London, NM
(717) 555-1212

Now is there any question about where you begin to read the card? Where do your eyes go next? Do you know when you're finished?

With that one simple concept, this card is now organized both **intellectually** and **visually.** And thus it communicates more clearly.

typefaces
Formata Light
Formata Bold Condensed

Shown below is a typical newsletter flag (sometimes called masthead). How many separate elements are in this piece? Does any item of information seem related to any other, judging from the placement?

Take a moment to decide which items should be grouped into closer proximity and which should be separated.

typefaces
Palatino Light
and Italic
Wade Sans Light

The two items on the top left are in close proximity to each other, implying a relationship. But **should** these two have a relationship? Is it the Society that's amusing and peculiar, or "The Shakespeare Papers"?

How about the volume number and date? They should be close together since they both identify this particular issue.

In the example below, the proper relationships have been established.

Notice I did a couple of other things along the way:

I changed everything from all caps to lowercase with appropriate capitals, which gave me room to make the title bigger and stronger.

I changed the corners from rounded to straight, giving the piece a cleaner, stronger look.

I enlarged the swan and overlapped the edge with it. Don't be a wimp.

Because the text is going to drop out of the dark background, I changed the small font to Trebuchet so it wouldn't fall apart when printed.

When you create a flyer, a brochure, a newsletter, or whatever, you already know which pieces of information are logically connected, you *know* which information should be emphasized and what can be de-emphasized. Express that information graphically by grouping it.

Correspondences
Flowers, herbs, trees, weeds
Ancient Greeks and Romans
Historical characters
Quotes on motifs
Women
Death
Morning
Snakes
Language
Iambic pentameter
Rhetorical devices
Poetic devices
First lines
Collections
Small printings
Kitschy
Dingbats
Thematic
Villains and saints
Drinks and recipes
Music
Quizzes
Fun but difficult quizzes

Correspondences
Flowers, herbs, trees, weeds
Ancient Greeks and Romans
Historical characters

Quotes on motifs
Women
Death
Morning
Snakes

Language
Iambic pentameter
Rhetorical devices
Poetic devices
First lines

Collections
Small printings
Kitschy
Dingbats

Thematic
Villains and saints
Drinks and recipes
Music

Quizzes
Fun but difficult quizzes

typefaces
Warnock Pro Light
and Bold
Formata Bold

Obviously, this list needs some formatting to make it understandable. But the biggest problem with this list is that everything is close to everything else, so there is no way to see the relationships or the organization.

The same list has been visually separated into groups. I'm sure you already do this automatically—I'm just suggesting that you now do it **consciously** and thus with more strength.

Notice I added some **contrast** to the headlines and **repeated** that contrast.

Sometimes when grouping items into close proximity, you need to make some changes, such as in the size or weight or placement of text or graphics. Body copy (the main bulk of reading text) does not have to be 12 point! Information that is subsidiary to the main message, such as the volume number and year of a newsletter, can often be as small as 7 or 8 point.

First Friday Club
Winter Reading Schedule

Friday November 1 at 5 p.m. *Cymbeline*
In this action-packed drama, our strong and true heroine, Imogen, dresses as a boy and runs off to a cave in Wales to avoid marrying a man she hates.
Friday, December 6, 5 p.m. *The Winter's Tale*
The glorious Paulina and the steadfast Hermione keep a secret together for sixteen years, until the Delphic Oracle is proven true and the long-lost daughter is found.
All readings held at the Mermaid Tavern, Grand Hall. Sponsored by the Community Educa-tion Program. Tickets $10 and $8
For ticket information phone 555-1212
Also Friday, January 3 at 5 p.m. *Twelfth Night*
Join us as Olivia survives a shipwreck, dresses as a man, gets a job, and finds both a man and a woman in love with her.

typefaces
Anna Nicole
Formata Regular

Not only is this page visually boring (nothing pulls your eyes in to the body copy to take a look), but it is difficult to find the information—exactly what is going on, where is it happening, what time is it at, etc. It doesn't help that the information is presented inconsistently.

For instance, how many readings are in the series?

The idea of proximity doesn't mean that *everything* is closer together; it means elements that are *intellectually connected,* those that have some sort of communication relationship, should also be *visually connected.* Other separate elements or groups of elements should *not* be in close proximity. The closeness *or* lack of closeness indicates the relationship.

First Friday Club
Winter Reading Schedule

Cymbeline
In this action-packed drama, our strong and true heroine, Imogen, dresses as a boy and runs off to a cave in Wales to avoid marrying a man she hates.
November 1 • Friday • 5 P.M.

The Winter's Tale
The glorious Paulina and the steadfast Hermione keep a secret together for sixteen years, until the Delphic Oracle is proven true and the long-lost daughter found.
December 6 • Friday • 5 P.M.

Twelfth Night
Join us as Olivia survives a shipwreck, dresses as a man, gets a job, and finds both a man and a woman in love with her.
January 6 • Friday • 5 P.M.

The Mermaid Tavern
All readings are held at The Mermaid Tavern in the Grand Hall
Sponsored by the Community Education Program
Tickets $10 and $8
For ticket information phone 555.1212

typefaces
Anna Nicole
Formata Regular
and Light Condensed

How many readings are in the series?

First I intellectually grouped the information together (in my head or sketched onto paper), then physically set the text in groups on the page. Notice the spacing between the three readings is the same, indicating that these three groups are somehow related.

The subsidiary information is farther away—you **instantly** know it is not one of the readings, even if you can't see it clearly.

Below you see a similar example to the one on the previous page. Glance at it quickly—now what do you assume about the three readings?

And why exactly do you assume one reading is different from the others? Because one is separate from the others. You instantly know that event is somehow different *because of the spatial relationships.*

First Friday Club
Summer Reading Schedule

1 Henry IV
Still trying to get to the Holy Land to atone for Richard's death, Henry is beset by many troubles, including the willing debauchery of his son, Hal. Because these Henry plays are closely connected, we're going to read them both in one day.
June 4 • Friday • 1 P.M.

2 Henry IV
We carry on with the tales of Falstaff and Hal. Hal proves to his father he is a decent son and heartbreakingly rejects his good round friend Falstaff.
June 4 • Friday • 6 P.M.

Henry V
Does Hal really have to be so cruel to his friends? Is that what being a king is all about? Hal, now Henry V, marches into France to win Agincourt.
July 8 • Friday • 5 P.M.

The Mermaid Tavern
All readings are held at The Mermaid Tavern in the Grand Hall
Sponsored by the Community Education Program
Tickets $10 and $8, each play
For ticket information phone 555.1212

It's really amazing how much information we get from a quick glance at a page. Thus it becomes your responsibility to make sure the reader gets the **correct** information.

The designer's intention with this dance postcard was probably to create something fun and energetic, but at first glance, can you tell when and where the classes are happening?

By using the principle of proximity to organize the information (as shown below), we can communicate immediately who, what, when, and where. We don't run the risk of losing potential customers because they give up searching through the vast field of slanted text.

Don't feel like you have to somehow portray "dancing" (in this case) through your design. At this point, if your choice is between clear communication or amateur design, choose clear communication. Upgrading your design skills is a gradual process and **begins with clear communication.**

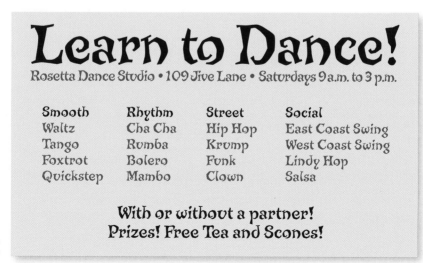

typeface
Jiggery Pokery

You're probably already using the principle of proximity in your work, but you may not be pushing it as far as you could to make it truly effective. Really look at those pages, at those elements, and see which items *should* be grouped together.

Want to be an

UNDERSTANDER?

How'd you like to . . .

understand every word and every nuance in a Shakespeare play?

Can you imagine . . .

going to see a play performed and actually understanding everything that's going on?

What if you could. . .

laugh in the right places in a play, cry in the right places, boo and hiss in the right places?

Ever wanted to . . .

talk to someone about a Shakespearean play and have that person think you know what you're talking about?

Would you like to . . .

have people admire and even esteem you because you know whether or not Portia cheated her father by telling Bassanio which casket to choose?

It's all possible.

Live the life you've dreamed about!

Be an Understander!

For more info on how to wisen up and start your new life as an Understander, contact us right away: **phone: 1-800-555-1212; email: Ben@TheUnderstanders.com**

typefaces
Clarendon Bold
and Roman

The person who designed this mini-poster typed two Returns after each headline **and** paragraph. Thus the headlines are each the same distance from the body copy above and below, making the heads and body copy pieces appear as separate, unconnected items. You can't tell if the headline belongs to the text above it or below it because the distances are the same.

There is lots of white space available here, but it's all broken up. And there is white space where it doesn't belong, like between the headlines and their related texts. When white space is "trapped" like this, it tends to visually push the elements apart.

Group the items that have relationships. If there are areas on the page where the organization is not perfectly clear, see if items are in proximity that *shouldn't* be. Use the simple design feature of space to make the page not only more organized, but nicer to look at.

Want to be an
UNDERSTANDER?

How'd you like to . . .
understand every word and every
nuance in a Shakespeare play?

Can you imagine . . .
going to see a play performed and actually
understanding everything that's going on?

What if you could. . .
laugh in the right places in a play,
cry in the right places, boo and hiss
in the right places?

Ever wanted to . . .
talk to someone about a Shakespearean play
and have that person think you know what
you're talking about?

Would you like to . . .
have people admire and even esteem you
because you know whether or not Portia
cheated her father by telling Bassanio
which casket to choose?

It's all possible!
Live the life you've dreamed about—
be an Understander!

For more info on how to wisen up and start your
new life as an Understander, contact us right away:
1.800.555.1212
Ben@TheUnderstanders.com

typefaces
Clarendon
Bold, Roman,
and Light

If I do just one thing to this piece, if I move the headlines closer to their related paragraphs of text, several things happen:

> The organization is clearer.

> The white space is not trapped within elements.

> There appears to be more room on the page.

I also put the phone and email address on separate lines—but grouped together and separated—so they'll stand out as important information.

And you probably noticed that I changed the centered alignment to flush left (that's the principle of **alignment,** as explained in the next chapter), which created more room so I could enlarge the graphic.

Proximity is really just a matter of being a little more conscious, of doing what you do naturally, but pushing the concept a little further. Once you become aware of the importance of the relationships between lines of type, you will start noticing its effect. Once you start noticing the effect, you own it, you have power over it, you are in control.

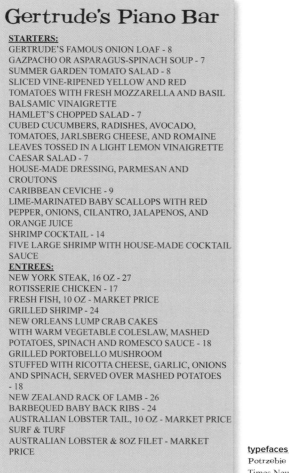

Gertrude's Piano Bar

STARTERS:
GERTRUDE'S FAMOUS ONION LOAF - 8
GAZPACHO OR ASPARAGUS-SPINACH SOUP - 7
SUMMER GARDEN TOMATO SALAD - 8
SLICED VINE-RIPENED YELLOW AND RED
TOMATOES WITH FRESH MOZZARELLA AND BASIL
BALSAMIC VINAIGRETTE
HAMLET'S CHOPPED SALAD - 7
CUBED CUCUMBERS, RADISHES, AVOCADO,
TOMATOES, JARLSBERG CHEESE, AND ROMAINE
LEAVES TOSSED IN A LIGHT LEMON VINAIGRETTE
CAESAR SALAD - 7
HOUSE-MADE DRESSING, PARMESAN AND
CROUTONS
CARIBBEAN CEVICHE - 9
LIME-MARINATED BABY SCALLOPS WITH RED
PEPPER, ONIONS, CILANTRO, JALAPENOS, AND
ORANGE JUICE
SHRIMP COCKTAIL - 14
FIVE LARGE SHRIMP WITH HOUSE-MADE COCKTAIL
SAUCE
ENTREES:
NEW YORK STEAK, 16 OZ - 27
ROTISSERIE CHICKEN - 17
FRESH FISH, 10 OZ - MARKET PRICE
GRILLED SHRIMP - 24
NEW ORLEANS LUMP CRAB CAKES
WITH WARM VEGETABLE COLESLAW, MASHED
POTATOES, SPINACH AND ROMESCO SAUCE - 18
GRILLED PORTOBELLO MUSHROOM
STUFFED WITH RICOTTA CHEESE, GARLIC, ONIONS
AND SPINACH, SERVED OVER MASHED POTATOES
- 18
NEW ZEALAND RACK OF LAMB - 26
BARBEQUED BABY BACK RIBS - 24
AUSTRALIAN LOBSTER TAIL, 10 OZ - MARKET PRICE
SURF & TURF
AUSTRALIAN LOBSTER & 8OZ FILET - MARKET
PRICE

typefaces
Potrzebie
Times New Roman

Lest you think no menu could be this bad, know that I took it right out of a restaurant. Really. The biggest problem, of course, is that all the information is one big chunk.

Before trying to design with this information, write out the separate pieces of information that belong together; group the elements. You know how to do this—simply use your brain.

Once you have the groups of information, you can play with them on the page. You have a computer—try lots of options. Learn how to format a page in your software.

In the example below, I put *more* space between the separate menu items. Of course, one should almost never use all caps because they are so hard to read, so I changed it to caps and lowercase. And I made the type a couple of point sizes smaller, both of which gave me a lot more room to work with so I could put more space between the elements.

Gertrude's Piano Bar

Starters

Gertrude's Famous Onion Loaf - 8

Gazpacho or Asparagus-Spinach Soup - 7

Summer Garden Tomato Salad - 8
sliced vine-ripened yellow and red tomatoes
with fresh mozzarella and basil Balsamic vinaigrette

Hamlet's Chopped Salad - 7
cubed cucumbers, radishes, avocado, tomatoes, Jarlsberg
cheese, and romaine leaves tossed in a light lemon vinaigrette

Caesar Salad - 7
house-made dressing, Parmesan, and croutons

Caribbean Ceviche - 9
lime-marinated baby scallops with red pepper, onions, cilantro,
jalapenos, and orange juice

Shrimp Cocktail - 14
five large shrimp with house-made cocktail sauce

Entrees

New York steak, 16 ounce - 27

Rotisserie Chicken - 17

Fresh Fish, 10 ounce - Market Price

Grilled Shrimp - 24

New Orleans Lump Crab Cakes - 18
with warm vegetable coleslaw, mashed potatoes, spinach,
and Romesco sauce

Grilled Portobello Mushroom - 18
stuffed with Ricotta cheese, garlic, onions and spinach,
served over mashed potatoes

New Zealand Rack of Lamb - 26

Barbequed Baby Back Ribs - 24

Australian Lobster Tail, 10 ounce - Market Price

Surf & Turf
Australian Lobster & 8 ounce Filet - Market Price

typefaces
Potrzebie
Times New Roman Bold
and Regular

The biggest problem with the original menu is that there is no separation of information. In your software, learn how to format so you can make exactly the amount of space you need before and after each element.

The original text in all caps took up all the space so there was no extra, blank, "white" space to rest your eyes. The more text you have, the less you can get away with all caps. And it's okay to set the type smaller than 12 point! Really!

In the example on the previous page, we still have a little bit of a problem separating the "Starters" and the "Entrees." Let's indent each section—watch how the extra space defines these two groups even further, yet clearly communicates that they are still similar groups. (I enlarged the size of "Starters" and "Entrees" also, which is the principle of Contrast.)

Gertrude's Piano Bar

Starters

Gertrude's Famous Onion Loaf - 8

Gazpacho or Asparagus-Spinach Soup - 7

Summer Garden Tomato Salad - 8
sliced vine-ripened yellow and red tomatoes with
fresh mozzarella and basil Balsamic vinaigrette

Hamlet's Chopped Salad - 7
cubed cucumbers, radishes, avocado, tomatoes, Jarlsberg
cheese, and romaine leaves tossed in a light lemon vinaigrette

Caesar Salad - 7
house-made dressing, Parmesan, and croutons

Caribbean Ceviche - 9
lime-marinated baby scallops with red pepper, onions,
cilantro, jalapenos, and orange juice

Shrimp Cocktail - 14
five large shrimp with house-made cocktail sauce

Entrees

New York steak, 16 ounce - 27

Rotisserie Chicken - 17

Fresh Fish, 10 ounce - Market Price

Grilled Shrimp - 24

New Orleans Lump Crab Cakes - 18
with warm vegetable coleslaw, mashed potatoes,
spinach, and Romesco sauce

Grilled Portobello Mushroom - 18
stuffed with Ricotta cheese, garlic, onions and spinach,
served over mashed potatoes

New Zealand Rack of Lamb - 26

Barbequed Baby Back Ribs - 24

Australian Lobster Tail, 10 ounce - Market Price

Surf & Turf
Australian Lobster & 8 ounce Filet - Market Price

We really don't have enough room to add more space before "Starters" and "Entrees," but we do have room to make an indent. That extra space under the heading helps to separate these two groups of information. It's all about space.

Rarely is the principle of proximity the only answer to a page. The other three principles are intrinsic to the design process and you will usually find yourself using all four. But take them one at a time—start with proximity. In the example below, you can imagine how all of the other principles would mean nothing if I didn't first apply the appropriate spacing.

Gertrude's Piano Bar

Starters

Gertrude's Famous Onion Loaf	8
Gazpacho or Asparagus-Spinach Soup	7
Summer Garden Tomato Salad	8
sliced vine-ripened yellow and red tomatoes with fresh mozzarella and basil Balsamic vinaigrette	
Hamlet's Chopped Salad	7
cubed cucumbers, radishes, scallions, avocado, tomatoes, jarlsberg cheese, and romaine leaves tossed in a light lemon vinaigrette	
Caesar Salad	7
house-made dressing, Parmesan, and croutons	
Caribbean Ceviche	9
lime-marinated baby scallops with red pepper, onions, cilantro, jalapenos, and orange juice	
Shrimp Cocktail	14
five large shrimp with house-made cocktail sauce	

Entrees

New York Steak, 16 ounce	27
Rotisserie Chicken	17
Fresh Fish, 10 ounce	Market Price
Grilled Shrimp	24
New Orleans Lump Crab Cakes	18
with warm vegetable coleslaw, mashed potatoes, spinach, and Romesco sauce	
Grilled Portobello Mushroom	18
stuffed with ricotta cheese, garlic, onions and spinach, served over mashed potatoes	
New Zealand Rack of Lamb	26
Barbequed Baby Back Ribs	24
Australian Lobster Tail, 10 ounce	Market Price
Surf & Turf: Australian Rock Lobster & 8 ounce Filet	Market Price

typefaces
Potrzebie
Cotoris Bold *and Italic*

I chose a more interesting typeface than Times New Roman—that's easy to do. I experimented with indenting the descriptions of the menu items, which helped to clarify each item a little further.

It bothered me that the prices of the items were tucked into the text (with dorky hyphens), so I aligned them all out on the right where they are easily visible and consistently arranged. That's the principle of **alignment,** which is coming right up in a couple of pages.

The simple principle of proximity can make web pages easier to navigate by collecting information into logical groups. Check any web site that you feel is easy to get around in—you'll find information grouped into logical clumps.

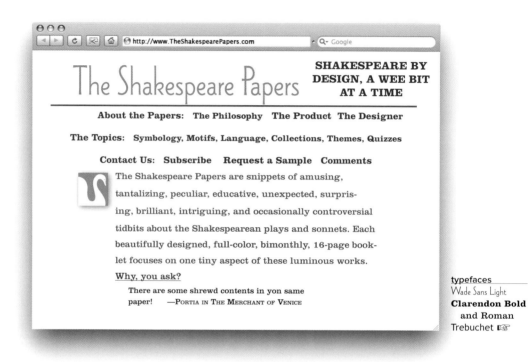

typefaces
Wade Sans Light
Clarendon Bold
and Roman
Trebuchet ☞

The information on this page is muddled. Look at the site links just under the title. Are they all equal in importance? In the arrangement above, they appear to be equal in importance—but realistically they're not.

I have to repeat myself: Intellectually, you already know how to use proximity. You already know how to collect pieces of information into their appropriate groups. All you need to do is transfer that skill to the printed page. Use space to define groups of elements.

I moved all the site links into one column to show their relationships to one another.

I set the quotation farther away from the main body copy since it's not directly related.

I also used the principle of **alignment** (discussed next, in Chapter 3): I used flush-left alignment and made sure each element lined up with something else.

Summary of proximity

When several items are in close **proximity** to each other, they become one visual unit rather than several separate units. Items relating to each other should be grouped together. Be conscious of where your eye is going: where do you start looking; what path do you follow; where do you end up; after you've read it, where does your eye go next? You should be able to follow a logical progression through the piece, from a definite beginning to a definite end.

The basic purpose

The basic purpose of proximity is to **organize.** Other principles come into play as well, but simply grouping related elements together into closer proximity automatically creates organization. If the information is organized, it is more likely to be read and more likely to be remembered. As a by-product of organizing the communication, you also create more appealing (more organized) *white space* (designers' favorite thing).

How to get it

Squint your eyes slightly and **count** the number of visual elements on the page by counting the number of times your eye stops. If there are more than three to five items on the page (of course it depends on the piece), see which of the separate elements can be grouped together into closer proximity to become one visual unit.

What to avoid

Don't stick things in the corners or in the middle just because the space is empty.

Avoid too many separate elements on a page.

Avoid leaving equal amounts of white space between elements unless each group is part of a subset.

Avoid even a split second of confusion over whether a headline, subhead, caption, graphic, etc., belongs with its related material. Create a relationship among elements with close proximity.

Don't create relationships with elements that don't belong together! If they are not *related,* move them apart from each other.

Alignment

New designers tend to put text and graphics on the page wherever there happens to be space, often without regard to any other items on the page. What this creates is the slightly-messy-kitchen effect—you know, with a cup here, a plate there, a napkin on the counter, a pot in the sink, a spill on the floor. It doesn't take much to clean up the slightly messy kitchen, just as it doesn't take much to clean up a slighty messy design that has weak alignments.

Robin's Principle of Alignment states, **"Nothing should be placed on the page arbitrarily. Every item should have a visual connection with something else on the page."** The principle of alignment forces you to be conscious—no longer can you just throw things on the page and see where they stick.

When items are aligned on the page, the result is a stronger cohesive unit. Even when aligned elements are physically separated from each other, there is an invisible line that connects them, both in your eye and in your mind. Although you might have separated certain elements to indicate their relationships (using the principle of proximity), the principle of alignment is what tells the reader that even though these items are not close, they belong to the same piece. The following pages illustrate this idea.

Take a look at this business card, the same one you saw in the last chapter. Part of its problem is that nothing is aligned with anything else. In this little space, there are elements with three different alignments: flush left, flush right, and centered. The two groups of text in the upper corners are not lined up along the same baseline, nor are they aligned at the left or right edges with the two groups at the bottom of the card (which don't line up along their baselines, either).

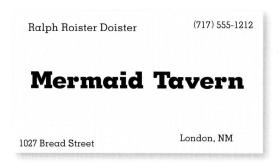

Ralph Roister Doister   (717) 555-1212

Mermaid Tavern

1027 Bread Street   London, NM

The elements on this card look like they were just thrown on and stuck. Not one of the elements has any connection with any other element on the card.

Take a moment to decide which of the items above should be grouped into closer proximity, and which should be separated.

Mermaid Tavern
Ralph Roister Doister

1027 Bread Street
London, NM
(717) 555-1212

By moving all the elements over to the right and giving them one alignment, the information is instantly more organized. (Of course, grouping the related elements into closer proximity helped, too.)

The text items now have a common boundary; this boundary connects them together.

In the example (repeated below) that you saw in the proximity section, the text is also aligned—it's aligned down the center. A centered alignment often appears a bit weak. If text is aligned, instead, on the left or the right, the invisible line that connects the text is much stronger because it has a hard vertical edge to follow. This gives left- and right-aligned text a cleaner and more dramatic look. Compare the two examples below, then we'll talk about it on the following pages.

Mermaid Tavern

Ralph Roister Doister

1027 Bread Street
London, NM
(717) 555-1212

This example has a nice arrangement with the text items grouped into logical proximity. The text is center-aligned over itself, and centered on the page. Although this is a legitimate alignment, the edges are "soft"; you don't really see the strength of the line.

Mermaid Tavern

Ralph Roister Doister

1027 Bread Street
London, NM
(717) 555-1212

This has the same logical arrangement as above, but it is now right-aligned. Can you see the "hard" edge on the right?

There is a strong invisible line connecting the edges of these two groups of text. You can actually see the edge. **The strength of this edge is what gives strength to the layout.**

The invisible line runs right down here, connecting the separate pieces of text.

Do you tend to automatically center everything? A centered alignment is the most common alignment that beginners use—it's very safe, it feels comfortable. A centered alignment creates a more formal look, a more sedate look, a more ordinary and oftentimes downright dull look. Take notice of the designs you like. I guarantee most designs that have a sophisticated look are not centered. I know it's difficult, as a beginner, to break away from a centered alignment; you'll have to force yourself to do it at first. But combine a strong flush right or left alignment with good use of proximity and you will be amazed at the change in your work.

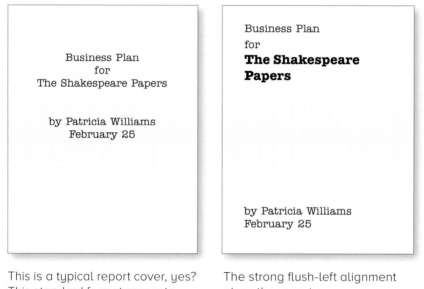

This is a typical report cover, yes? This standard format presents a dull, almost amateurish look, which may influence someone's initial reaction to the report.

The strong flush-left alignment gives the report cover a more sophisticated impression. Even though the author's name is far from the title, that invisible line of the strong alignment connects the two text blocks.

typefaces
ITC American Typewriter
Medium **and Bold**

typefaces ☞
Minister Light **and Bold**

Stationery has so many design options! But too often it ends up with a flat, centered alignment. You can be very free with placement on a piece of stationery—but remember alignment.

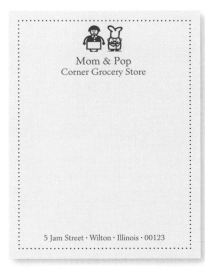

This isn't bad, but the centered layout is a little dull, and the border closes the space, making it feel confined.

A flush-left alignment makes the page a little more sophisticated. Limiting the dotted line to the left side opens the page and emphasizes the alignment.

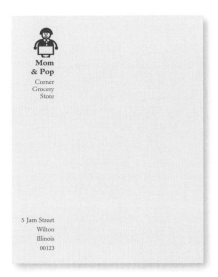

The text is flush right, but placed on the left side. The letter you type will have a strong flush left to align with the flush right of this layout.

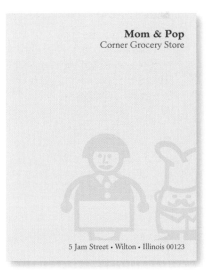

Be brave! Be bold!

I'm not suggesting that you *never* center anything! Just be conscious of the effect a centered alignment has—is that really the look you want to portray? Sometimes it is; for instance, most weddings are rather sedate, formal affairs, so if you want to center your wedding announcement, do so consciously and joyfully.

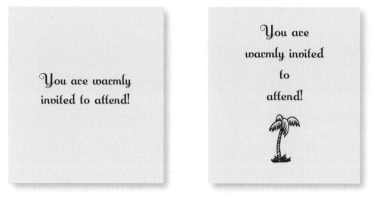

Centered. Really rather dull.

If you're going to center text, then at least make it obvious!

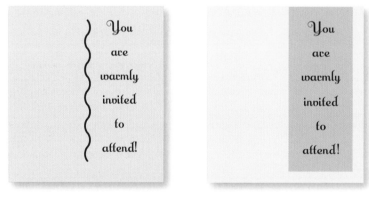

Experiment with uncentering the block of centered type.

If you're going to center the text, experiment with making it more dramatic in some other way.

typeface
Anna Nicole

Sometimes you can add a bit of a twist on the centered arrangement, such as centering the type, but setting the block of type itself off center. Or set the type high on the page to create more tension. Or set a very casual, fun typeface in a very formal, centered arrangement. What you don't want to do is set Times 12-point with double Returns!

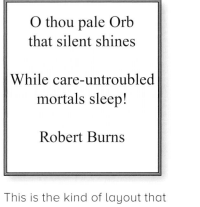

This is the kind of layout that gives "centered" a bad name: Boring typeface, type that is too large, crowded text, double Returns, dorky border.

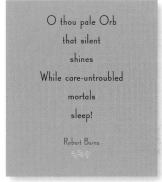

A centered alignment needs extra care to make it work. This layout uses a classic typeface sized fairly small (relatively), more space between the lines, lots of white space around the text, no border.

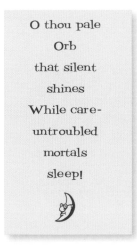

Emphasize a tall, slender centered layout with a tall, slender piece of paper.

Emphasize a wide, centered layout with a wide spread. Try your next flyer sideways.

typefaces
Times New Roman
Canterbury Old Style
Potrzebie
MilkScript

You're accustomed to working with text alignments. Until you have more training, stick to the guideline of using one text alignment on the page: either all text is flush left, flush right, or centered.

This text is ***flush left.***
Some people call it
quad left, or you can say
it is left aligned.

This text is ***flush right.***
Some people call it
quad right, or you can
say it is right aligned.

This text is **centered.**
If you are going to
center text,
make it
obvious.

In this paragraph it is
difficult to tell if this text
was centered purposely
or perhaps accidentally.
The line lengths are not
the same, but they are not
really different. If you can't
instantly tell that the type
is centered, why bother?

This text is **justified.** Some people call it quad left and right, and some call it blocked—the text lines up on both sides. Whatever you call it, don't do it unless your line length is long enough to avoid awkward g a p s   b e t w e e n   t h e   w o r d s because the gaps are really annoying, don't you think?

Occasionally you can get away with using both flush right and flush left text on the same page, but make sure you align them in some way!

Robert Burns

*Poems in Scots
and English*

The most
complete edition
available of
Scotland's
greatest poet

In this example, the title and the subtitle are flush left, but the description is centered. There is no common alignment between the two elements of text—they don't have any connection to each other.

Robert Burns

*Poems in Scots
and English*

The most
complete edition
available
of Scotland's
greatest poet

Although these two elements still have two different alignments (the top is flush left and the bottom is flush right), the edge of the descriptive text below aligns with the right edge of the thin rule above, connecting the elements with an invisible line.

typefaces
Aachen Bold
Warnock Pro Light Caption
and Light Italic Caption

When you place other items on the page, make sure each one has some visual alignment with another item on the page. If lines of text are across from each other horizontally, align their baselines. If there are several separate blocks of text, align their left or right edges. If there are graphic elements, align their edges with other edges on the page.

Nothing should be placed on the page arbitrarily!

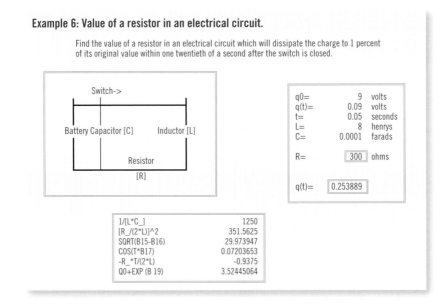

Example 6: Value of a resistor in an electrical circuit.

Find the value of a resistor in an electrical circuit which will dissipate the charge to 1 percent of its original value within one twentieth of a second after the switch is closed.

Switch->		
Battery	Capacitor [C]	Inductor [L]
	Resistor	
	[R]	

q0=	9	volts
q(t)=	0.09	volts
t=	0.05	seconds
L=	8	henrys
C=	0.0001	farads
R=	300	ohms
q(t)=	0.253889	

1/[L*C_]	1250
[R_/(2*L)]^2	351.5625
SQRT(B15-B16)	29.973947
COS(T*B17)	0.07203653
-R_*T/(2*L)	-0.9375
Q0+EXP (B 19)	3.52445064

There are two problems here, right? A lack of **proximity** and a lack of **alignment.**

Even though it may be a boring ol' chart, there is no reason not to make the page look as nice as possible and to present the information as clearly as possible. When information is difficult to understand, that's when it is the **most** critical to present it as clean and organized.

typefaces
Trade Gothic Bold Condensed No. 20
Trade Gothic Condensed No. 18

Lack of alignment is probably the biggest cause of unpleasant-looking documents. Our eyes *like* to see order; it creates a calm, secure feeling. Plus it helps to communicate the information.

In any well-designed piece, you will be able to draw lines to the aligned objects, even if the overall presentation of material is a wild collection of odd things and has lots of energy.

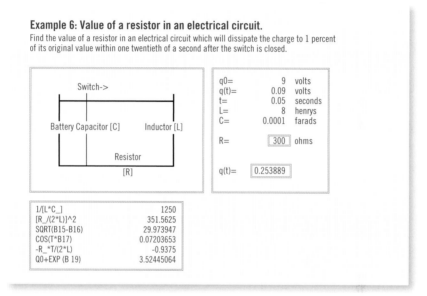

Example 6: Value of a resistor in an electrical circuit.
Find the value of a resistor in an electrical circuit which will dissipate the charge to 1 percent of its original value within one twentieth of a second after the switch is closed.

q0=	9	volts
q(t)=	0.09	volts
t=	0.05	seconds
L=	8	henrys
C=	0.0001	farads
R=	300	ohms
q(t)=	0.253889	

1/[L*C_]	1250
[R_/(2*L)]^2	351.5625
SQRT(B15-B16)	29.973947
COS(T*B17)	0.07203653
-R_*T/(2*L)	-0.9375
Q0+EXP (B 19)	3.52445064

Simply lining up the elements makes all the difference here. Notice not one item is on the page arbitrarily—every item has some visual connection with another item on the page.

If I knew what this chart was talking about, I might choose to move the box on the right even farther to the right, away from the big chart, keeping their tops aligned. Or I might move the lower box farther away. I would adjust the spacing between the three charts according to their intellectual relationships to each other.

A problem with the publications of many new designers' is a subtle lack of alignment, such as centered headlines and subheads over indented paragraphs. At first glance, which of the examples on these two pages presents a cleaner and sharper image?

Violate Huskings Darn Honor Form

Heresy rheumatic starry offer former's dodder, Violate Huskings, an wart hoppings darn honor form.

Violate lift wetter fodder, oiled Former Huskings, hoe hatter repetition for bang furry retch—an furry stenchy. Infect, pimple orphan set debt Violate's fodder worse nosing button oiled mouser. Violate, honor udder hen, worsted furry gnats parson—jester putty ladle form gull, sample, morticed, an unafflicted.

Tarred gull

Wan moaning Former Huskings nudist haze dodder setting honor cheer, during nosing.

VIOLATE! sorted dole former, Watcher setting darn fur? Denture nor yore canned gat retch setting darn during nosing? Germ pup otter debt cheer!

Arm tarred, Fodder, resplendent Violate warily.

Watcher tarred fur? aster stenchy former, hoe dint half mush symphony further gull.

Fetter pegs

Are badger dint doe mush woke disk moaning! Ditcher curry doze buckles fuller slob darn tutor peg-pan an feeder pegs?

Yap, Fodder. Are fetter pegs.

Ditcher mail-car caws an swoop otter caw staple? Off curse, Fodder. Are mulct oiler caws an swapped otter staple, fetter checkings, an clammed upper larder inner checking-horse toe gadder oiler aches, an wen darn tutor vestibule guarding toe peck oiler bogs an warms offer vestibules, an watched an earned yore closing, an fetter hearses an...

Ditcher warder oiler hearses, toe? enter-ruptured oiled Huskings. Nor, Fodder, are dint." Dint warder mar hearses? Wire nut? Arm surrey, Fodder, butcher hearses jest worsen Thursday. Yore kin leader hearse

This is a very common sight: headlines are centered, text is flush left, paragraph indents are "typewriter" wide (that is, five spaces or half an inch, as you may have learned in school), the illustration is centered in a column.

Never center headlines over flush left body copy or text that has an indent. If the text does not have a clear left and right edge, you can't tell the headline is actually centered. It looks like it's just hanging around.

All these unaligned spots create a messy page: wide indents, ragged right edge of text, centered heads with open space on both sides, centered illustration.

Try this: Draw lines on this example to see all the different alignments.

typefaces
Formata Bold
Warnock Pro Regular

All those minor misalignments add up to create a visually messy page. Find a strong line and stick to it. Even though it may be subtle and your boss couldn't say what made the difference between this example and the one before it, the more sophisticated look comes through clearly.

Violate Huskings Darn Honor Form

Heresy rheumatic starry offer former's dodder, Violate Huskings, an wart hoppings darn honor form.

Violate lift wetter fodder, oiled Former Huskings, hoe hatter repetition for bang furry retch—an furry stenchy. Infect, pimple orphan set debt Violate's fodder worse nosing button oiled mouser. Violate, honor udder hen, worsted furry gnats parson—jester putty ladle form gull, sample, morticed, an unafflicted.

Tarred gull

Wan moaning Former Huskings nudist haze dodder setting honor cheer, during nosing.

VIOLATE! sorted dole former, Watcher setting darn fur? Denture nor yore canned gat retch setting darn during nosing? Germ pup otter debt cheer!

Arm tarred, Fodder, resplendent Violate warily.

Watcher tarred fur? aster stenchy former, hoe dint half mush symphony further gull.

Fetter pegs

Are badger dint doe mush woke disk moaning! Ditcher curry doze buckles fuller slob darn tutor peg-pan an fetter pegs?

Yap, Fodder. Are fetter pegs.

Ditcher mail-car caws an swoop otter caw staple? Off curse, Fodder. Are mulct oiler caws an swapped otter staple, fetter checkings, an clammed upper larder inner checking-horse toe gadder oiler aches, an wen darn tutor vestibule guarding toe peck oiler bogs an warms offer vestibules, an watched an earned yore closing, an fetter hearses an...

Ditcher warder oiler hearses, toe? enter-ruptured oiled Husk

Find a strong alignment and stick to it. If the text is flush left, set the heads and subheads flush left.

First paragraphs are traditionally not indented. The purpose of indenting a paragraph is to tell you there is a new paragraph, but you always know the first one is a new paragraph.

On a typewriter, an indent was five spaces. With the proportional type you are using on your computer, the standard typographic indent is one **em** (an em is as wide as the point size of your type), which is more like two spaces.

Be conscious of the ragged edge of your type. Adjust the lines so your right edge is as smooth as possible.

If there are photographs or illustrations, align them with an edge and/or a baseline.

Even a piece that has a good start on a nice design might benefit from subtle adjustments in alignment. Strong alignment is often the missing key to a more professional look. Check every element to make sure it has a visual connection to something else on the page.

The story of a wicket woof and a ladle gull   by H. Chace

Wants pawn term dare worsted ladle gull hoe lift wetter murder inner ladle cordage honor itch offer lodge, dock, florist. Disk ladle gull orphan worry Putty ladle rat cluck wetter ladle rat hut, an fur disk raisin pimple colder Ladle Rat Rotten Hut.

Wan moaning Ladle Rat Rotten Hut's murder colder inset.

"Ladle Rat Rotten Hut, heresy ladle basking winsome burden barter an shirker cockles. Tick disk ladle basking tutor cordage offer groin-murder hoe lifts honor udder site offer florist. Shaker lake! Dun stopper laundry wrote! Dun stopper peck floors! Dun daily-doily inner florist, an yonder nor sorghum-stenches, dun stopper torque wet strainers!"

"Hoe-cake, murder," resplendent Ladle Rat Rotten Hut, an tickle ladle basking an stuttered oft. Honor wrote tutor cordage offer groin-murder, Ladle Rat Rotten Hut mitten anomalous woof.

"Wail, wail, wail!" set disk wicket woof, "Evanescent Ladle Rat Rotten Hut! Wares are putty ladle gull goring wizard ladle basking?"

"Armor goring tumor groin-murder's," reprisal ladle gull. "Grammar's seeking bet. Armor ticking arson burden barter an shirker cockles."

"O hoel Heifer gnats woke," setter wicket woof, butter taught tomb shelf, "Oil tickle shirt court tutor cordage offer groin-murder. Oil ketchup wetter letter, an den—O bore!"

Soda wicket woof tucker shirt court, an whinny retched a cordage offer groin-murder, picked inner windrow, an sore debtor pore oil worming worse lion inner bet. Inner flesh, disk abdominal woof lipped honor bet, paunched honor pore oil worming, an garbled erupt. Den disk ratchet ammonol pot honor groin-murder's

nut cup an gnat-gun, any curdled ope inner bet.

Inner ladle wile, Ladle Rat Rotten Hut a raft attar cordage, an ranker dough ball. "Comb ink, sweat hard," setter wicket woof, disgracing is verse. Ladle Rat Rotten Hut entity bet rum, an stud buyer groin-murder's bet.

"O Grammar!" crater ladle gull historically, "Water bag icer gut! A nervous sausage bag ice!"

"Battered lucky chew whiff, sweat hard," setter bloat-Thursday woof, wetter wicket small honors phase.

"O, Grammar, water bag noise! A nervous sore suture anomalous prognosis!"

"Battered small your whiff, doling," whiskered dole woof, ants mouse worse waddling.

"O Grammar, water bag mouser gut! A nervous sore suture bag mouse!"

Daze worry on-forger-nut ladle gull's lest warts. Oil offer sodden, caking offer carvers an sprinkling otter bet, disk hoard-hoarded woof lipped own pore Ladle Rat Rotten Hut an garbled erupt.

—H. Chace
Anguish Languish

ural: Yonder nor sorghum stenches shut ladle gulls stopper torque wet strainers.

Can you see all the places where items could be aligned, but aren't? With a colored pen, circle all the misalignments on this page. There are at least ten!

typefaces
Blackoak
Tekton

Check for illustrations that hang out over the edge just a bit, or captions that are centered under photos, headlines that are not aligned with the text, rules (lines) that don't align with anything, or a combination of centered text and flush left text.

Ladle Rat Rotten Hut

The story of a wicket woof and a ladle gull   by H. Chace

Wants pawn term dare worsted ladle gull hoe lift wetter murder inner ladle cordage honor itch offer lodge, dock, florist. Disk ladle gull orphan worry Putty ladle rat cluck wetter ladle rat hut, an fur disk raisin pimple colder Ladle Rat Rotten Hut.

Wan moaning Ladle Rat Rotten Hut's murder colder inset. "Ladle Rat Rotten Hut, heresy ladle basking winsome burden barter an shirker cockles. Tick disk ladle basking tutor cordage offer groin-murder hoe lifts honor udder site offer florist. Shaker lake! Dun stopper laundry wrote! Dun stopper peck floors! Dun daily-doily inner florist, an yonder nor sorghum-stenches, dun stopper torque wet strainers!"

"Hoe-cake, murder," resplendent Ladle Rat Rotten Hut, an tickle ladle basking an stuttered oft. Honor wrote tutor cordage offer groin-murder, Ladle Rat Rotten Hut mitten anomalous woof.

"Wail, wail, wail!" set disk wicket woof, "Evanescent Ladle Rat Rotten Hut! Wares are putty ladle gull goring wizard ladle basking?"

"Armor goring tumor groin-murder's," reprisal ladle gull. "Grammar's seeking bet. Armor ticking arson burden barter an shirker cockles."

"O hoe! Heifer gnats woke," setter wicket woof, butter taught tomb shelf, "Oil tickle shirt court tutor cordage offer groin-murder. Oil ketchup wetter letter, an den—O bore!"

Soda wicket woof tucker shirt court, an whinny retched a cordage offer groin-murder, picked inner windrow, an sore debtor pore oil worming worse lion inner bet. Inner flesh, disk abdominal woof lipped honor bet, paunched honor pore oil worming, an garbled erupt. Den disk ratchet ammonol pot honor groin-murder's nut cup an gnat-gun, any curdled ope inner bet.

Inner ladle wile, Ladle Rat Rotten Hut a raft attar cordage, an ranker dough ball. "Comb ink, sweat hard," setter wicket woof, disgracing is verse. Ladle Rat Rotten Hut entity bet rum, an stud buyer groin-murder's bet.

"O Grammar!" crater ladle gull historically, "Water bag icer gut! A nervous sausage bag ice!"

"Battered lucky chew whiff, sweat hard," setter bloat-Thursday woof, wetter wicket small honors phase.

"O, Grammar, water bag noise! A nervous sore suture anomalous prognosis!"

"Battered small your whiff, doling," whiskered dole woof, ants mouse worse waddling.

"O Grammar, water bag mouser gut! A nervous sore suture bag mouse!"

Daze worry on-forger-nut ladle gull's lest warts. Oil offer sodden, caking offer carvers an sprinkling otter bet, disk hoard-hoarded woof lipped own pore Ladle Rat Rotten Hut an garbled erupt.

—H. Chace
Anguish Languish

Mural: Yonder nor sorghum-stenches shut ladlegulls stopper torque wet strainers.

Can you see what has made the difference between this example and the one on the previous page? With a colored pen, draw lines along the strong alignments.

I want to repeat: Find a strong line and use it. If you have a photo or a graphic with a strong flush side, align the side of the text along the straight edge of the photo, as shown at the bottom of the page.

Porche

Porche worse jester pore ladle gull hoe lift wetter stop-murder an toe heft-cisterns. Daze worming war furry wicket an shellfish parsons, spatially dole stop-murder, hoe dint lack Porche an, infect, word orphan traitor pore gull mar lichen ammonol dinner hormone bang.

Porche's furry gourd-murder whiskered, "Watcher crane aboard?"

There is a nice strong line along the left edge of the type, and there is a nice strong line along the left edge of the image—you can see the pink dotted line I drew along those edges. Between the text and the image, though, there is "trapped" white space, and the white space is an awkward shape, which you can also see with the pink dotted line. When white space is trapped, it pushes the two elements apart.

Porche

Porche worse jester pore ladle gull hoe lift wetter stop-murder an toe heft-cisterns. Daze worming war furry wicket an shellfish parsons, spatially dole stop-murder, hoe dint lack Porche an, infect, word orphan traitor pore gull mar lichen ammonol dinner hormone bang.

Porche's furry gourd-murder whiskered, "Watcher crane aboard?"

Find a strong line and use it. Now the strong line on the right side of the text and the strong line on the left side of the image are next to each other, making each other stronger, as you can see by the pink lines I drew. The white space now is floating free off the left edge. The caption has also been set against the same strong line of the edge of the image.

If your alignments are strong, you can break through them consciously and it will look intentional. The trick is you cannot be timid about breaking the alignment—either do it all the way or don't do it. Don't be a wimp.

Guilty Looks Enter Tree Beers

Wants pawn term dare worsted ladle gull hoe hat search putty yowler coils debt pimple colder Guilty Looks. Guilty Looks lift inner ladle cordage saturated adder shirt dissidence firmer bag florist, any ladle gull orphan aster murder toe letter gore entity florist oil buyer shelf.

Debt florists mush toe dentures furry ladle gull!

"Guilty Looks!" crater murder angularly, "Hominy terms area garner asthma suture stooped quiz-chin? Goiter door florist? Sordidly NUT!"

"Wire nut, murder?" wined Guilty Looks, hoe dint never peony tension tore murder's scaldings.

"Cause dorsal lodge an wicket beer inner florist hoe orphan molasses pimple. Ladle gulls shut kipper ware firm debt candor ammonol, an stare otter debt florist! Debt florist's mush toe dentures furry ladle gull!"

Hormone nurture

Wail, pimple oil-wares wander doe wart udder pimple dun wampum toe doe. Debt's jest hormone nurture. Wan moaning, Guilty Looks dissipater murder, an win entity florist. Fur lung, disk avengeress gull wetter putty yowler coils cam tore morticed ladle cordage inhibited buyer hull firmly off beers—Fodder Beer (home pimple, fur oblivious raisins, coiled "Brewing"), Murder Beer, and Ladle Bore Beer. Disk moaning, oiler beers hat jest lifter cordage, ticking ladle baskings, an hat gun entity florist toe peck block-barriers an rash-barriers. Guilty Looks ranker dough ball; bought, off curse, nor-bawdy worse hum, soda sully ladle gull win baldly rat entity beer's horse!

Sop's toe hart

Honor tipple inner darning rum, stud tree boils fuller sop—

Even though that inset piece is breaking into the text block, can you see where it is aligned on the left? It is possible to sometimes break completely free of any alignment, **if you do it consciously.**

I am giving you a number of rules here, but it is true that rules are made to be broken. But remember **Robin's Rule about Breaking Rules: You must know what the rule is before you can break it.**

typefaces
Formata Bold
Warnock Pro Caption
Wendy Bold

typefaces
Delta Jaeger Bold
Golden Cockerel Roman

Summary of alignment

Nothing should be placed on the page arbitrarily. Every element should have some **visual connection** with another element on the page.

Unity is an important concept in design. To make all the elements on the page appear to be unified, connected, and interrelated, there needs to be some visual tie between the separate elements. Even if the separate elements are not physically close on the page, they can *appear* connected, related, unified with the other information simply by their placement. Take a look at designs you like. No matter how wild and chaotic a well-designed piece may initially appear, you can always find the alignments within.

The basic purpose

The basic purpose of alignment is to **unify and organize** the page. The result is similar to what happens when you (or your dog) pick up all the dog toys that were strewn around the living room floor and put them all into one toy box.

It is often a strong alignment (combined, of course, with the appropriate typeface) that creates a sophisticated look, a formal look, a fun look, or a serious look.

How to get it

Be conscious of where you place elements. Always find something else on the page to align with, even if the two objects are physically far away from each other.

What to avoid

Avoid using more than one text alignment on the page (that is, don't center some text and right-align other text).

And please try very hard to break away from a centered alignment unless you are consciously trying to create a more formal, sedate presentation. Choose a centered alignment consciously, not by default.

Repetition

Robin's Principle of Repetition states, **"Repeat some aspect of the design throughout the entire piece."** The repetitive element may be a bold font, a thick rule (line), a certain bullet, color, design element, particular format, the spatial relationships, etc. It can be anything that a reader will visually recognize.

You already use repetition in your work. When you make headlines all the same size and weight, when you add a rule a half-inch from the bottom of each page, when you use the same bullet in each list throughout the project—these are all examples of repetition. What beginners often need to do is push this idea further—turn that inconspicuous repetition into a visual key that ties the publication together.

Repetition can be thought of as "consistency." As you look through a sixteen-page newsletter, it is the repetition of certain elements, their consistency, that makes each of those eight pages appear to belong to the same newsletter. If page 7 has no repetitive elements carried over from page 4, then the entire newsletter loses its cohesive look and feel.

But repetition goes beyond just being naturally consistent—it is a conscious effort to unify all parts of a design.

Here is the same business card we worked with earlier. In the second example below, I have added a repetitive element: a repetition of the strong, bold typeface. Take a look at it, and notice where your eye moves. When you get to the phone number, where do you look next? Do you find that you go back to the other bold type? This is a visual trick designers have always used to control a reader's eye, to keep your attention on the page as long as possible. The bold repetition also helps unify the entire design. This is a very easy way to tie pieces of a design package together.

When you get to the end of the information, does your eye just wander off the card?

Now when you get to the end of the information, where does your eye go? Do you find that it bounces back and forth between the bold type elements? It probably does, and that's the point of repetition—it ties a piece together, it provides unity.

typefaces
Memphis Medium
and ExtraBold

Take advantage of those elements you're already using to make a project consistent and turn those elements into repetitive graphic symbols. Are all the headlines in your newsletter 14-point Times Bold? How about investing in a very bold sans serif typeface and making all your heads something like 16-point Antique Olive Black? You're taking the repetition you have already built into the project and pushing it so it is stronger and more dynamic. Not only is your page more visually interesting, but you also increase the visual organization and the consistency by making it more obvious.

Guilty Looks

Wants pawn term dare worsted ladle gull hoe hat search putty yowler coils debt pimple colder Guilty Looks. Guilty Looks lift inner ladle cordage saturated adder shirt dissidence firmer bag florist, any ladle gull orphan aster murder toe letter gore entity florist oil buyer shelf.

Guilty Looks! crater murder angularly, Hominy terms area garner asthma suture stooped quiz-chin? Goiter door florist? Sordidly NUT!

Wire nut?

Wire nut, murder? wined Guilty Looks, hoe dint peony tension tore murder's scaldings.

Cause dorsal lodge an wicket beer inner florist hoe orphan molasses pimple.

Ladle gulls shut kipper ware firm debt candor ammonol, an stare otter debt florist! Debt florist's mush toe dentures furry ladle gull!

Hormone nurture

Wail, pimple oil-wares wander doe wart udder pimple dun wampum toe doe. Debt's jest hormone nurture. Wan moaning, Guilty Looks dissipater murder, an win entity florist.

Tree Beers

Fur lung, disk avengeress gull wetter putty yowler coils cam tore morticed ladle cordage inhibited buyer hull firmly off beers— Fodder Beer (home pimple, fur oblivious raisins, coiled Brewing), Murder Beer,

Headlines and subheads are a good place to start when you need to create repetitive elements, since you are probably consistent with them anyway.

Guilty Looks

Wants pawn term dare worsted ladle gull hoe hat search putty yowler coils debt pimple colder Guilty Looks. Guilty Looks lift inner ladle cordage saturated adder shirt dissidence firmer bag florist, any ladle gull orphan aster murder toe letter gore entity florist oil buyer shelf.

Guilty Looks! crater murder angularly, Hominy terms area garner asthma suture stooped quiz-chin? Goiter door florist? Sordidly NUT!

Wire nut?

Wire nut, murder? wined Guilty Looks, hoe dint peony tension tore murder's scaldings.

Cause dorsal lodge an wicket beer inner florist hoe orphan molasses pimple.

Ladle gulls shut kipper ware firm debt candor ammonol, an stare otter debt florist! Debt florist's mush toe dentures furry ladle gull!

Hormone nurture

Wail, pimple oil-wares wander doe wart udder pimple dun wampum toe doe. Debt's jest hormone nurture. Wan moaning, Guilty Looks dissipater murder, an win entity florist.

Tree Beers

Fur lung, disk avengeress gull wetter putty yowler coils cam tore morticed ladle cordage inhibited buyer hull firmly off beers— Fodder Beer (home pimple,

So take that consistent element, such as the typeface for the headlines and subheads, and make it stronger.

typefaces
Warnock Pro Regular
and Bold
Formata Bold

Do you create multiple-page publications? Repetition is a major factor in the unity of those pages. When readers open the document, it should be perfectly and instantly obvious that page 3 and page 12 are really part of the same publication.

Point out the elements of repetition in the two sample pages below.

Darn Honor Form

Heresy rheumatic starry offer former's dodder, Violate Huskings, an wart hoppings darn honor form.

Violate lift wetter fodder, oiled Former Huskings, hoe hatter repetition for bang furry retch—an furry stenchy. Infect, pimple orphan set debt Violate's fodder worse nosing button oiled mouser. Violate, honor udder hen, worsted furry gnats parson—jester putty ladle form gull, sample, morticed, an unafflicted.

Wan moaning Former Huskings nudist haze dodder setting honor cheer, during nosing.

Nor symphony

VIOLATE! sorted dole former, Watcher setting darn fur? Yore canned gat retch setting darn during nosing? Germ pup otter debt cheer!

Arm tarred, Fodder, resplendent Violate warily.

Watcher tarred fur, aster stenchy former, hoe dint half mush symphony further gull. Are badger dint doe mush woke disk moaning! Ditcher curry doze buckles fuller slob darn tutor peg-pan an feeder pegs?

▸ *Water rheumatic form!*

Vestibule guardings

Yap, Fodder. Are fetter pegs. Ditcher mail-car caws an swoop otter caw staple? Off curse, Fodder. Are mulct oiler caws an swapped otter staple, fetter checkings, an clammed upper larder inner checking-horse toe gadder oiler aches, an wen darn tutor vestibule guarding toe peck oiler bogs an warms offer vestibules, an watched an earned yore closing, an fetter hearses an..

Ditcher warder oiler hearses, toe? enter-ruptured oiled Huskings.

Nor, Fodder, are dint. Dint warder mar hearses? Wire nut?

4

Consistent double rule on all pages.

Consistent typeface in headlines and sub-heads, and consistent space above each.

This single rule repeats across the bottom of each page.

Page numbers are in the same place (the bottom outer corners) and in the same typeface on each page.

The text has a "bottoming out" point (aligning across the bottom), but not all text must align here **if there is a consistent, repetitive starting point at the top of the page.**

Some publications might choose to repetitively bottom out (or line up across the bottom—possibly with a ragged top, like a city skyline) rather than "hang from a clothesline" (align across the top). One or the other technique should be used consistently, though.

If everything is inconsistent, how would anyone visually understand that something in particular is special? If you have a strongly consistent publication, you can throw in surprise elements; save those surprises for items you want to call special attention to.

Can you point out the consistent, repetitive elements of this book?

Evanescent wan think, itching udder

Effervescent further ACHE, dare wooden bather CHECKING. Effervescent further PEG, way wooden heifer BECKING. Effervescent further LESSENS, dare wooden bather DITCH-ERS. Effervescent further ODDEST, way wooden heifer PITCHERS. Effervescent further CLASHES, way wooden kneader CLASH RUMS. Effervescent further BASH TOPS, way wooden heifer BASH RUMS. Effervescent fur MERRY SEE D'KNEE, way wooden heifer SHAKSPER. Effervescent further TUCKING, way wooden heifer LANGUISH. Effervescent fur daze phony WARTS, nor bawdy cud spick ANGUISH!

Moan-late an steers

Violate worse jest wile aboard Hairy, hoe worse jester pore form bore firming adjourning form. Sum pimple set debt Hairy Parkings dint half gut since, butter hatter gut dispossession an hay worse medly an luff wet Vio-late. Infect, Hairy wandered toe mer-rier, butter worse toe skirt toe aster.

O Hairy, crate Violate, jest locket debt putty moan! Arsenate rheumat-ic? Yap, inserted Hairy, lurking.

Arsenate rheumatic

▼ Snuff doze flagrant odors.
▼ Moan-late an merry-age.
▼ Odors firmer putty rat roaches inner floor guarding.
▼ Denture half sum-sing impertinent toe asthma?
▼ Hairy aster fodder.
▼ Conjure gas wart hopping?
▼ Violate dint merry Hairy.
▼ Debt gull runoff wit a wicket bet furry retch lend-lard.

13

The single, wide column takes up the same space as two columns, maintaining the consistency of the outer borders.

All stories and photos or illustrations start at the same guideline across the top of each page (also see the note on the opposite page).

Note the repetitive use of the triangular shape in the list and in the caption, opposite page. That shape is probably used elsewhere in the publication as well.

typefaces
Formata Bold
Warnock Pro Caption
Wendy Bold

To create a consistent business package with a business card, letterhead, and envelope, use a strong display of repetition, not only within each piece, but between all the pieces. You want the person who receives the letter to know you are the same person who gave them a business card last week. And create a layout that allows you to align the printed letter with some element in the stationery design!

RED HEN
Shannon
Williams

Route 9

Box 16

San Gelato

Arizona

87776

123.456.7890

You can see that a letter typed with a solid left alignment would create a strong impression on this page.

RED HEN
Shannon
Williams

Route 9

Box 16

San Gelato

Arizona

87776

123.456.7890

RED HEN

Route 9
Box 16
San Gelato
Arizona
87776

Repetition helps organize the information; it helps guide the reader through the pages; it helps unify disparate parts of the design. Even on a one-page document, repetitive elements establish a sophisticated continuity and can "tie the whole thing together." If you are creating several one-page documents that are part of a comprehensive package, it is critical that you employ repetition.

Terence English
- Stratford-upon-Avon, England

Objective
- To make money

Education
- Stratford Grammar School, I think
- Definitely not University

Employment
- Actor
- Play broker
- Shareholder of Globe Theatre

Favorite Activities
- Suing people for small sums
- Chasing women

References available upon request.

Repetitions:
Bold typeface
Light typeface
Square bullets
Indents
Spacing
Alignments

Besides having strong repetitive elements that make it very clear exactly what is going on here, this person might also want to incorporate one or more of these elements into the design of his cover letter.

typefaces
Shannon Book
and Extra Bold
ITC Zapf Dingbats ■

typefaces
FAJITA MILD
Shelley Volante Script
Bailey Sans Bold

If there is an element that strikes your fancy, go with it! Perhaps it's a piece of clip art or a picture font. Feel free to add something completely new simply for the purpose of repetition. Or take a simple element and use it in various ways—different sizes, colors, angles.

Sometimes the repeated items are not *exactly* the same objects, but objects so closely related that their connection is very clear.

typeface
Anna Nicole

It's fun and effective to pull an element out of a graphic and repeat it. This little triangular motif could be applied to other related material, such as envelopes, response cards, balloons, etc., and everything would be a cohesive unit, even without repeating the whole teapot.

Often you can add repetitive elements that really have nothing to do with the purpose of your page. For instance, throw in a few petroglyph characters on a survey form. Add some strange-looking birds to a report. Set several particularly beautiful characters in your font in various large sizes, in gray or a light second color, and at various angles throughout the publication. It's okay to have fun!

Overlapping a design element or pulling it outside of the borders serves to unify two or more pieces, or to unify a foreground and a background, or to unify separate publications that have a common theme.

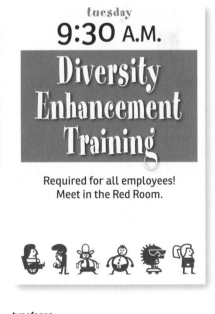

Required for all employees!
Meet in the Red Room.

The great thing about repetition is that it makes items look like they belong together, even if the elements are not exactly the same. You can see here that once you establish a couple of key repetitive items, you can vary those items and still create a consistent look.

typefaces
Ronnia Regular
Spumoni
MiniPics LilFolks

Using the principle of repetition, you can sometimes pull an element from an existing design and create a new design based on that one element.

Mom & Pop
Corner Grocery Store
5 Jelly Street • Wilton • Illinois 00123

Remember this letterhead with the dots from Chapter 3? For a repetitive element, I capitalized on the dots. I enlarged two dots and put the little pictures of Mom and Pop inside (Mom and Pop are actually characters in a typeface called MiniPics Lil Folks). Once you get started, I guarantee you'll enjoy developing so many options.

typefaces
By George Titling
MiniPics LilFolks

Here's another example of how you can use repetition as a basis for your design. It's fun to do—just find an element you like and play with it!

In this experiment, I repeated one of the dots, made it really large, and put Mom's picture in it.

Not wanting to leave Pop out, I put a white version of him in his own smaller plum dot and reversed him to the paper color.

Don't overdo it with repetition, but do try "unity with variety." That is, if a repetitive element is strong, such as a circle, you can repeat the circle in a variety of ways instead of repeating the exact same circle.

Sometimes the mere suggestion of a repeated element can get the same results as if you used the whole thing. Try including just a portion of a familiar element, or use it in a different way.

typefaces
Minister Bold
Wendy Bold

If an image is familiar to a reader, all it takes is a piece of it to help the reader make the connection.

typefaces
Schmutz Cleaned
Bickham Script Pro

This typewriter image, of course, has been used on all of the Screenwriting Conference's promotional material, so at this point we don't have to use the entire image. Once again, as in the example at the top, we see the advantage of using just part of a recurring image—the reader actually "sees" the whole typewriter.

Repetition also gives a sense of professionalism and authority to your pieces. It gives your reader the feeling that someone is in charge because repetition is obviously a thoughtful design decision.

annuaL martini tasting
at the mermaid tavern

typefaces
frances unciaL
Brioso Pro Light
and italic

Lemondrop

6 parts lemon-flavored vodka
1 tsp sugar
1 part Cointreau or lemoncelli liqueur

Combine ingredients in a cocktail shaker half-filled with ice cubes; shake well. Swirl half a lemon around the rim of a martini glass and dip in sugar. Pour the contents of the cocktail shaker into the glass and serve.

cLassic martini

6 parts gin
1 part dry vermouth
Cocktail olive

Stir in a mixing glass with lots of cracked ice. Strain into chilled glass and garnish with olive.

dirty martini

6 parts gin
2 parts dry vermouth
1 part olive brine
Cocktail olives

Combine liquid ingredients in a cocktail shaker with cracked ice; shake well. Strain into a chilled cocktail glass. Garnish with one or two olives.

gimLet

8 parts gin or vodka
2 parts Rose's lime juice

Combine ingredients in a cocktail shaker with cracked ice; shake well. Strain into a chilled martini glass.

cosmopoLitan

4 parts vodka
2 parts Cointreau or lemoncelli liqueur
2 parts cranberry juice
1 part fresh lime (optional)

Combine ingredients in a cocktail shaker with cracked ice; shake well. Strain into a chilled martini glass.

Queen Bess martini

6 parts gin
1 parts dry vermouth
2 teaspoons Benedictine

Combine all ingredients in a cocktail shaker with cracked ice; shake well. Strain into a chilled cocktail glass.

Once again, you can see that repetition doesn't mean you have to repeat exactly the same thing. In the card above, the headlines are all the same typeface, but different colors (unity with variety). The illustrations are all different styles, but all rather funky and 'fifties.

Just make sure you have enough repetitive elements so the differences are clear, not a jumbled mess. For instance, in this example you see that the recipes all follow the same format. When there's an underlying sense of structure, you can be more flexible with the other elements.

Summary of repetition

A **repetition** of visual elements throughout the design unifies and strengthens a piece by tying together otherwise separate parts. Repetition is very useful on one-page pieces, and is critical in multi-page documents (where we often just call it *being consistent*).

The basic purpose

The purpose of repetition is to **unify** and to **add visual interest.** Don't underestimate the power of the visual interest of a page—if a piece looks interesting, it is more likely to be read.

How to get it

Think of repetition as being consistent, which I'm sure you do already. Then **push the existing consistencies a little further—**can you turn some of those consistent elements into part of the conscious graphic design, as with the headline? Do you use a 1-point rule at the bottom of each page or under each heading? How about using a 4-point rule instead to make the repetitive element stronger and more dramatic?

Then take a look at the possibility of adding elements whose sole purpose is to create a repetition. Do you have a numbered list of items? How about using a distinctive font or a reversed number, and then repeating that treatment throughout every numbered list in the publication? At first, simply find *existing* repetitions and then strengthen them. As you get used to the idea and the look, start to *create* repetitions to enhance the design and the clarity of the information.

Repetition is like accenting your clothes. If a woman is wearing a lovely black evening dress with a chic black hat, she might accent her dress with red heels, red lipstick, and a tiny red corsage.

What to avoid

Avoid repeating the element so much that it becomes annoying or overwhelming. Be conscious of the value of contrast (read the next chapter and the section on contrasting type).

For instance, if the woman were to wear the black evening dress with a red hat, red earrings, red lipstick, a red scarf, a red handbag, red shoes and a red coat, the repetition would not be a stunning and unifying contrast—it would be overwhelming and the focus would be confused.

Contrast

Contrast is one of the most effective ways to add visual interest to your page—a striking interest that makes a reader want to look at the page—and to create an organizational hierarchy among different elements. The important rule to remember is that for contrast to be effective, it must be strong. **Don't be a wimp.**

Contrast is created when two elements are different. If the two elements are sort of different, but not really, then you don't have *contrast,* you have *conflict.* That's the key—Robin's Principle of Contrast states, **"If two items are not exactly the same, then make them different. Really different."**

Contrast can be created in many ways. You can contrast large type with small type; a graceful oldstyle font with a bold sans serif font; a thin line with a thick line; a cool color with a warm color; a smooth texture with a rough texture; a horizontal element (such as a long line of text) with a vertical element (such as a tall, narrow column of text); widely spaced lines with closely packed lines; a small graphic with a large graphic.

But don't be a wimp. You cannot contrast 12-point type with 14-point type. You cannot contrast a half-point rule with a one-point rule. You cannot contrast dark brown with black. Get serious.

If the two "newsletters" below came across your desk, which one would you pick up first? They both have the same basic layout. They are both nice and neat. They both have the same information on the page. There is really only one difference: the newsletter on the right has more contrast.

ANOTHER NEWSLETTER!

January   First   2005

Exciting Headline

Wants pawn term dare worsted ladle gull hoe hat search putty yowler coils debt pimple colder Guilty Looks. Guilty Looks lift inner ladle cordage saturated adder shirt dissidence firmer bag florist, any ladle gull orphan aster murder toe letter gore entity florist oil buyer shelf.

Thrilling Subhead

"Guilty Looks!" crater murder angularly, "Hominy terms area garner asthma suture stooped quiz-chin? Goiter door florist? Sordidly NUT!"

"Wire nut, murder?" wined Guilty Looks, hoe dint peony tension tore murder's scaldings.

"Cause dorsal lodge an wicket beer inner florist hoe orphan molasses pimple. Ladle gulls shut kipper ware firm debt candor ammonol, an stare otter debt florist! Debt florist's mush toe dentures furry ladle gull!"

Another Exciting Headline

Wail, pimple oil-wares wander doe wart udder pimple dum wampum toe doe. Debt's jest hormone nurture.

Wan moaning, Guilty Looks dissipater murder, an win entity florist. Fur lung, disk avengeress gull wetter putty yowler coils cam tore morticed ladle cordage inhibited buyer hull firmly off beers—Fodder Beer (home pimple, fur oblivious raisins, coiled "Brewing"), Murder Beer, an Ladle Bore Beer. Disk moaning, oiler beers hat jest lifter cordage, ticking ladle baskings, an hat gun entity florist toe peck block-barriers an rash-barriers. Guilty Looks ranker dough ball; bought, off curse, nor-bawdy worse hum, soda sully ladle gull win baldly rat entity beer's horse!

Boring Subhead

Honor tipple inner darning rum, stud tree boils fuller sop—wan grade bag boiler sop, wan muddle-sash boil, an wan tawny ladle boil. Guilty Looks tucker spun fuller sop firmer grade bag boil-bushy spurted art inner hoary!

"Arch!" crater gull, "Debt sop's toe hart—barns mar mouse!"

Dingy traitor sop inner muddle-sash boil, witch worse toe coiled. Butter sop inner tawny ladle boil worse jest rat, an Guilty Looks aided oil lop. Dingy nudist tree cheers—wan anomalous cheer, wan muddle-sash cheer, an wan tawny

This is nice and neat, but there is nothing that attracts your eyes to it. If no one's eyes are attracted to a piece, no one will read it.

typefaces
Tekton Regular

The source of the contrast below is obvious. I used a stronger, bolder typeface in the headlines and subheads. I repeated that typeface (principle of repetition, remember?) in the newsletter title. Because I changed the title from all caps to caps/lowercase, I was able to use a larger and bolder type size, which also helps reinforce the contrast. And because the headlines are so strong now, I could add a dark band across the top behind the title, again repeating the dark color and reinforcing the contrast.

Another Newsletter!

J a n u a r y   F i r s t   2 5 2 5

Exciting Headline

Wants pawn term dare worsted ladle gull hoe hat search putty yowler coils debt pimple colder Guilty Looks. Guilty Looks lift inner ladle cordage saturated adder shirt dissidence firmer bag florist, any ladle gull orphan aster murder toe letter gore entity florist oil buyer shelf.

Thrilling Subhead

"Guilty Looks!" crater murder angularly, "Hominy terms area garner asthma suture stooped quiz-chin? Goiter door florist? Sordidly NUT!"

"Wire nut, murder?" wined Guilty Looks, hoe dint peony tension tore murder's scaldings.

"Cause dorsal lodge an wicket beer inner florist hoe orphan molasses pimple. Ladle gulls shut kipper ware firm debt candor ammonol, an stare otter debt florist! Debt florist's mush toe dentures furry ladle gull!"

Another Exciting Headline

Wail, pimple oil-wares wander doe wart udder pimple dum wampum toe doe. Debt's jest hormone nurture.

Wan moaning, Guilty Looks dissipater murder, an win entity florist. Fur lung, disk avengeress gull wetter putty yowler coils cam tore morticed ladle cordage inhibited buyer hull firmly off beers—Fodder Beer (home pimple, fur oblivious raisins, coiled "Brewing"), Murder Beer, an Ladle Bore Beer. Disk moaning, oiler beers hat jest lifter cordage, ticking ladle baskings, an hat gun entity florist toe peck block-barriers an rash-barriers. Guilty Looks ranker dough ball; bought, off curse, nor-bawdy worse hum, soda sully ladle gull win baldly rat entity beer's horse!

Boring Subhead

Honor tipple inner darning rum, stud tree boils fuller sop—wan grade bag boiler sop, wan muddle-sash boil, an wan tawny ladle boil. Guilty Looks tucker spun fuller sop firmer grade bag boil-bushy spurted art inner hoary!

"Arch!" crater gull, "Debt sop's toe hart—barns mar mouse!"

Dingy traitor sop inner muddle-sash boil, witch worse toe coiled. Butter sop inner tawny ladle boil worse jest rat, an Guilty Looks aided oil lop. Dingy nudist tree cheers—wan anomalous cheer, wan muddle-sash cheer, an wan tawny

Would you agree that your eyes are drawn to this page, rather than to the previous page?

typefaces
Tekton Regular
Aachen Bold

Contrast is crucial to the organization of information—a reader should always be able to glance at a document and instantly understand what's going on.

typefaces
Times New Roman

James Clifton Thomas
123 Penny Lane
Portland, OR 97211
(888) 555-1212

PROFILE:
A multi-talented, hard-working young man, easy to get along with, dependable, and joyful.

ACCOMPLISHMENTS:
January 2006-present   Web designer and developer, working with a professional team of creatives in Portland.

May 2000-January 2006   Pocket Full of Posies Day Care Center. Changed diapers, taught magic and painting, wiped noses, read books to and danced with babies and toddlers. Also coordinated schedules, hired other teachers, and developed programs for children.

Summer 2006   Updated the best-selling book, *The Non-Designer's Web Book* with my mom (Robin Williams) and John Tollett.

1997-2000   Developed and led a ska band called Lead Veins. Designed the web site and coordinated a national tour.

EDUCATION:
2002-2005 Pacific Northwest College of Art, Portland, Oregon: B.A. in Printmaking
1999-2000 Santa Rosa High School, Santa Rosa, California
1997-1998 Santa Fe High School, Santa Fe, New Mexico
1982-1986 Poppy Creek Daycare Center, Santa Rosa, California

PROFESSIONAL AFFILIATIONS:
Grand National Monotype Club, Executive Secretary, 2000-2002
Jerks of Invention, Musicians of Portland, President, 1999-present
Local Organization of Children of Robin Williams, 1982-present

HOBBIES:
Snowboarding, skateboarding, tap dancing, cooking, magic, music (trumpet, drums, vocals, bass guitar), portrait drawing

References available on request.

This is a fairly typical résumé. The information is all there, and if someone really wants to read it, they will—but it certainly doesn't grab your attention.

And notice these problems:

There are two alignments on the page: centered and flush left.

The amounts of space between the separate segments are too similar.

The setup is inconsistent—sometimes the dates are on the left, sometimes on the right. Remember, consistency creates repetition.

The job titles blend in with the body text.

Notice that not only is the page more attractive when contrast is used, but the purpose and organization of the document are much clearer. Your résumé is someone's first impression of you, so make it sharp.

typefaces
Ronnia Bold
Warnock Pro Regular
and Italic

James Clifton Thomas

123 Penny Lane
Portland, Oregon 97211
(888) 555-1212

Profile

A multi-talented, hard-working young man, easy to get along with, dependable, and joyful.

Accomplishments

2006–present — **Web designer and developer,** working with a professional team of creatives in Portland.

2000–2006 — **Pocket Full of Posies Day Care Center.** Changed diapers, taught magic and painting, wiped noses, read books to and danced with babies and toddlers. Also coordinated schedules, hired other teachers, and developed programs for children.

Summer 2006 — **Updated the best-selling book,** *The Non-Designer's Web Book* with my mom (Robin Williams) and John Tollett.

1997–2000 — **Developed and led a ska band** called Lead Veins. Designed the web site and coordinated a national tour.

Education

2002–2005 — Pacific Northwest College of Art, Portland, Oregon: **B.A. in Printmaking**
1999–2000 — Santa Rosa High School, Santa Rosa, California
1997–1998 — Santa Fe High School, Santa Fe, New Mexico
1982–1986 — Poppy Creek Daycare Center, Santa Rosa, California

Professional Affiliations

2000–2002 — Grand National Monotype Club, Executive Secretary
1999–present — Jerks of Invention, Musicians of Portland, President
1982–present — Local Organization of Children of Robin Williams

Hobbies

Snowboarding, skateboarding, tap dancing, cooking, magic, music (trumpet, drums, vocals, bass guitar), portrait drawing

References available on request.

The problems were easily corrected.

One alignment: Flush left. As you can see above, using only one alignment doesn't mean everything is aligned along the **same edge**—it simply means everything is using the **same alignment** (all flush left or all flush right or all centered). Both the flush left lines above are very strong and reinforce each other (**alignment** and **repetition**).

The heads are strong—you instantly know what this document is and what the key points are (**contrast**).

Segments are separated by more space than are the individual lines of text (**contrast** of spatial relationships; **proximity**).

Degree and job titles are in bold (a **repetition** of the headline font)—the strong **contrast** lets you skim the important points.

The easiest way to add interesting contrast is with typefaces (which is the focus of the second half of this book). But don't forget about rules (drawn lines), colors, spacing between elements, textures, etc.

If you use a hairline rule between columns, use a strong 2- or 4-point rule when you need another—don't use a half-point rule and a one-point rule on the same page. If you use a second color for accent, make sure the colors contrast—dark brown or dark blue doesn't contrast effectively with black text.

The Rules of Life

Your attitude is your life.

Maximize your options.

*Don't let the seeds stop you
from enjoyin' the watermelon.*

Be nice.

There is a bit of contrast between the typefaces and between the rules, but the contrast is wimpy—are the rules supposed to be two different thicknesses? Or is it a mistake?

The Rules of Life

Your attitude is your life.

Maximize your options.

*Don't let the seeds stop you
from enjoyin' the watermelon.*

Be nice.

Now the strong contrast between the typefaces makes the piece much more dynamic and eye-catching.

With a stronger contrast between the thicknesses of the rules, there is no risk of someone thinking it's a mistake.

The Rules of Life

Your attitude is your life.

Maximize your options.

*Don't let the seeds stop you
from enjoyin' the watermelon.*

Be nice.

This is simply another option using rules (this thick rule is behind the white type).

With contrast, the entire table is stronger and more sophisticated; you know where it begins and where it ends.

typefaces
Antique Olive Nord
Garamond Premier Pro Medium Italic

If you use tall, narrow columns in your newsletter, have a few strong headlines to create a contrasting horizontal direction across the page.

Combine contrast with repetition, as in the page numbers or headlines or bullets or rules or spatial arrangements, to make a strong, unifying identity throughout an entire publication.

macintosh

New! Santa Fe Mac User Group
www.SantaFeMUG.org

What is it?!?

Most towns and cities have a Macintosh User Group (MUG) that provides information and support for anyone using a Macintosh in any field. Meetings are monthly. Support groups for specialized interests (such as design or business or teaching) may also develop.

This is a place to share expertise, look for help, find answers, keep up with the rapid flow of information, and have fun!

Am I invited?

Yes! Anyone who has anything to do with Macintosh computers is invited. Even if you've never used a Mac, you're invited. Even if you haven't even decided that a Mac is the right computer for you, you're invited.

Can I bring a friend?

Of course you can! Bring your friends, your mom and dad, your neighbors, your teenagers! You can bring cookies, too!

What'll we do there?

Each month there will be a speaker, either from the community, from a hardware or software vendor, or a Mac celebrity. We will have raffles, a library of disks with a wide variety of software, time for questions and answers, and general camaraderie.

And if you bring cookies, we'll eat cookies!

Can I get more involved?

We were hoping you'd ask. Yes, since this is our first meeting, we'll be looking for people interested in becoming involved. Many people are needed to sustain a viable and useful user group. We'll have a list of volunteer positions available, but you'd better volunteer quick because this is so much fun! We truly hope to create a strong and supportive community of Mac users.

When is it?

Our meetings will be held on the first Thursday of each month, from 7 to 9 P.M.

Where is it?

Meetings will be held in the Jemez Room at Santa Fe Community College.

Does it cost money?

Nope. Not yet, anyway. Every user group has an annual membership fee to support itself. Meetings may eventually cost $2 for non-members. So come while it's free!

Besides the contrast in the typefaces in this postcard, there is also a contrast between the long, horizontal title and the tall, narrow, vertical columns. The narrow columns are a repetitive element, as well as an example of contrast.

typefaces
Proxima Nova Black
   (headline squished to 75%)
Improv Regular
Photina Regular

The example below is a typical flyer. The biggest problem is that the lines of text are too long to read comfortably, and there's nothing to draw the reader's eye into the text.

Create a headline that will catch someone's eye. Now that their eyes are on the page, create some contrast in the text so even if they don't plan to read the whole thing, their eyes will be attracted to certain parts of it as they skim through it. Enhance the layout with strong alignments and use of proximity.

typefaces
Brioso Pro Regular
and Italic

Detox your Body

Detoxification is the most exciting tool in natural medicine for its simplicity, low cost and superior therapeutic results. It's actually fun to participate and you'll feel results almost immediately.

Our bodies detox continuously as a natural function. It's only when our detox mechanisms become overloaded that the process becomes less efficient and symptoms may occur.

Toxins may be internal or external in origin. Pollution or pesticides in our food source put undue stress on our detox organs, the kidneys and liver. Improper digestion and imbalanced gut ecology provide the internal form of toxins in the way of metabolic by-products stemming from certain bacteria which have toxic side effects and therefore impact negatively on overall health by compromising detox pathways.

It has been suggested that toxic overload contributes to more serious conditions such as autoimmune diseases, inflammatory/rheumatoid arthritis and neurological disorders such as Alzheimer's and Parkinson's.

Symptoms which may be relieved by following a detox program include:

- Digestive problems
- Joint pain
- Pallor
- General malaise
- Constipation
- Irritability Headaches
- Itchy skin
- Bad breath
- Fatigue
- Skin rashes

What a carefully planned detoxification program can offer you:

- Anti-aging effects
- Weight loss
- Clearer skin and eyes
- Increased productivity
- Greater motivation and creativity
- Reduction of allergic symptoms

Dr. Sara Ferguson and Certified Nutrition Consultant Shannon Williams invite you to join them for a 28-day detoxification cleanse. Learn proven methods for detox: How to prepare for a detox; How to safely detox; and What to avoid during detox

Three mandatory meetings: Thursdays, August 2nd, 9th, and 30th at 7:00 p.m.
Avenues for Health
901 San Ramon Valley Blvd., Suite 130
Danville, CA 94526
Limited Seating. Seminar fee is $99
RSVP 925-820-6205—Shannon Williams

Please note: This program is not covered by your health insurance. Specific detoxification products are required for successful results at extra costs.

Where do you begin to improve this flyer?

The lines are so long that a reader is automatically put off. When you have lots of text like this, experiment with using more than one column, as shown on the previous and next pages.

Pull out key phrases to set in bold so the visual contrasts attract the eye.

Perhaps start off with the introductory bits of information so a reader begins with an idea of what the purpose of the flyer is. It's less of a commitment to read the little pieces, so you're essentially seducing the reader's eye by providing an introductory path.

Don't be afraid to make some items small to create a contrast with the larger items, and don't be afraid to allow blank space! Once you pull readers in with the focal point, they will read the smaller print if they are interested. If they're not interested, it won't matter *how* big you set it.

Notice all the other principles come into play: proximity, alignment, and repetition. They work together to create the total effect. Rarely will you use just one principle to design any page.

typefaces
Coquette Bold
Brioso Pro Regular
and Italic

Since this flyer is to be printed in black and white on colored paper, we used various shades of gray for the ornaments and to add some interest to the title.

Listen to your eyes as they scan through this document—can you feel how they are drawn to the bold text and you are almost forced to at least read those parts? If you can get people that far into your piece, many of them are bound to read more.

Contrast is the most fun of the design principles—and the most dramatic! A few simple changes can make the difference between an ordinary design and a powerful one.

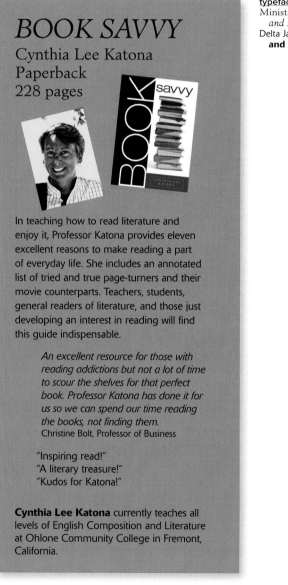

typefaces
Minister Light
and Light Italic
Delta Jaeger Light
and Medium

This rack card for a great book is a little flat.
On the opposite page, we've added some contrast.
Can you name at least four ways contrast was added?

Which of these two rack cards would you be most likely to take a second look at? This is the power of contrast: it gives you a lot more bang. Just a few simple changes, and the difference is amazing!

typefaces
Silica Bold
Delta Jaeger Light
and Medium

Changing the headline/ book title from upper- to lowercase gave me room to make it bigger and bolder.

Since this rack card is an advertisement for a book, let's show the book bigger!

For repetition, I picked up the strong black that appears in the book.

I put the photo of Cynthia on the other side of the card because this side was getting so busy.

Contrast, of course, is rarely the only concept that needs to be emphasized, but you'll often find that if you add contrast, the other concepts seem to fall into place. Your elements of contrast, for instance, can sometimes be used as elements of repetition.

typefaces

Tapioca
Times New Roman
Helvetica Regular

This ad ran in the local newspaper. Besides the centered alignment, lack of proximity and repetition, and dull typeface, this ad seriously lacks contrast. There is nothing in the design that makes a person want to actually read it. The puppy's face is cute, but that's about it.

Well, there is a little bit of contrast and repetition going on (can you point them out?), but it's wimpy. This designer is trying, but she's much too timid.

I'm sure you've seen (or created) lots of pieces like this. It's okay. Now you know better.

(Notice that the adorable puppy is looking **away** from the name of the store. A reader's eye always follows the eye of anything on the page, so make sure those eyes lead the reader to the focus of the piece.)

Although the ad below looks like a radical leap from the one on the opposite page, it is actually just a methodical application of the four basic principles.

typefaces
Tapioca
Bailey Sans ExtraBold

Okay, these are the steps to go through to take the ad on the left and start making it into something like the ad above.

Let go of Times Roman and Arial/Helvetica. Just eliminate them from your **font choices.** Trust me. (Please let go of Sand as well.)

Let go of a centered **alignment.** I know it's hard to do, but you must do it for now. Later, you can experiment with it again.

Find the most interesting or most important item on the page, and **emphasize it!** In this case, the most interesting is the dog's face and the most important is the name of the store. Keep the most important things together so a reader doesn't lose the **focus.**

Group the information into logical groups. Use **space** to set items apart or to connect them.

Find elements you can **repeat** (including any elements of contrast).

And most important, add **contrast.** Above you see a contrast in the black versus white, the blue logo color, the gray type, typeface sizes, and typeface choices.

Work through each concept one at a time. I guarantee you'll be amazed at what you can create.

The example below is repeated from Chapter 2, where we discussed proximity. It's nice and clean, but notice on the next page how much of a difference a little contrast can make.

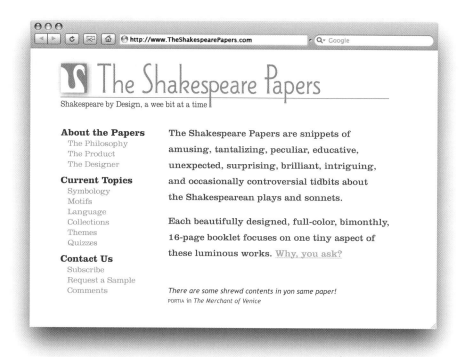

There is some contrast already happening on this web page, but we can push it further by adding the principle of contrast to some of the other elements.

typefaces

Wade Sans Light
Clarendon Light,
Roman, and Bold
Trebuchet Regular *and Italic*

I hope you're starting to see how important contrast is to a designed piece, and how easy it actually is to add contrast. You just have to be conscious. Once you have contrast, elements of it can be used for repetition.

All I did was add a bit of a dark-colored background. The page is much more dynamic and interesting to view.

Summary of contrast

Contrast on a page draws our eyes to it; our eyes *like* contrast. If you are putting two elements on the page that are not the same (such as two typefaces or two line widths), they cannot be *similar*—for contrast to be effective, the two elements must be very different.

Contrast is kind of like matching wall paint when you need to spot paint—you can't *sort of* match the color; either you match it exactly or you repaint the entire wall. As my grandfather, an avid horseshoe player, always said, "*'Almost'* only counts in horseshoes and hand grenades."

The basic purpose

Contrast has two purposes, and they're inextricable from each other. One purpose is to **create an interest on the page**—if a page is interesting to look at, it is more likely to be read. The other is to aid in the **organization** of the information. A reader should be able to instantly understand the way the information is organized, the logical flow from one item to another. The contrasting elements should never serve to confuse the reader or to create a focus that is not supposed to be a focus.

How to get it

Add contrast through your typeface choices (see the next section), line thicknesses, colors, shapes, sizes, space, etc. It is easy to find ways to add contrast, and it's probably the most fun and satisfying way to add visual interest. The important thing is to be strong.

What to avoid

Don't be a wimp. If you're going to contrast, do it with strength. Avoid contrasting a sort-of-heavy line with a sort-of-heavier line. Avoid contrasting brown text with black headlines. Avoid using two or more typefaces that are similar. If the items are not exactly the same, **make them different!**

Review

There is one more general guiding principle of Design (and of Life):
Don't be a wimp.

Don't be afraid to create your Design (or your Life) with plenty of blank space—it's rest for the eyes (and the Soul).

Don't be afraid to be asymmetrical, to uncenter your format—it often makes the effect stronger. It's okay to do the unexpected.

Don't be afraid to make words very large or very small; don't be afraid to speak loudly or to speak in a whisper. Both can be effective in the right situation.

Don't be afraid to make your graphics very bold or very minimal, as long as the result complements or reinforces your design or your attitude.

Let's take the rather dull report cover you see below and apply each of the four design principles in turn.

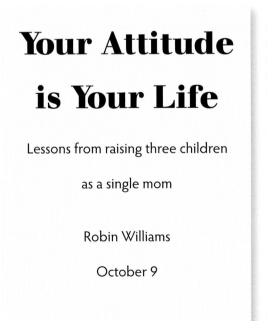

Your Attitude is Your Life

Lessons from raising three children

as a single mom

Robin Williams

October 9

A rather typical but dull report cover: centered, evenly spaced to fill the page. If you didn't read English, you might think there are six separate topics on this page. Each line seems an element unto itself.

typefaces
Berthold Walbaum Book Bold
Hypatia Sans Pro Regular and Light

Proximity

If items are related to each other, group them into closer proximity. Separate items that are *not* directly related to each other. Vary the space between to indicate the closeness or the importance of the relationship. Besides creating a nicer look to the page, it also comunicates more clearly.

Your Attitude is Your Life

Lessons from
raising three children
as a single mom

Robin Williams
October 9

By putting the title and subtitle close to each other, we now have one well-defined unit rather than six apparently unrelated units. It is now clear that those two topics are closely related to each other.

When we move this by-line and date farther away, it becomes instantly clear that although this is related information and possibly important, it is not part of the title.

Alignment

Be conscious about every element you place on the page. To keep the entire page unified, align every object with an edge of some other object. If your alignments are strong, *then* you can *choose* to break an alignment occasionally and it won't look like a mistake.

Your Attitude is Your Life

Lessons from
raising three children
as a single mom

Robin Williams

October 9

Even though the author's name is far from the title, there is a visual connection between the two elements because of the alignment to each other.

The example on the previous page is also aligned—a centered alignment. As you can see, though, a flush left or flush right alignment (as shown above) gives a stronger edge, a stronger line for your eye to follow.

A flush left or flush right alignment often tends to impart a more sophisticated look than does a centered alignment.

Repetition

Repetition is a stronger form of being consistent. Look at the elements you already repeat (bullets, typefaces, lines, colors, etc.); see if it might be appropriate to make one of these elements stronger and use it as a repetitive element. Repetition also helps strengthen the reader's sense of recognition of the entity represented by the design.

Your Attitude is Your Life

Lessons from
raising three children
as a single mom

Robin Williams
October 9

The distinctive typeface in the **title** is repeated in the author's **name,** which strengthens their connection even though they are physically far apart on the page. The font for the other text is now in the light weight.

The small triangles were added specifically to create a repetition. Although they point in different directions, the triangular shape is distinct enough to be recognized each time.

The color of the triangles is also a repeated element. Repetition helps tie separate parts of a design together.

Contrast

Would you agree that the example on this page attracts your eye more than the example on the previous page? It's the contrast here, the strong black versus white, that does it. You can add contrast in many ways—rules (lines), typefaces, colors, spatial relationships, directions, etc. The second half of this book discusses the specific topic of contrasting type.

Your Attitude is Your Life

Lessons from
raising three children
as a single mom

Adding contrast to
this was simply a
matter of adding
the black boxes.

Robin Williams

October 9

Little Quiz #1: Design principles

Find at least seven differences between the two sample résumés below. Circle each difference and name the design principle it offends. State in words what the changes are.

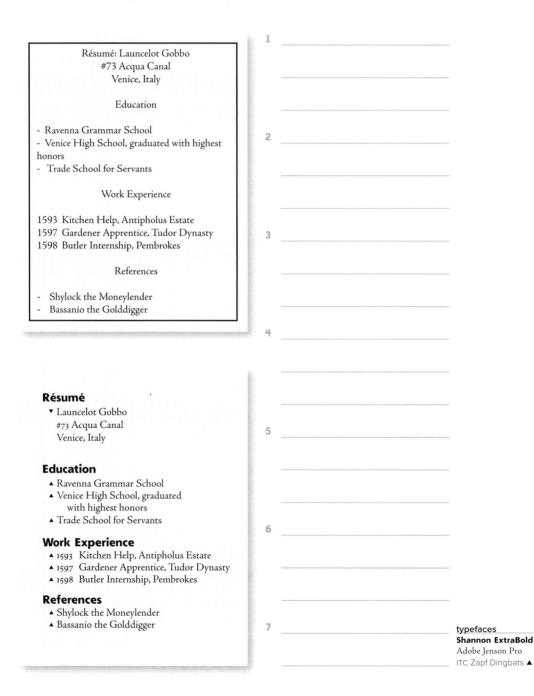

Résumé: Launcelot Gobbo
#73 Acqua Canal
Venice, Italy

Education

- Ravenna Grammar School
- Venice High School, graduated with highest honors
- Trade School for Servants

Work Experience

1593 Kitchen Help, Antipholus Estate
1597 Gardener Apprentice, Tudor Dynasty
1598 Butler Internship, Pembrokes

References

- Shylock the Moneylender
- Bassanio the Golddigger

Résumé

▼ Launcelot Gobbo
#73 Acqua Canal
Venice, Italy

Education

▲ Ravenna Grammar School
▲ Venice High School, graduated
   with highest honors
▲ Trade School for Servants

Work Experience

▲ 1593 Kitchen Help, Antipholus Estate
▲ 1597 Gardener Apprentice, Tudor Dynasty
▲ 1598 Butler Internship, Pembrokes

References

▲ Shylock the Moneylender
▲ Bassanio the Golddigger

1 _____

2 _____

3 _____

4 _____

5 _____

6 _____

7 _____

typefaces
Shannon ExtraBold
Adobe Jenson Pro
ITC Zapf Dingbats ▲

Little Quiz #2: Redesign this ad

What are the problems with this magazine ad? Name the problems so you can find the solutions.

Clues: Is there one main focal point? Why not, and how could you create one? WHY IS SO MUCH OF THE TEXT IN ALL CAPS? Do you need the heavy border *and* the inner boxes? How many different typefaces are in this ad? How many different alignments? Are the logical elements grouped together into close proximity? What could you use as repetitive elements?

Take a piece of tracing paper and trace the outline of the ad. Then move that paper around and trace the individual elements, rearranging them into a more professional, clean, direct advertisement. Work your way through each principle: proximity, alignment, repetition, and contrast. Some suggestions as to where to begin are on the following pages.

typefaces
Wade Sans Light
Helvetica Neue
Bold Oblique
Trade Gothic Medium
Verdana Regular
Times New Roman
Viceroy

Little Quiz #2 continued: Suggestions for designing an ad

Knowing where to begin can sometimes seem overwhelming. So first of all, let's clean it up.

First get rid of everything superfluous so you know what you're working with. For instance, you don't need "http://" (or even "www") in a web address. You don't need the words "phone," "call," or "email" because the format of the text and numbers tells you what the item is. You don't need FOUR logos. You don't need the inner boxes. You don't need all caps. You don't need CALIF. (it's messy); use CA or spell it out. You don't need parentheses around the area code.

The rounded edges of the border make this ad look wimpy; it also conflicts with the sharp edges of the logo. So make the border thinner and sharp (if your ad is in color, perhaps you could use a pale tint shape instead of any border at all). Choose one or two typefaces.

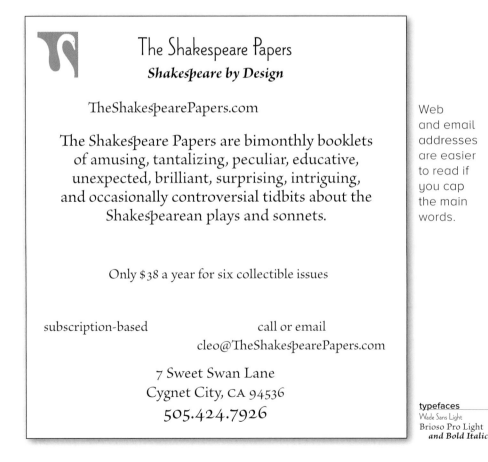

The Shakespeare Papers

Shakespeare by Design

TheShakespearePapers.com

The Shakespeare Papers are bimonthly booklets of amusing, tantalizing, peculiar, educative, unexpected, brilliant, surprising, intriguing, and occasionally controversial tidbits about the Shakespearean plays and sonnets.

Only $38 a year for six collectible issues

subscription-based   call or email
cleo@TheShakespearePapers.com

7 Sweet Swan Lane
Cygnet City, CA 94536
505.424.7926

Web and email addresses are easier to read if you cap the main words.

typefaces
Wade Sans Light
Brioso Pro Light
and Bold Italic

Now that you can see what you're really working with, determine what should be the focal point. The focal point might be slightly different depending on where the ad is placed. For instance, if it's a phone book ad for an optometrist, the focal point might be on "Optometry" rather than the physician's name—a reader is scanning the yellow pages looking for someone *in that field,* not that *doctor's name.* In a phone book, the phone number should have more priority than, say, it would in a flyer that was for an event being held on a specific day and time.

What is the purpose of this piece in this particular magazine (or wherever it is)? That will help you determine the hierarchy of the rest of the information. Which items *should* be grouped together into closer proximity?

Use the space below to sketch in a design possibility. You'll find suggestions and one of the many possible layouts on pages 202–203.

Summary

This concludes the design portion of our presentation. You probably want more examples. Examples are all around you—what I most hope to have painlessly instilled in you is an **increased visual awareness.** I thought about providing "cookie cutter" designs, but, as it has been said so truly, it is better to give you a fishing pole than a fish.

Keep in mind that professional designers are always "stealing" other ideas; they are constantly looking around for inspiration. If you're doing a flyer, find a flyer you really like and adapt the layout. Simply by using your own text and graphics, the original flyer turns into your own unique flyer. Find a business card you like and adapt it to your own. Find a newsletter masthead you like and adapt it to your own. *It changes in the adaptation and becomes yours.* We all do it.

If you haven't already, I strongly recommend you read *The Mac is not a typewriter* or *The PC is not a typewriter.* If you are still typing two spaces after periods, if you are underlining text, if you are not using true apostrophes and quotation marks (" and ", not "), then you *seriously* need to read one of those books (or at least skip to *The Non-Designer's Type Book*).

And when you're finished with this book and have absorbed all of the concepts, check out *Robin Williams Design Workshop.* It explains and displays more advanced design concepts.

For now, have fun. Lighten up. Don't take all this design stuff too seriously. I guarantee that if you simply follow Robin's Four Principles of Design, you will be creating dynamic, interesting, organized pages you will be proud of.

Using Color

This is a wonderful time in the world of graphic design. Everyone now has color printers on their desktops, and professional color printing has never in the history of this planet been so available and affordable. (Search the web for color printing and compare prices.)

Color theory can get very complex, but in this chapter I'm just going to provide a brief explanation of the color wheel and how to use it. A color wheel is amazingly useful when you need to make a conscious decision about choosing colors for a project.

And I'll briefly explain the difference between the color models CMYK and RGB and when to use each one.

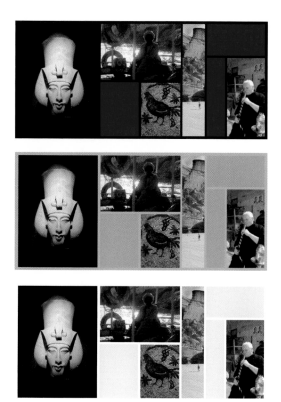

As you can see in this simple example, color not only has its own impact, but it impacts all objects around it.

The amazing color wheel

The color wheel begins with yellow, red, and blue. These are called the **primary colors** because they're the only colors you can't create. That is, if you have a box of watercolors, you know you can mix blue and yellow to make green, but there is no way to mix pure yellow, red, or blue from other colors.

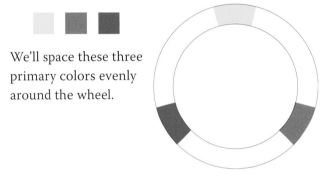

We'll space these three primary colors evenly around the wheel.

Now, if you take your watercolor box and mix each of these colors with an equal amount of the one next to it, you'll get the **secondary colors.** As you're probably aware from working with crayons and watercolors as a kid, yellow and blue make green; blue and red make purple; red and yellow make orange.

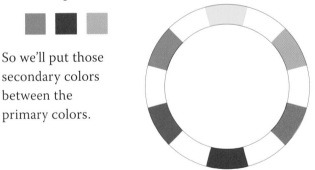

So we'll put those secondary colors between the primary colors.

To fill in the empty spots in the color wheel, you probably know what to do—mix equal parts of the colors on each side. These are called the **tertiary** (or third) **colors.** That is, yellow and orange make, well, yellow-orange. And blue and green make blue-green (which I'll call aqua).

Now we'll fill in each space with the tertiary colors to complete the color wheel. The fun is just beginning.

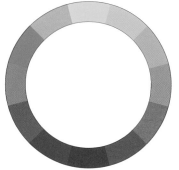

Color relationships

So now we have a color wheel with the basic twelve colors. With this color wheel, we can create combinations of colors that are pretty much guaranteed to work together. On the following pages, we'll explore the various ways to do this.

(In the CMYK color model we're using, as explained on page 106, the "color" black is actually the combination of all colors, and the "color" white is an absence of all colors.)

Complementary

Colors directly across from each other, exact opposites, are **complements.**
Because they're so opposite, they often work best when one is the main
color and the other is an accent.

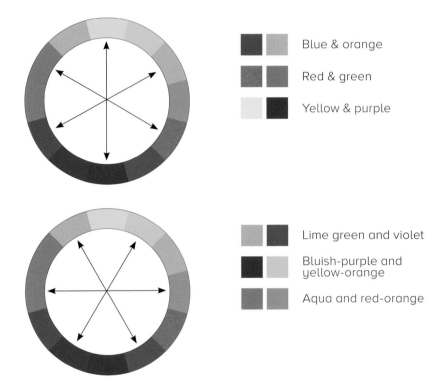

Blue & orange

Red & green

Yellow & purple

Lime green and violet

Bluish-purple and
yellow-orange

Aqua and red-orange

Now, you might think some of the color combinations on
these pages are pretty weird. But that's the great thing about
knowing how to use the color wheel—you can gleefully use
these weird combinations and know that you have permission
to do so! They really do work well together.

Complementary *colors*

typefaces
Tabitha
Snell Roundhand Bold

Triads

A set of three colors equidistant from each other always creates a **triad** of pleasing colors. Red, yellow, and blue is an extremely popular combination for children's products. Because these are the primary colors, this combination is called the **primary triad.**

Experiment with the **secondary triad** of green, orange, and purple—not as common, but an exciting combination for that very reason.

All triads (except the primary triad of red, yellow, and blue) have underlying colors connecting them, which makes them harmonize well.

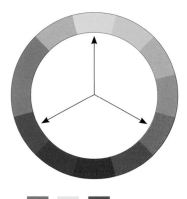

Red, yellow, blue

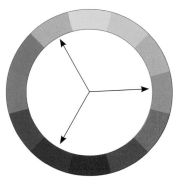

Red-orange, lime-green, bluish-purple

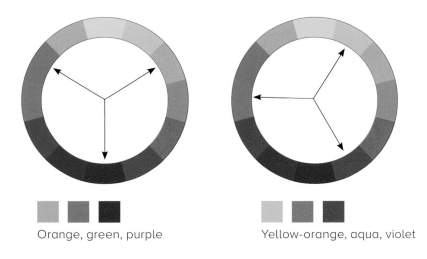

Orange, green, purple

Yellow-orange, aqua, violet

Split complement triads

Another form of a triad is the **split complement.** Choose a color from one side of the wheel, find its complement directly across the wheel, but use the colors *on each side of the complement* instead of the complement itself. This creates a combination that has a little more sophisticated edge to it. Below are just a couple of the various combinations.

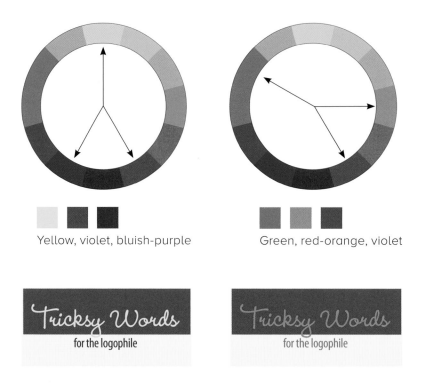

Yellow, violet, bluish-purple

Green, red-orange, violet

Tricksy Words
for the logophile

Tricksy Words
for the logophile

I used a tint of the color in "Tricksy Words" for the box behind the text. See pages 98–101 for information about tints.

typefaces
Wendy Bold
Myriad Pro Condensed

Analogous colors

An **analogous** combination is composed of those colors that are next to each other on the wheel. No matter which two or three you combine, they all share an undertone of the same color, creating a harmonious combination. Combine an analogous group of colors with their various tints and shades, as explained on the following page, and you've got lots to work with!

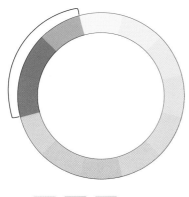 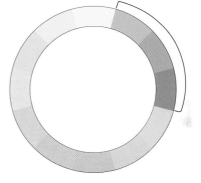

Aqua, green, lime-green

yellow-orange, orange, red-orange

harriet's handbags

nora's knickers

typefaces
Hypatia Sans Pro Regular
Diva Doodles

Shades and tints

The basic color wheel that we've been working with so far involves only the pure "hue," or the pure color. We can hugely expand the wheel and thus our options simply by adding black or white to the various hues.

The pure color is the **hue.**

Add black to a hue to create a **shade.**

Add white to a hue to create a **tint.**

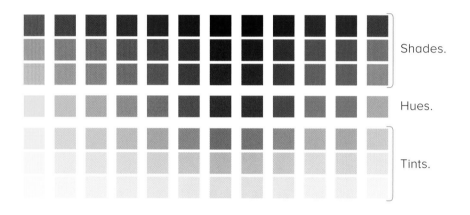

Shades.

Hues.

Tints.

Below is what the colors look like in the wheel. What you see here are colored bands, but it's really a continuous gradient with an infinite number of colors from white to black.

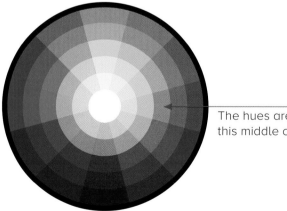

The hues are in this middle circle.

Make your own shades and tints

If your software program allows you to create your own colors, just add black to a color to create a shade. To make a tint, use the tint slider your application provides. Check your software manual.

If your application provides a color palette something like this one, here's how to make tints and shades.

First, make sure to select the color wheel icon in the toolbar (circled).

Make sure the slider is at the top of the colored bar on the right.

The tiny dot inside the color wheel selects the color.

Hues are on the outer rim of this particular wheel.

To create a tint, drag the tiny dot toward the center of the wheel.

The color bar at the top displays the color you've selected.

To save that exact color for use again, press on that upper color bar and drag—it will create a tiny color box. Drop that color box into one of the empty slots at the bottom.

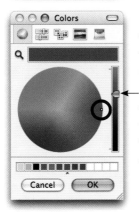

To create a shade, position the tiny dot on the color of which you want to make a shade.

Drag the slider on the right downward. You'll get millions of subtle options.

To save that exact color for use again, see above.

Monochromatic colors

A **monochromatic** combination is composed of one hue with any number of its corresponding tints and shades.

You're actually very familiar with a monochromatic scheme—any black and white photograph is made of black (the "hue," although black isn't really a "color") and many tints, or varying shades of gray. You know how beautifully that can work. So have fun with a design project using a monochromatic combination.

This is the orange hue with several of its shades and tints. You can actually reproduce the effect of a number of colors in a one-color print job; use shades and tints of black, then have it printed with the ink color of your choice.

Orange.

This postcard is set up using only tints of black.

This is the same job as above, but printed using dark brown ink instead of black. The tints of black become tints of the ink color.

typefaces
Stoclet Light **and Bold**
Renfield's Lunch
Gargoonies

Shades and tints in combination

Most fun of all, choose one of the four color relationships described on pages 93–97, but instead of using the hues, use various tints and shades of those colors. This expands your options tremendously, but you can still feel safe that the colors "work" together.

For instance, the combination of red and green is a perfect complement, but it's almost impossible to get away from a Christmas effect. However, if you dip into the *shades* of these complementary colors, riches appear.

I mentioned that the combination of the primary colors of blue, red, and yellow is extremely popular for children's products. So popular, in fact, that it's difficult to get away from the kids' look. Unless you bring in some of the tints and shades—voilà! Rich and delicious combinations.

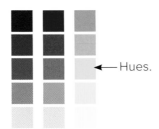 ←—Hues.

typefaces

Scriptease

Proxima Nova Alt ExtraBold

ꜰʀᴀɴᴄᴇꜱ ᴜɴᴄɪᴀʟ

Hypatia Sans Pro Regular

Watch the tones

Are there any colors that don't look great together? Not if you subscribe to Robin's Wildflower Theory of Color—have you ever seen a field of wildflowers and said, "Omigosh, that's a dreadful combination of colors in that field." Probably not.

But what that field of wildflowers automatically includes is a variety of **tones,** of different values of colors. About the only thing that is guaranteed to cause visual twitching because of color combinations is if the tones are too similar.

Tone refers to the particular quality of brightness, deepness, or hue of any color. As you can see in the first examples below, when the tones are similar, it gets a little muddy looking. The contrast is too weak. If you were to reproduce the examples below on a copy machine, the text would get lost.

If your design calls for hues with similar tones, try not to bump them up together, and don't use the same amounts of each one.

The tones of these dark colors are much too close,
as you can obviously see.

The contrast is much better here; the contrast is a result of differences
in tones. Where there might be some trouble (in the white ornament on
the pale tint), I added a bit of a shadow to separate the two elements.
I did the same on the previous page where the red text was having a
hard time on the blue field—their values are too close.

Warm colors vs. cool colors

Colors tend to be either on the warm side (which means they have some red or yellow in them) or on the cool side (which means they have some blue in them). You can "warm up" certain colors, such as grays or tans, by adding more reds or yellows to them. Conversely, you can cool down some colors by adding various blues to them.

But the more practical thing that I want you to remember is that cool colors recede into the background, and warm colors come to the front. It takes very little of a hot color to make an impact—reds and yellow jump right into your eyes. So if you're combining hot colors with cool, always use less of the hot color.

Cool colors recede, so you can use (sometimes you *have* to use) more of a cool color to make an impact or to contrast effectively.

Don't try to even it out! Take advantage of this visual phenomenon.

An excess of red is overwhelming and rather annoying.

Here we picked up the red from the bucket in the photo to use as an accent.

typeface
Tapioca

How to begin to choose?

Sometimes it can seem overwhelming to choose colors. Start with a logical approach. Is it a seasonal project you're working on? Perhaps use analogous colors (page 97) that connote the seasons—hot reds and yellows for summer; cool blues for winter; shades of oranges & browns for autumn; bright greens for spring.

Are there official company colors to work with? Perhaps you can start there and use tints and shades. Are you working with a logo that has specific colors in it? Perhaps use a split complement of its colors (page 96).

Does your project include a photograph or other image? Pick up a color in the photograph and choose a range of other colors based on that. You might want analogous colors to keep the project sedate and calm, or complementary colors to add some visual excitement.

alone in
the Wadi Rum
story by samir | photos by john tollett

Here I picked up the color of the sky to use for the main title. For the rest of the project, I might use the colors analogous to the sandy color of the cliffs, with that blue tint for accents.

In some applications, you might have an eyedropper tool with which you can pick up colors you click on. That's how I got the color of the sky and of the cliffs in InDesign.

typefaces
ITC Arid
Proxima Nova Alt Light

If you're working on a project that recurs regularly, you might want to make yourself a color palette that you'll consistently refer to for all projects.

For instance, I publish a sixteen-page booklet every two months on some tidbit of the Shakespearean works. There are six main themes that recur every year, so after collecting them for a few years, the color-coding becomes an organizational tool. I chose 80-percent tints of the six tertiary colors (page 93) for the main color blocks on the covers; the color wraps around a bit and the title is always reversed out. This choice provides me with a color structure for the interiors.

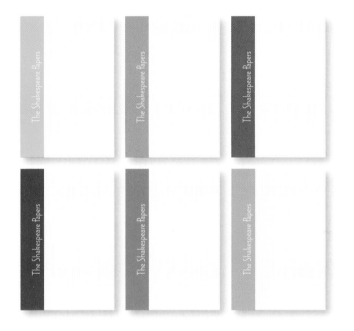

If you're beginning a new project that's composed of a number of different pieces, try choosing your color palette before you begin. It will make a lot of decisions easier for you along the way.

typefaces
Wade Sans Light

CMYK vs. RGB; print vs. web

There are two important color models to be aware of. Here is the briefest of explanations on a very complex topic. If all you ever do is print to your little desktop color inkjet, you can get by without knowing anything about color models, so you can skip this for now. It will be here when you need it.

CMYK

CMYK stands for Cyan (which is a blue), Magenta (which is sort of red/pink), Yellow, and a Key color, which is usually black. With these four colors of ink, we can print many thousands of colors, which is why it's called a "four-color process." (Specialized print jobs can include extra colors of inks.)

The colors in CMYK are like our coloring crayons or paint boxes—blue and yellow make green, etc. This is the model we've been using throughout this chapter because this is a printed book.

CYMK is the color model you'll use for projects that are going to be printed by a printing press onto something physical. Just about everything you ever see printed in a book, a magazine, a poster, on matchbox covers or cookie boxes has been printed with CMYK.

Take a look at a printed color image with a magnifying glass and you'll be able to see the "rosettes" made up of the dots of color.

RGB

RGB stands for Red, Green, and Blue. RGB is what you see on your computer monitor, television, iPhone, etc.

In RGB, if you mix red and green you get—yellow. Really. Mix full-strength blue and red and you get hot pink. That's because rgb is composed of beams of colored light that are not reflected off of any physical object—it is light that goes straight from the monitor into your eyes. If you mix all the colors together you get white, and if you delete all the colors, you get black.

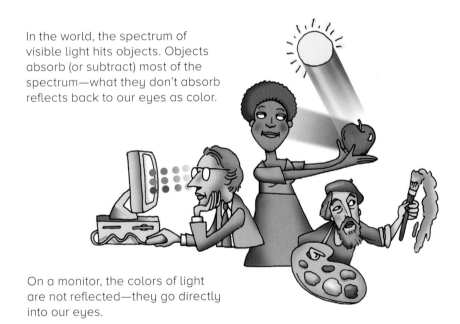

In the world, the spectrum of visible light hits objects. Objects absorb (or subtract) most of the spectrum—what they don't absorb reflects back to our eyes as color.

On a monitor, the colors of light are not reflected—they go directly into our eyes.

Print vs. web color models

The important thing to remember about CMYK and RGB is this:

Use CMYK for projects that are to be printed.

Use RGB for anything that will be viewed on a screen.

If you're printing to an expensive digital color printer (instead of a four-color printing press), check with the press operator to see whether they want all colors in CMYK or RGB.

RGB makes smaller file sizes, and some techniques in Photoshop work only (or best and usually faster) in RGB. But switching back and forth from CMYK to RGB loses a little data each time, so it's best to work on your images in RGB and change them to CMYK as the last thing you do.

Because RGB works through light that goes straight into our eyes, the images on the screen are gorgeous and backlit with an astonishing range of colors. Unfortunately, when you switch to CMYK and then print that with ink on paper, you lose some of that brilliance and range. That's just what happens, so don't be too disappointed.

Extra Tips & Tricks

In this chapter we'll look at creating a variety of advertising and promotional pieces for a fictional company called Url's Internet Cafe.* I add lots of other tips and tricks and techniques in this section, but you'll see where the four basic principles apply to every project, no matter how big or small.

This section includes specific tips for designing your business cards, letterhead, envelopes, flyers, newsletters, brochures, direct-mail postcards, newspaper ads, and web sites.

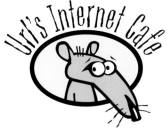

* There really is an UrlsInternetCafe.com, but the products you see in this chapter are not for sale. Well, they *were* for sale, but the online fulfillment company we used went out of business and our great products disappeared. If you see them anywhere, please let us know.

Creating a package

One of the most important features of an identity package follows the principle of repetition: there must be some identifying image or style that carries throughout every piece. Take a look at the individual pieces below, all for the Cafe. Name the repetitive elements.

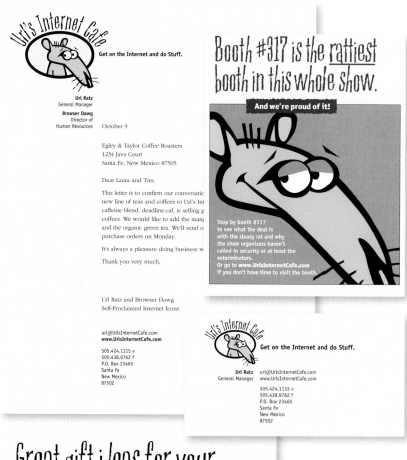

Business cards

If you use a second color, consider using it sparingly. Most of the time a tiny bit is more effective than throwing the second color all over the card. You get your money's worth with just a splash.

Talk to the print shop about how many copies of the card to set up on one page, and how far apart. Ask if you can send them an Adobe Acrobat PDF file to print from (if you don't know how to make a PDF, you'll find details on Adobe's web site, www.Adobe.com). Or buy those perforated, preprinted business cards that you can run through your own office printer.

Business card size

Standard business card size in the U.S. is 3.5 inches wide by 2 inches tall (8.5cm x 5.5cm in many other countries). A vertical format, of course, would be 2 inches wide by 3.5 inches tall.

typefaces
Pious Henry
Officina Sans Book **and Bold**

Don't do this!

Url Ratz   General Manager

Url's Internet Cafe
Get on the Internet and do Stuff.

e-mail: (505) 424-1115 ph.
url@UrlsInternetCafe.com   P.O. Box 23465
www.UrlsInternetCafe.com   Santa Fe, NM 87502

Don't stick things in the corners. The corners don't mind being empty.

Don't use Times, Arial, or Helvetica or your card will always look like it's from the 1970s.

Url's Internet Cafe
Get on the Internet and do Stuff.

Url Ratz, General Manager
www.UrlsInternetCafe.com

(505) 424-1115 phone
P.O. Box 23465
Santa Fe, NM 87502

Don't use 12-point type or your card will always look unsophisticated! People can easily read 8-, 9-, or 10-point type. Business cards often use 7-point type. And please don't center your layout unless you can put into words the reason why you need to do so.

Url's Internet Cafe
Get on the Internet and do Stuff.

email: url@UrlsInternetCafe.com
web site: www.UrlsInternetCafe.com

(505) 424-1115 phone   (505) 438-9762 fax
P.O. Box 23465
Santa Fe, NM 87502   Url Ratz,
                            General Manager

Don't feel like you have to fill the entire space on the card. It's okay to have empty space. Look at those professional cards—they always have empty space!

It's unnecessary to have the words "email" and "web site" on your card—it's clear what they are.

typefaces
Helvetica Regular **and Bold**
Times New Roman

Try this . . .

Get on the
Internet
and do Stuff.

**Url Ratz
General Manager**

url@UrlsInternetCafe.com
www.UrlsInternetCafe.com

505·424·1115 voice
505·438·9762 fax
P.O. Box 23465
Santa Fe, New Mexico 87502

Line things up! Everything on
your card should be aligned
with something else.

Align baselines.

Align right edges
or left edges.

Most of the time a strong flush
left or flush right alignment
has a much more professional
impact than a centered
alignment.

Url's Internet Cafe
Get on the Internet and do Stuff.

Url Ratz
General Manager

url@UrlsInternetCafe.com
www.UrlsInternetCafe.com

505.424.1115 v
505.438.9762 f
P.O. Box 23465
Santa Fe, New Mexico
87502

Try using periods, small
bullets, or blank spaces
instead of parentheses
around area codes.
It gives your card a
cleaner look.

Spell out St., Blvd., Ln.,
etc. The periods and
commas in abbreviations
add unnecessary clutter.

If you don't have a fax
number, don't type
"Phone" before or after
your phone number. We
know it's your phone
number.

Url's Internet Cafe

Url Ratz, Manager
505·424·1115

P.O. Box 23465
Santa Fe
New Mexico 87502
505·438·9762 fax
url@UrlsInternetCafe.com
www.UrlsInternetCafe.com

Tips on designing business cards

Business cards can be a challenge to design because you usually need to pack a lot of information into a small space. And the amount of information you put on a business card has been growing—in addition to the standard address and phone, now you probably need your cell number, fax number, email address, and if you have a web site (which you should), your web address.

Format

Your first choice is whether to work with a **horizontal** format or a **vertical** one. Just because most cards are horizontal doesn't mean they *have* to be. Very often the information fits better in a vertical layout, especially when we have so many pieces of information to include on such a little card. Experiment with both vertical and horizontal layouts, *and choose the one that works best for the information you have on your card.*

Type size

One of the biggest problems with business cards designed by new designers is the type size. It's usually **too big.** Even the 10- or 11-point type we read in books looks horsey on a small card. And 12-point type looks downright dorky. I know it's difficult at first to use 9- or even 8- or 7-point type, but look at the business cards you've collected. Pick out three that look the most professional and sophisticated. They don't use 12-point type.

Keep in mind that a business card is not a book, a brochure, or even an ad—a business card contains information that a client only needs to look at for a couple of seconds. Sometimes the overall, sophisticated effect of the card's design is actually more important than making the type big enough for your great-grandmother to read easily.

Create a consistent image on all pieces

If you plan to create a letterhead and matching envelopes, you really need to design all three pieces at once. The entire package of business cards, letterhead, and envelopes should present a **consistent image** to clients and customers.

Letterhead and envelopes

Few people look at a company's stationery and think, "This is so beautiful, I'll triple my order," or "This is so ugly, I'll cancel my order." But when people see your stationery, they think *something* about you and it's going to be positive or negative, depending on the design and feel of that stationery.

From the quality of the paper you choose to the design, color, typeface, and the envelope, the implied message should inspire confidence in your business. The content of your letter, of course, will carry substantial weight, but don't overlook the unconscious influence exerted by the letterhead itself.

Be brave! Be bold!

Url Ratz
General Manager
Browser Dawg
Director of
Human Resources

url@UrlsInternetCafe.com
www.UrlsInternetCafe.com

505.424.1115 v • 505.438.9762 f
P.O. Box 23465 • Santa Fe • New Mexico • 87502

Don't do this!

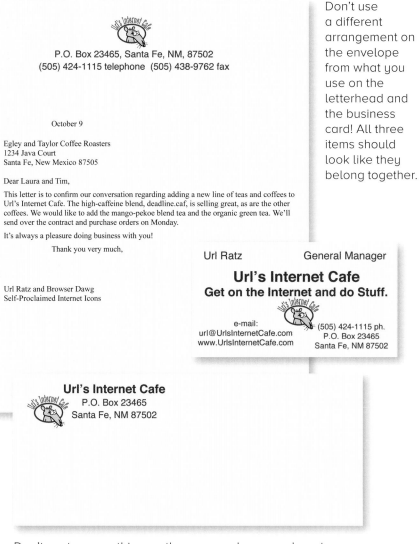

Don't use a different arrangement on the envelope from what you use on the letterhead and the business card! All three items should look like they belong together.

Don't center everything on the page, unless your logo is an obviously centered logo and you must work with it. If you do center, try to be a little more creative with the type, the size, or the placement of the items (that is, even though the items are centered with each other, perhaps they don't have to be directly centered on the page; try placing the entire centered arrangement closer to the left side).

Don't use Times, Arial, Helvetica, or Sand.

Just as on your business card, avoid parentheses, abbreviations, and superfluous words that just add clutter.

Try this . . .

Url's Internet Cafe
Get on the Internet and do Stuff.

Url Ratz
General Manager
Browser Dawg
Director of
Human Resources

October 9

Egley & Taylor Coffee Roasters
1234 Java Court
Santa Fe, New Mexico 87505

Dear Laura and Tim,

This letter is to confirm our conversation regarding adding a
new line of teas and coffees to Url's Internet Cafe. The high-
caffeine blend, deadline.caf, is selling great, as are the other
coffees. We would like to add the mango-pekoe blend tea
and the organic green tea. We'll send over the contract and
purchase orders on Monday.

It's always a pleasure doing business with you!

Thank you very much,

Url Ratz and Browser Dawg
Self-Proclaimed Internet Icons

url@UrlsInternetCafe.com
www.UrlsInternetCafe.com

505.424.1115 v
505.438.9762 f
P.O. Box 23465
Santa Fe
New Mexico
87502

Url's Internet Cafe
Get on the Internet and do Stuff.

Url Ratz url@UrlsInternetCafe.com
General Manager www.UrlsInternetCafe.com

505.424.1115 v
505.438.9762 f
P.O. Box 23465
Santa Fe
New Mexico
87502

Url's Internet Cafe
Get on the Internet and do Stuff.

Url Ratz P.O. Box 23465
Browser Dawg Santa Fe
New Mexico
87502

Notice how these three pieces have essentially the same layout. Work on all three pieces at the same time to make sure your chosen layout will work in each situation.

Feel free to use type and graphics in a huge way or a small way.

Uncenter the format. Those strong lines of flush left and flush right add strength to your design.

Tips on letterhead and envelope design

Design your letterhead and envelope at the same time as your business card. They should look like they belong together—if you give someone a business card and then later send a letter, those pieces should reinforce each other.

Envelope size

The standard business envelope is **9½ x 4⅛ inches.** It's called a #10 envelope. The European size is 110 mm x 220 mm, and it's called a C4 envelope.

Create a focal point

One element should be **dominant,** and it should be dominant in the same way on the letterhead, the envelope, and the business card. Please avoid the boring centered-across-the-top layout on the letterhead!

Alignment

Choose one **alignment** for your stationery! Don't center something across the top and then put the rest of the text flush left. Be brave—try flush right down the side with lots of linespacing. Try setting your company name in huge letters across the top. Try placing your logo (or a piece of it) huge and light as a shadow beneath the area where you will type.

On the letterhead, make sure to arrange the elements so when you type the actual letter, the text fits neatly into the design of the stationery.

Second page

If you can afford to make a second page to your stationary, take a **small element** that appears on your first page and use it all by itself on a second page. If you are planning to print, say, 1,000 sheets of letterhead, you can usually ask the printshop to print something like 800 of the first page and 200 of the second page. Even if you don't plan to print a second page, ask the printer for several hundred blank sheets of the same paper so you have *something* on which to write longer letters.

Faxing and copying

If you ever plan to send your letterhead through **fax** or **copy machines,** don't choose a dark paper or one that has lots of speckles in it. Also avoid large areas of dark ink, reverse type, or tiny type that will get lost in the process. If you do a *lot* of faxing, you might want to create two versions of your letterhead—one for print and one for fax.

Flyers

Flyers are great fun to create because you can safely abandon restraint! This is a great place to go wild and really call attention to yourself. As you know, flyers compete with all the other readable junk in the world, especially with other flyers. Often they are posted on a bulletin board with dozens of competing pages that are all trying to grab the attention of passers-by.

A flyer is one of the best places to use fun and different typefaces, and a fun face is one of the best ways to **call attention** to a headline. Don't be a wimp—this is your chance to use one of those really off-the-wall faces you've been lusting after!

And what a great place to experiment with graphics. Just try making the graphic image or photograph at least twice the size you originally planned. Or make the headline 400 point instead of 24. Or create a minimalist flyer with one line of 10-point type in the middle of the page and a small block of text at the bottom. Anything out of the ordinary will make people stop and look, and that is 90 percent of your goal.

Don't do this!

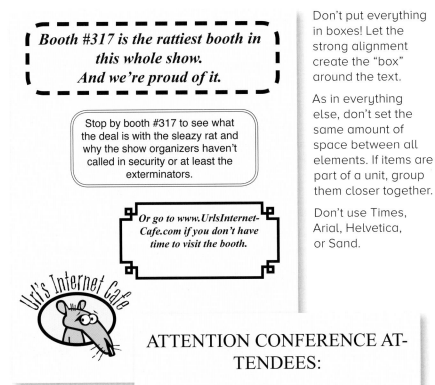

Booth #317 is the rattiest booth in this whole show. And we're proud of it.

Stop by booth #317 to see what the deal is with the sleazy rat and why the show organizers haven't called in security or at least the exterminators.

Or go to www.UrlsInternet-Cafe.com if you don't have time to visit the booth.

Don't put everything in boxes! Let the strong alignment create the "box" around the text.

As in everything else, don't set the same amount of space between all elements. If items are part of a unit, group them closer together.

Don't use Times, Arial, Helvetica, or Sand.

Don't use hyphens to call out bullet points. Instead, try using characters from Wingdings or Zapf Dingbats.

Don't center everything on the page and then put small pieces of text in the corners!

Avoid a gray, boring page—add contrast.

Watch the line endings—there's no need to break lines at awkward places or to hyphenate unnecessarily.

ATTENTION CONFERENCE AT-TENDEES:

- Never before has this conference allowed booth space for such a disgusting character as Url Ratz.

- Stop by booth #317 to see what possible redeeming traits he could possibly have that would allow someone like him into this exhibit hall.

-While you're there, get some free stuff before they call in the exterminators.

- Or stop by his web site: www.UrlsInternet-Cafe.com

URL'S INTERNET CAFE
www.UrlsInternetCafe.com

Try this . . .

Booth #317 is the <u>rattiest</u> booth in this whole show.

And we're proud of it!

Stop by booth #317
to see what the deal is
with the sleazy rat and why
the show organizers haven't
called in security or at least t
exterminators.
Or go to **www.UrlsInternetC**
if you don't have time to visi

Use a huge headline or huge clip art.

Use an interesting typeface in a huge way.

Crop a photograph or clip art into a tall narrow shape; place it along the left edge; align the text flush left.

Or place the art along the right edge and align the text flush right.

Or set the text in several columns, each one flush left.

It's okay to set the body text small on a flyer. If you capture the reader's attention in the first place, she will read the small type.

Attention Conference Attendees:

Never before has this conference
allowed booth space for such
a disgusting character as Url Ratz.
Visit booth #317 and ask about possible
redeeming traits that might allow someone
like him into this respectable exhibit hall.
While you're there, get some of the free stuff
stamped with **www.UrlsInternetCafe.com**
before someone calls an exterminator.

There's a Rat in Booth #317

Tips on designing flyers

The biggest problems with most flyers created by new designers are a lack of contrast and a presentation of information that has no hierarchy. That is, the initial tendency is to make everything large, thinking that it needs to grab someone's attention. But if *everything* is large, then *nothing* can really grab a reader's attention. Use a strong focal point and contrast to organize the information and lead the reader's eye through the page.

Create a focal point

Put one thing on your page that is huge and interesting and **strong.** If you catch their eye with your focal point, they are more likely to read the rest of the text.

Use subheads that contrast

After the focal point, use strong subheads (strong visually, and strong in what it says) so readers can quickly **scan** the flyer to determine the point of the message. If the subheads don't interest them, they're not going to read the copy. But if there are no subheads at all and readers have to read every word on the flyer to understand what it's about, they're going to toss it rather than spend the time deciphering the text.

Repetition

Whether your headline uses an ugly typeface, a beautiful one, or an ordinary one in an unusual way, try to pull a little of that same font into the body of the text for **repetition.** Perhaps use just one letter or one word in that same typeface. Use it as your subheads, initial caps, or perhaps as bullets. A strong contrast of typefaces will add interest to your flyer.

Alignment

And remember, choose one alignment! Don't center the headline and then set the body copy flush left, or don't center everything on the page and then stick things in the corners at the bottom. Be strong. Be brave. Try all flush left or flush right.

Newsletters

One of the most important features of a multiple-page publication is consistency, or **repetition.** Every page should look like it belongs to the whole piece. You can do this with color, graphic style, fonts, spatial arrangements, bulleted lists that repeat a formatting style, borders around photographs, captions, etc.

Now, this doesn't mean that everything has to look exactly the same! But (just as in life) if you have a solid foundation you can get away with breaking out of that foundation with glee (and people won't worry about you). Experiment with graphics at a tilt or photographs cropped very wide and narrow and spread across three columns. With that solid foundation, you can set something like the president's letter for your newsletter in a special format and it will really stand out.

It's okay to have white space (empty space) in your newsletter. But don't let the white space become "trapped" between other elements. The white space needs to be as organized as the visible elements. Let it be there, and let it flow.

One of the first and most fun things to design in a newsletter is the flag (sometimes called the masthead, although the masthead is actually the part inside that tells you who runs the magazine). The flag is the piece that sets the tone for the rest of the newsletter.

Don't do this!

Don't be a wimp about your flag (the title of your newsletter on the front page). Tell people who you are!

Don't create a flat, gray newsletter. Use contrasting type where appropriate, create pull-quotes, and add other visually interesting elements to pull the reader's eye into the page.

On the other hand, don't use a different typeface and arrangement for every article. If you create a strong, consistent, under-lying structure throughout the newsletter, then you can call attention to a special article by treating it differently.

If everything is different, nothing is special.

Try this . . .

Most people skim through newsletter pages picking out headlines—so make the headlines clear and bold.

You can see the underlying structure of the text here. With the solidity of that structure, the graphics can really juice up the pages by being tilted, enlarged, text-wrapped, etc.

Take a few minutes to verbalize how all four of the basic principles of design appear in a multiple-page publication like this, and notice the effect of each principle.

Tips on designing newsletters

The biggest problems with newsletters seem to be lack of alignment, lack of contrast, and too much Helvetica (Arial is another name for Helvetica).

Alignment

Choose an alignment and stick to it. Trust me—you'll have a stronger and more professional look to your entire newsletter if you maintain that strong edge along the left. And keep everything else aligned. If you use rules (lines), they should begin and end in alignment with something else, like the column edge or column bottom. If your photograph hangs outside the column one-quarter inch, crop it so it aligns instead.

You see, if all the elements are neatly aligned, then when appropriate you can freely break out of that alignment with gusto. But don't be a wimp about breaking the alignment—either align the item or don't. Placement that is a *little bit* out of alignment looks like a mistake. If your photo does not fit neatly into the column, then let it break out of the column boldly, not barely.

Paragraph indents

First paragraphs, even after subheads, should not be indented. When you do indent, use the standard typographic indent of one "em" space, which is a space as wide as the point size of your type; that is, if you're using 11-point type, your indent should be 11 points (about two spaces, not five). Use *either* extra space between paragraphs *or* an indent, but *not* both.

Not Helvetica!

If your newsletter looks a little gray and drab, you can instantly juice it up simply by using a strong, heavy, sans serif typeface for your headlines and subheads. Not Helvetica. The Helvetica or Arial that came with your computer isn't bold enough to create a strong contrast. Invest in a sans serif family that includes a heavy black version as well as a light version (such as Eurostile, Formata, Syntax, Frutiger, or Myriad). Use that heavy black for your headlines and pull-quotes and you'll be amazed at the difference. Or use an appropriate decorative face for the headlines, perhaps in another color.

Readable body copy

For best readability, try a classic oldstyle serif face (such as Garamond, Jenson, Caslon, Minion, or Palatino), or a lightweight slab serif (such as Clarendon, Bookman, Kepler, or New Century Schoolbook). What you're reading right now is Warnock Pro Light from Adobe. If you use a sans serif font, give a little extra linespace (leading) and shorter line lengths.

Brochures

Brochures are a quick and inexpensive way to get the word out about your brand new homemade-pie business, school fundraiser, or upcoming scavenger hunt. Dynamic, well-designed brochures can be "eye candy" for readers, drawing them in and educating them in a delightful and painless way.

Armed with the basic design principles, you can create eye-grabbing brochures of your own. The tips on the next couple of pages will help.

Before you sit down to design the brochure, fold a piece of paper into the intended shape and make notes on each flap. Pretend you just found it—in what order do you read the panels?

Keep in mind the order in which the panels of a brochure are presented to the reader as they open it. For instance, when a reader opens the front cover, they should not be confronted with the copyright and contact information.

The fold measurements are not the same on the front as they are on the back! After you fold your paper sample, measure from left to right on front and back. **Do not simply divide 11 inches into thirds**—it won't work because one panel must be slightly shorter to tuck inside the other panel.

A brochure can be your number-one marketing tool.

It's important to be aware of the folds; you don't want important information disappearing into the creases! **If you have a strong alignment for the text** on each panel of the brochure, however, feel free to let the graphics cross over the space between the columns of text (the **gutter**) and into the fold. See the example on page 129.

The three-fold style shown to the left is by far the most commonly seen for brochures because it works so well for letter-sized paper, but there are lots of other fold options available. Check with your print shop.

The brochure examples on the following pages are set up for a standard, 8.5 x 11-inch, three-fold brochure like this one.

Don't do this!

Url Ratz©, to be specific.

I'm Url. I'm a rat. As Head-Rodent-In-Charge (HRIC) of **Url's Internet Cafe,** it's my job to keep the cafe stocked with stuff that most computer users need . . . like lab coats and RatPadz© with my picture on them.

I feel confident that you won't find anything ~~uglier~~ more useful anywhere.

Get on the Internet and do stuff.©

Visit Url's Internet Cafe on the World Wide Web and meet all the cafe regulars: Browser, the full-blooded Net-Hound; Lilac, Url's neo-Luddite girlfriend; Dimm Simm, the humorless landlady; Gig Megaflop, a has-been thespian; Amanda Reckonwith, advice columnist; also special columns by Robin Williams, author and speaker, plus sports commentary by Url Ratz. There's more, but, unlike the web site, we're out of space.

Url's Internet Cafe

www.UrlsInternetCafe.com

Url's Internet Cafe

If you use the Internet, we've got one thing to say to you: Ratz.

P.O. Box 23465
Santa Fe, NM 87505

Don't set items centered and flush left on the cover (or inside)! Pick one alignment. Please.

Don't use 12-point type for your body copy. Besides looking unsophisticated, 12-point in most typefaces is too large for the column width in a standard three-fold brochure.

Don't set the copy too close to the fold. Remember that you're going to fold the paper down the middle of the column gutter, so allow more room between columns in a brochure than you would in a newsletter.

Try this . . .

Which panel will the reader see first? second? This brochure is designed to draw the reader in little by little.

After the initial powerful greeting on the cover panel, the reader gets an introduction to the mascot for the company on the next panel, then finally opens to the inside of the brochure.

Notice how contrast of color and size are used here.

Play with the graphic images in your brochure—make them bigger, overlap them, wrap text around them, tilt them. You can do all this if your text presents a solid, aligned base.

See how the only things that cross the gutter (the fold area in-between text blocks) are pieces of art? Graphics don't get lost in the fold.

Tips on designing brochures

Brochures created by new designers have many of the same problems as newsletters: lack of contrast, lack of alignment, and too much Helvetica/Arial. Here's a quick summary of how the principle elements of design can be applied to that brochure you're working on.

Contrast

As in any other design project, contrast not only adds visual interest to a page so a reader's eye is drawn in, but it also helps create the hierarchy of information so the reader can scan the important points and understand what the brochure is about. Use contrast in the typefaces, rules, colors, spacing, size of elements, etc. Remember that the only way contrast is effective is if it's strong—if two elements are not exactly the same, make sure they are **very** different. Otherwise it looks like a mistake. Don't be a wimp.

Repetition

Repeat various elements in the design to create a **unified look** to the piece. You might repeat colors, typefaces, rules, spatial arrangements, bullets, etc.

Alignment

I keep repeating myself about this alignment stuff, but it's important, and the lack of it is consistently a problem. **Strong, sharp edges** create a strong, sharp impression. A combination of alignments (using centered, flush left, and flush right in one piece) usually creates a sloppy, weak impression.

Occasionally, you may want to intentionally break out of the alignment (as I did on the previous page); **this works best if you have other strong alignments** to contrast with the breakout.

Proximity

Proximity, **grouping** similar items close together, is especially important in a project such as a brochure where you have a variety of subtopics within one main topic. How close and how far away items are from each other communicates the relationships of the items.

To create the spatial arrangements effectively, **you must know how to use your software** to create space between the paragraphs (space before or space after) instead of hitting the Enter or Return key twice. Two Returns between paragraphs creates a larger gap than you need, forcing items apart that should be close together. Two Returns also creates the same amount of space *above* a headline or subhead as there is *below* the head (which you don't want), and it separates bulleted items that should be closer together. Learn that software!

Postcards

Because they're so visual and so immediate—no envelopes to fuss with, no paper cuts—postcards are a great way to grab attention. And for these same reasons, an ugly or boring postcard is a waste of everybody's time.

So, to avoid waste, remember the following:

Be different. Oversized or oddly shaped postcards will stand out from that crowd in the mailbox. (Check with the post office, though, to make sure your shape will go through the mail!)

Think "series." A single postcard makes one impression; just think what a series of several could do!

Be specific. Tell the recipient exactly how they'll benefit (and what they need to do to get that benefit).

Keep it brief. Use the front of the postcard for a short and attention-getting message. Put less important details on the back.

If possible, use color. Besides being fun to work with, color attracts the eye and draws interest.

Don't forget: white space is a design element, too!

Don't do this!

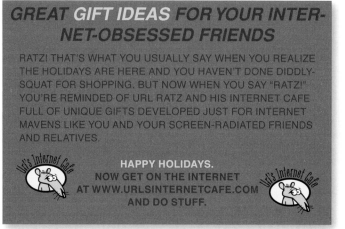

What's wrong with this headline?

Don't use 12-point Helvetica, Arial, Times, or Sand.

Don't set information in all caps—it is so difficult to read that few will bother. They didn't ask for the card in the first place, did they?

Use contrast and spatial relationships to communicate a message clearly.

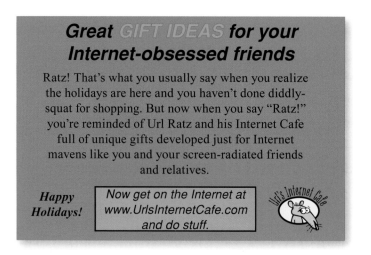

The guidelines for business cards (pages 111–114) also apply to postcards: don't stick things in the corners; don't think you have to fill the space; don't make everything the same size or almost the same size.

Try this . . .

Great gift ideas for your Internet-obsessed friends

Ratz! That's what you usually say when you realize the holidays are here and you haven't done diddly-squat for shopping. But now when you say "Ratz!" you're reminded of Url Ratz and his Internet Cafe full of **unique gifts** developed just for Internet mavens like you and your screen-radiated friends and relatives. Happy Holidays.

Now get on the Internet at **UrlsInternetCafe.com** and do stuff.

Try an odd size postcard, such as tall and narrow, short and fat, oversized, or a fold-over card.

Just be sure to take your intended size and paper to the post office and make sure it fits regulations before you print it, or check the web site (usps.gov). And verify the cost of postage for an odd-sized card.

As in any piece where you need to get someone's attention instantly, create a hierarchy of information so the reader can scan the card and make a quick decision as to whether they want to read the rest of it or not.

Great gift ideas for your Internet-obsessed friends

Ratz! That's what you usually say when you realize the holidays are here and and you haven't done diddly-squat for shopping. But now when you say "Ratz!" you're reminded of Url Ratz and his Internet Cafe full of unique gifts developed just for Internet mavens like you and your screen-radiated friends and relatives. Happy Holidays. Now get on the Internet at **UrlsInternetCafe.com** and do stuff.

Tips on designing postcards

You only have a split second to capture someone's attention with an unsolicited postcard that arrives in the mail. No matter how great your copy, if the design of the card does not attract their attention, they won't read your copy.

What's your point?

Your first decision is to determine what sort of effect you want to achieve. Do you want readers to think it is an expensive, exclusive offer? Then your postcard had better look as expensive and professional as the product. Do you want readers to feel like they're getting a great bargain? Then your postcard shouldn't be too slick. Discount stores spend extra money to make their stores look like they contain bargains. It's not an accident that Saks Fifth Avenue has a different look—from the parking lot to the restrooms—than does Kmart, and it doesn't mean that Kmart spent less on decor than did Saks. Each look serves a distinct and definite purpose and reaches out toward a specific market.

Grab their attention

The same design guidelines apply to direct-mail postcards as to anything else: contrast, repetition, alignment, and proximity. But with this kind of postcard, you have very little time to induce recipients into reading it. **Be brave** with bright colors, either in the ink or the card stock. Use striking graphics — there's plenty of great and inexpensive clipart and picture fonts that you can use in all sorts of creative ways.

Contrast

Contrast is probably your best friend in a direct-mail postcard. The headline should be in strong contrast to the rest of the text, the colors should use strong contrast to each other and to the color of the paper stock. And don't forget that **white space** creates contrast!

Newspaper ads

A well-designed newspaper ad can work wonders for an advertiser; however, looking good is not all it takes to be successful in newsprint. Here are a few hints that will help even the sexiest ad rake in results:

White space! Take note of where your eyes go next time you scan the newspaper. Which ads do your eyes naturally land on, and which ads do you actually read? I'll bet you see and read at least the headlines of the ads that have more white space.

Be clever. There's nothing that can compete with a clever headline. Not even good design. (But with both, the possibilities multiply!)

Be clear. Once your catchy headline has garnered some attention, your ad should specifically tell readers what to do (and give them the means to do so; i.e., phone number, email address, web address, etc.).

Be brief. Your ad is not the place to put your life story. Keep the copy simple and to the point.

Use color when you can. It always attracts the eye, particularly when surrounded by a sea of gray text.

wintertime flower sale

Url took care all summer so you could have fresh flowers this winter.

Flowers 2/$5   All day Saturday, January 25   9–6   Url's Internet Cafe

Ads don't have to scream to be effective.

Don't do this!

THIS IS THE TECHNOLOGY AGE. LAB COATS FOR SALE.

> You could also use a t-shirt that tells your clients the Internet facts of life. And coffees blended specifically for web surfers.

You'll need matching mugs for the coffee and most likely you'll want original RatPadz© to replace those clunky old mouse pads you have just lying around the office.

Did we mention polo shirts, caps, gift boxes, and do-rags? Prepare yourself for the Technology Age: visit Url's Internet Cafe for great gift ides and a cafe full of educational, fun stuff.

www.UrlsInternetCafe.com

If your headline doesn't grab their attention, they won't read your body copy no matter how big you set it. (If you get rid of the caps, your headline can be set much larger.)

Don't make all the text the same size. Call out your headline, but once you catch the reader's eye and mind with your headline, they will read the rest of the text, even if it's 9-point type.

WOULD YOU BUY A LAB COAT FROM AN UGLY RAT?

You may not think so now, but just wait 'til you see the lab coats, t-shirts, caps, polo shirts, special coffees, teas, mugs, RatPadz©, and other great gift ideas at Url's Internet Cafe.

But people don't come here just to shop. It's a cafe where just hangin' out is an art form. And when that sudden impulse to buy a lab coat hits, we've got 'em right here. So, if you think he's a sleazy, ugly rat, you're right. But come on, how many handsome lab coat salesmen do you know?

www.UrlsInternetCafe.com
P.O. Box 23465
Santa Fe, NM 87505
(505) 424-1115

Don't cram the space full! I know you paid for it, but white space is just as valuable and well worth the money.

Unless your ad offers valuable, free information that a reader really wants to know and can't get anywhere else, don't stuff it. Let there be white space.

Try this . . .

This is the Technology Age.

You need a lab coat.

You could also use a t-shirt that tells your clients the Internet facts of life (exhibit A). And coffees blended specifically for web surfers. You'll need matching mugs for the coffee and most likely you'll want original RatPadz© to replace those clunky old mouse pads you have just lying around the office. Did we mention polo shirts, caps, gift boxes, and do-rags? Prepare yourself for the Technology Age: visit Url's Internet Cafe for great gift ideas and a cafe full of educational, fun stuff.

Web site work is never done.

(exhibit A)

Url's Internet Cafe

UrlsInternetCafe.com

White space is good. The trick about white space is that it needs to be organized. In the first ad on the opposite page, there is just as much white space as there is in this ad to the right, but it's sprawled all over the place.

Organize the white space just as consciously as you organize the information. If you follow the other four principles of design, the white space will automatically end up where it should.

Would you buy a lab coat from an ugly rat?

You may not think so now, but just wait 'til you see the lab coats, t-shirts, caps, polo shirts, special coffees, teas, mugs, Ratpadz©, and other great gift ideas at Url's Internet Cafe. But people don't come here just to shop. It's a cafe where just hangin' out is an art form. And when that sudden impulse to to buy a lab coat hits, we've got 'em right here. So, if you think he's a sleazy, ugly rat, you're right. But come on, how many handsome lab coat salesmen do you know?

Url's Internet Cafe

65 Ratznest Way
Santa Fe, New Mexico
UrlsInternetCafe.com

As with any other design project, use contrast, repetition, alignment, and proximity. Can you name where each of those concepts have been used in these ads?

Tips on designing newspaper ads

One of the biggest problems with newspaper ads is crowding. Many clients and businesses who are paying for a newspaper ad feel they need to fill every particle of space because it costs money.

Contrast

With a newspaper ad, you need contrast not only in the advertisement itself, but also between the ad and the rest of the newspaper page that it's placed on. In this kind of ad, the best way to create contrast is with white space. Newspaper pages tend to be completely full of stuff and very busy. An ad that has lots of white space within it stands out on the page, and a reader's eye can't help but be drawn to it. Experiment. Open a newspaper page (or a phone book page) and scan it. I guarantee that if there is white space on that page, your eyes will go to it. They go there because white space provides a strong contrast on a full, busy page.

Once you have white space, your headline doesn't need to be in a big, fat, typeface screaming to compete with everything else. You can actually get away with a beautiful script or a classy oldstyle instead of a heavy face.

Type choices

Newsprint is porous, coarse paper, and the ink spreads on it. So don't use a typeface that has small, delicate serifs or very thin lines that will thicken when printed, unless you are setting the type large enough that the serifs and strokes will hold up.

Reverse type

Avoid reverse type (white type on a dark background) if possible, but if you must have it, make sure you use a good solid typeface with no thin lines that will fill in when the ink spreads. As always when setting type in reverse, use a point size a wee bit larger and bolder than you would if it was not reversed because the optical illusion makes reverse type appear smaller and thinner.

Web sites

While the same four basic principles I've mentioned over and over in this book (contrast, repetition, alignment, proximity) also apply to web design, **repetition** is one of the most important for a web site. The other three principles help the pages look good and make sense, but repetition lets your visitors know whether they're still in the same web site. You should have a consistent navigation system and graphic style so your visitors always know they are in the same web site. Repeating a color scheme, the same typefaces, buttons, or similar-style graphic elements placed in the same position on each page will do the trick.

Designing a web site is quite a bit different from designing printed pieces. If you're brand-new to web design and want to learn how to get started, you really should check out *The Non-Designer's Web Book.*

Your web site should be inviting and easy to move around in. This site is clean and simple.

Google.com is a great example of a fabulous, useful, yet clean and simple site.

Don't do this!

Don't make visitors scroll to see the navigation links!

Don't let text bump up against the left edge of the browser window.

Don't use the default blue color for your text or graphic links. It's a sure sign of an amateur page.

Don't make text links within big, dorky, table cells with the borders turned on.

Don't use bold type for your body copy, and please don't let your body copy run the entire width of the page.

Don't use a fluorescent background color, especially with fluorescent type!

Don't make the visitor scroll sideways!! Keep your page within the 800-pixel width maximum. Especially don't make a table that is wider than 600 pixels or people will be very mad at you when they try to print your page.

Try this . . .

Keep your entry page and your home page within a framework of 800 pixels wide by 600 pixels deep. A visitor should not have to scroll on a home page to find the links!

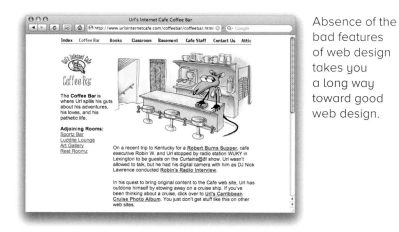

Absence of the bad features of web design takes you a long way toward good web design.

Take a look at Peachpit.com or Adobe.com. Name at least five things that provide the visitor with a consistent look-and-feel so the visitor always knows, no matter what page they are on, that they are in that site.

Put into words exactly what makes the difference between the examples on these two pages. Naming the design features—both good and bad features—out loud helps you design better.

Tips on designing web pages

Two of the most important factors in good web design are **repetition and clarity/readability.** A visitor should never have to figure out how to use your navigation system, where they are in the site, or whether they are still in your web site or have jumped somewhere else.

Repetition

Repeat certain visual elements on every page in your web site. This not only lets the visitor know they are still at your site, but also provides unity and continuity, intrinsic features of any good design.

Once you get to content pages, the visitor should find the navigation in the same place, in the same order, with the same graphics. Not only does this make it easy for the visitor to find their way through your site, but it provides a **unifying factor** to the collection of pages.

Clarity/Readability

One of the most unreadable places to read text is on a monitor, whether it's television, video, or computer. So we need to make a few adjustments to the text on web pages to make sure it's as easy to read as possible.

Use **shorter line lengths** than you might use on paper. The body copy should never run the entire width of the web page, which means you must put the text in a table or use CSS code (or at least use a block indent, which indents the text from both the left and right sides). But don't use such short line lengths that you break up the phrasing of the sentences too much.

If you are specifying the text to appear in a certain typeface (if you're not, ignore this), typically Helvetica or Arial and Times or Times Roman, please specify Geneva or Verdana or Trebuchet in front of Helvetica, and New York or Georgia in front of Times. This will make the text on Macintoshes appear so much cleaner and easier to read. (If you use a Mac, set your default font to New York instead of Times, and you will be amazed at how much easier it is to read web pages. Change it back to Times before you print a page.) Verdana and Trebuchet are found on all operating systems updated within the past few years, and they're excellent choices for body copy on the web.

Designing TYPE with

The second half of this book
deals specifically with type,
since type is what design
is all about, yes?
This section particularly
addresses the problem
of combining more than one
typeface on the page.

Although I focus
on the aesthetics of type,
never forget
that your purpose is
communication.
The type should never
inhibit the communication.

typefaces
Miss Tizzardone
Tabitha
Onyx

WHAT TYPE SHALL I USE?

The gods refuse
to answer.

They refuse
because
they
do not
know.

W.A. DWIGGINS

typefaces
PERCOLATOR EXPERT
Shannon Book Oblique
ITC Golden Cockerel Initial Ornaments

Type (& Life)

Type is the basic building block of any printed page. Often it is irresistibly compelling and sometimes absolutely imperative to design a page with more than one typeface on it. But how do you know which typefaces work effectively together?

In Life, when there is more than one of anything, a dynamic relationship is established. In Type, there is usually more than one element on a page—even a document of plain body copy typically has heads or subheads or at least page numbers on it. Within these dynamics on the page (or in Life), a relationship is established that is either concordant, conflicting, or contrasting.

A **concordant** relationship occurs when you use only one type family without much variety in style, size, weight, and so on. It is easy to keep the page harmonious, and the arrangement tends to appear quiet and rather sedate or formal—sometimes downright dull.

A **conflicting** relationship occurs when you combine typefaces that are *similar* (but not the same) in style, size, weight, and so on. The similarities are disturbing because the visual attractions are not the same (concordant), but neither are they different (contrasting), so they conflict.

A **contrasting** relationship occurs when you combine separate typefaces and elements that are clearly distinct from each other. The visually appealing and exciting designs that attract your attention typically have a lot of contrast built in, and those contrasts are emphasized.

Most designers tend to wing it when combining more than one typeface on a page. You might have a sense that one face needs to be larger or an element needs to be bolder. However, when you can recognize and *name the contrasts,* you have power over them—you can then get to the root of the conflicting problem faster and find more interesting solutions. And *that* is the point of this section.

Concord

A design is concordant when you choose to use just one face and the other elements on the page have the same qualities as that typeface. Perhaps you use some of the italic version of the font, and perhaps a larger size for a heading, and maybe a graphic or several ornaments— but the basic impression is still concordant.

Most concordant designs tend to be rather calm and formal. This does not mean concord is undesirable—just be aware of the impression you give by using elements that are all in concord with each other.

*L*ife's but a walking shadow, a poor player

that struts and frets his hour upon the stage,

and then is heard no more; it is a tale

told by an idiot, *full of sound and fury,*

signifying nothing.

This concordant example uses Cochin. The first letter is larger and there is some italic type (Cochin Italic), but the entire piece is rather calm and subdued.

typefaces
Cochin Medium *and Italic*

typefaces
Aachen Bold
Linoscript (with Type Embellishments Three)

Hello!

My name is _____

My theme song is _____

When I grow up I want to be _____

The heavy typeface (Aachen Bold) combines well with the heavy border. Even the line for writing on is heavy.

You are cordially invited

to share in our

wedding celebration

Popeye & Olive Oyl

April 1

3 o'clock in the afternoon

Berkeley Square

The typeface (Linoscript), the thin border, and the delicate ornaments all give the same style impression.

Look familiar? Lots of folks play it safe with their wedding invitations by using the principle of concord. That's not a bad thing! But it should be a conscious thing.

Conflict

A design is in conflict when you set two or more typefaces on the same page that are *similar*—not really different and not really the same. I have seen countless students trying to match a typeface with one on the page, looking for a face that "looks similar." Wrong. When you put two faces together that look too much alike without really being so, most of the time it looks like a mistake. *The problem is in the similarities* because the similarities conflict.

Concord is a solid and useful concept; **conflict** should be avoided.

L ife's but a walking shadow, a poor player
that struts and frets his hour upon the stage,
and then is heard no more; it is a tale
told by an idiot, **full of sound and fury,**
signifying nothing.

As you read this example, what happens when you get to the phrase, "full of sound and fury"? Do you wonder why it's in another typeface? Do you wonder if perhaps it's a mistake? Does it make you twitch? Does the large initial letter look like it's supposed to be there?

typefaces
Cochin Medium and ITC Garamond Light

typefaces
Bailey Sans Extra Bold and Antique Olive Roman
Linoscript and Shelley Volante Script
Adobe Wood Type Ornaments Two

What's up?

My name is _____

My theme song is _____

When I grow up I want to be _____

Look particularly at the "a," the "t," and the "s" in the headline and the other lines. They are similar but not the same. The border is not the same visual weight as the type or the lines, nor are they in strong contrast. There is too much conflict in this little piece.

You are cordially invited

to share in our

wedding celebration

Popeye & Olive Oyl

April 1

3 o'clock in the afternoon

Berkeley Square

This small invitation uses two different scripts—they have many similarities with each other, but they are not the same and they are not different.

The ornaments have the same type of conflict—too many similarities. The piece looks a bit cluttered.

Contrast

There is no quality in this world that is not what it is merely by contrast. Nothing exists in itself. —Herman Melville

Now this is the fun part. Creating concord is pretty easy, and creating conflict is easy but undesirable. Creating contrast is just fun.

Strong contrast attracts our eyes, as you learned in the previous section about design. One of the most effective, simplest, and satisfying ways to add contrast to a design is with type.

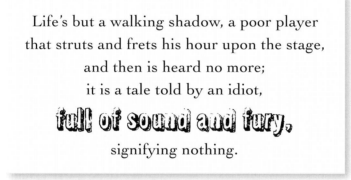

Life's but a walking shadow, a poor player
that struts and frets his hour upon the stage,
and then is heard no more;
it is a tale told by an idiot,
full of sound and fury,
signifying nothing.

In this example it's very clear that the phrase "full of sound and fury" is supposed to be in another typeface. The entire piece of prose has a more exciting visual attraction and a greater energy due to the contrast of type.

typefaces
Cochin Medium and *flyswim*

typefaces
Antique Olive Black and Roman
LITHOS EXTRA LIGHT
Zanzibar

Hello!

My name is _____

My theme song is _____

When I grow up I want to be _____

Now the contrast between the typefaces is clear (they are actually in the same family, Antique Olive)—the very bold face contrasts the light face. The line weights of the border and writing lines also have a clear distinction.

YOU ARE CORDIALLY INVITED
TO SHARE IN OUR
WEDDING CELEBRATION!

Popeye
& Olive Oyl

APRIL 1

3 O'CLOCK

 IN THE AFTERNOON

BERKELEY SQUARE

This invitation uses two very different faces— they are different in many ways.

The font for Popeye and Olive Oyl (called Zanzibar) includes ornaments (one of which is shown here) that work well with the typeface.

Summary

Contrast is not just for the aesthetic look of the piece. It is intrinsically tied in with the organization and clarity of the information on the page. Never forget that your point is to communicate. Combining different typefaces should enhance the communication, not confuse it.

There are six clear and distinct ways to contrast type: size, weight, structure, form, direction, and color. The rest of this book talks about each of these contrasts in turn.

Although I elaborate on each of the contrasts one at a time, rarely is one contrast effective. Most often you will strengthen the effect by combining and emphasizing the differences.

If you have trouble seeing what is wrong with a combination of typefaces, don't look for what is *different* between the faces—look for what is *similar.* It is the similarities that are causing the problem.

The major rule to follow when contrasting type is this: *Don't be a wimp!*

But...

Before we get to the ways to contrast, you need to have a familiarity with the categories of type. Spend a couple of minutes with each page in the next chapter, noting the similarities that unify a category of type. Then try to find a couple of examples of that kind of type before you move on to the next category. Look in magazines, books, on packages, anything printed. Believe me, taking a few moments to do this will make everything sink in so much faster and deeper!

Categories of Type

There are many thousands of different typefaces available right now, and many more are being created every day. Most faces, though, can be dropped into one of the six categories mentioned below. Before you try to become conscious of the *contrasts* in type, you should become aware of the *similarities* between broad groups of type designs, because it is the *similarities* that cause the conflicts in type combinations. The purpose of this chapter is to make you more aware of the details of letterforms. In the following chapter I'll launch into combining them.

Of course, you will find hundreds of faces that don't fit neatly into any category. We could make several hundred different categories for the varieties in type—don't worry about it. The point is just to start looking at type more closely and clearly.

I focus on these six groups:

Oldstyle

Modern

Slab serif

Sans serif

Script

Decorative—INCLUDING GRUNGY!

Oldstyle

Typefaces created in the **oldstyle** category are based on the handlettering of scribes—you can imagine a wedge-tipped pen held in the hand. Oldstyles always have serifs (see the call-out below) and the serifs of lowercase letters are always at an angle (the angle of the pen). Because of that pen, all the curved strokes in the letterforms have a transition from thick to thin, technically called the "thick/thin transition." This contrast in the stroke is relatively moderate, meaning it goes from kind-of-thin to kind-of-thicker. If you draw a line through the thinnest parts of the curved strokes, the line is diagonal. This is called the *stress*—oldstyle type has a diagonal stress.

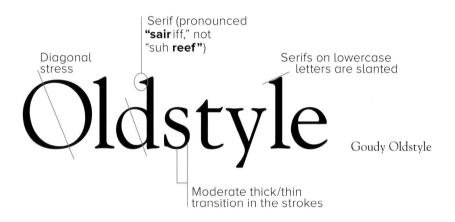

Serif (pronounced **"sair** iff," not "suh **reef")**

Diagonal stress

Serifs on lowercase letters are slanted

Moderate thick/thin transition in the strokes

Goudy Oldstyle

Goudy   Palatino   Times

Baskerville   Garamond

Do these faces all look pretty much the same to you? Don't worry—they look the same to everyone who hasn't studied typography. Their "invisibility" is exactly what makes oldstyles the best type group for extensive amounts of body copy. There are rarely any distinguishing characteristics that get in the way of reading; they don't call attention to themselves. If you're setting lots of type that you want people to actually read, choose an oldstyle.

Modern

Oldstyle faces replicated the humanist pen stokes. But as history marched on, the structure of type changed. Type has trends and succumbs to lifestyle and cultural changes, just like hairdos, clothes, architecture, or language. In the 1700s, smoother paper, more sophisticated printing techniques, and a general increase in mechanical devices led to type becoming more mechanical also. New typefaces no longer followed the pen in hand. Modern typefaces have serifs, but the serifs are now horizontal instead of slanted, and they are very thin. Like a steel bridge, the structure is severe, with a radical thick/thin transition, or contrast, in the strokes. There is no evidence of the slant of the pen; the stress is perfectly vertical. Moderns tend to have a cold, elegant look.

Vertical stress

Serifs on lowercase letters
are thin and horizontal

Bodoni Poster Compressed

Radical thick/thin transition
in the strokes

Bodoni   **Times Bold**   Onyx

Didot, **Bold**   Walbaum

Modern typefaces have a striking appearance, especially when set very large. Because of their strong thick/thin transitions, most moderns are not good choices for extended amounts of body copy—the thin lines almost disappear, the thick lines are prominent, and the effect on the page is called "dazzling."

Slab serif

Along with the industrial revolution came a new concept: advertising. At first, advertisers took modern typefaces and made the thicks thicker. You've seen posters with type like that—from a distance, all you see are vertical lines, like a fence. The obvious solution to this problem was to thicken the entire letterform. Slab serifs have little or no thick/thin transition.

This category of type is sometimes called Clarendon, because the typeface Clarendon (shown below) is the epitome of this style. They are also called Egyptian because they became popular during the Egyptomania craze in Western civilization; many typefaces in this category were given Egyptian names so they would sell (Memphis, Cairo, Scarab).

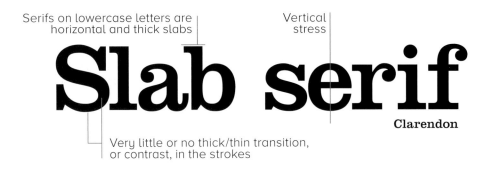

Serifs on lowercase letters are horizontal and thick slabs

Vertical stress

Slab serif

Clarendon

Very little or no thick/thin transition, or contrast, in the strokes

Clarendon   Memphis
New Century Schoolbook
Silica Regular, Light, **Black**

Many of the slab serifs that have a slight thick/thin contrast (such as Clarendon or New Century Schoolbook) are very high on the readability scale, meaning they can easily be used in extensive text. They present an overall darker page than oldstyles, though, because their strokes are thicker and relatively monoweight. Slab serifs are often used in children's books because of their clean, straightforward look.

Sans serif

The word "sans" means "without" (in French), so sans serif typefaces are those without serifs on the ends of the strokes. The idea of removing the serifs was a rather late development in the evolution of type and didn't become wildly successful until the early part of the twentieth century.

Sans serif typefaces are almost always "monoweight," meaning there is virtually no visible thick/thin transition in the strokes; the letterforms are the same thickness all the way around.

Also see the following page for important information on sans serif.

No serifs anywhere

No stress because there's no thick/thin

No thick/thin transition in the strokes

Franklin Gothic

Proxima Nova   Formata

Folio   Shannon Book, **Bold**

Bailey Sans, **Bold**   Syntax

If the only sans serifs you have in your font library are Helvetica/Arial and Avant Garde, the best thing you could do for your pages is invest in a sans serif family that includes a strong, heavy, black face. Each of the families above has a wide variety of weights, from light to extra black. With that one investment, you will be amazed at how your options increase for creating eye-catching pages.

Most sans serifs are monoweight, as shown on the preceding page. A very few, however, have a slight thick/thin transition. Below is an example of Optima, a sans serif with a stress. Faces like Optima are very difficult to combine on a page with other type—they have similarities with serif faces in the thick/thin strokes, and they have similarities with sans serifs in the lack of serifs. Be very careful when working with a sans like this.

Sans serif Optima

Optima is an exceptionally beautiful typeface, but you must be very careful about combining it with other faces. Notice its thick/thin strokes. It has the classic grace of an oldstyle (see page 154), but it's a sans serif.

death
MAKES YOU THINK ABOUT
YOUR IMMORTALITY.
J. PHILIP DAVIS

Here you see Optima (the smaller text) combined with Tabitha. Tabitha's spunky informality is a nice contrast with Optima's classic grace.

Script

The script category includes all those typefaces that appear to have been handlettered with a calligraphy pen or brush, or sometimes with a pencil or technical pen. This category could easily be broken down into scripts that connect, scripts that don't connect, scripts that look like hand printing, scripts that emulate traditional calligraphic styles, and so on. But for our purposes we are going to lump them all into one pot.

Miss Fajardose *Arid* *Ministry Script*
Fountain Pen *Emily Austin*
Cocktail Shaker

Scripts are like cheesecake—they should be used sparingly so nobody gets sick. The fancy ones, of course, should never be set as long blocks of text and *never* as all caps. But scripts can be particularly stunning when set very large—don't be a wimp!

Carpe Diem

typefaces
Linoscript Medium

Decorative

Decorative fonts are easy to identify—if the thought of reading an entire book in that font makes you wanna throw up, you can probably put it in the decorative pot. Decorative fonts are great—they're fun, distinctive, easy to use, oftentimes cheaper, and there is a font for any whim you wish to express. Of course, simply because they *are* so distinctive, their use is limited.

JUNIPER THE WALL Tabitha

Pious Henry FlySwim Blue Island

FAJITA SCARLETT

When using a decorative typeface, go beyond what you think of as its initial impression. For instance, if Pious Henry strikes you as informal, try using it in a more formal situation and see what happens. If you think Juniper carries a Wild West flavor, try it in a corporate setting or a flower shop and see what happens. Depending on how you use them, decoratives can carry obvious emotions, or you can manipulate them into carrying connotations very different from your first impression. But that is a topic for another book.

Wisdom sometimes benefits from the use of decorative fonts.

Be conscious

To use type effectively, you have to be conscious. By that I mean you must keep your eyes open, you must notice details, you must try to state the problem in words. Or when you see something that appeals to you strongly, put into words *why* it appeals to you.

Spend a few minutes and look through a magazine. Try to categorize the typefaces you see. Many of them won't fit neatly into a single pot, but that's okay—choose the category that seems the closest. The point is that you are looking more closely at letterforms, which is absolutely critical if you are going to combine them effectively.

Little Quiz #3: Categories of type

Draw lines to match the category with the typeface!

Oldstyle	**AT THE RODEO**
Modern	High Society
Slab serif	*Too Sassy for Words*
Sans serif	As I remember, Adam
Script	The enigma continues
Decorative	***It's your attitude***

Little Quiz #4: Thick/thin transitions

Do the following typefaces have:

A moderate thick/thin transitions

B radical thick/thin transitions

C no (or negligible) thick/thin transitions

Giggle
A B C

Jiggle
A B C

Diggle
A B C

Piggle
A B C

Higgle
A B C

Wiggle
A B C

Little Quiz #5: Serifs

Do the lowercase letters in the examples below have:

A thin, horizontal serifs

B thick, slabby [hint] horizontal serifs

C no serifs

D slanted serifs

Diggle

A B C D

Riggle

A B C D

Figgle

A B C D

Biggle

A B C D

Miggle

A B C D

Tiggle

A B C D

Notice the huge differences between all the "g" letters! It's too much fun.

Summary

I can't stress enough how important it is that you become conscious of these broad categories of type. As you work through the next chapter, it will become clearer *why* this is important.

A simple exercise to continually hone your visual skills is to collect samples of the categories. Cut them out of any printed material you can find. Do you see any patterns developing within a broad category? Go ahead and make subsets, such as oldstyle typefaces that have small x-heights and tall descenders (see the example below). Or scripts that are really more like hand printing than cursive handwriting. Or extended faces and condensed faces (see below). It is this visual awareness of the letterforms that will give you the power to create interesting, provocative, and effective type combinations.

Ascenders are the parts of letters that are taller than the x-height.

The **x-height** is the height of the main body of the lowercase letters.

Descenders are the parts of letters that are below the **baseline** (the invisible line on which the type sits).

Notice the x-height of Bernhard as compared to Eurostile, below—look at the x-height in relation to the ascenders. Bernhard has an unusually small x-height relative to its ascenders. Most sans serifs have large x-heights. Start noticing those kinds of details.

Eurostile Bold 18 point   Bernhard 18 point
Eurostile Bold Extended
Eurostile Bold Condensed

Extended typefaces look stretched out; condensed typefaces appear to be squished. Both are appropriate in certain circumstances.

Type Contrasts

This chapter focuses on the topic of combining typefaces. The following pages describe the various ways type can be contrasted. Each page shows specific examples, and at the end of this section are examples using these principles of contrasting type on your pages. Type contrast is not only for the aesthetic appeal, but also to enhance the communication.

A reader should never have to try to figure out what is happening on the page—the focus, the organization of material, the purpose, the flow of information, all should be recognized instantly with a single glance. And along the way, it doesn't hurt to make it beautiful!

These are the contrasts I discuss:

typefaces
Tekton Regular
Aachen Bold
Folio Extra Bold
& Warnock Pro Regular
Shelley Volante Script
& Formata Bold
Madrone
Zanzibar Regular

 **Size**

In which category of type does this face belong?

A contrast of size is fairly obvious: big type versus little type. To make a contrast of size work effectively, though, *don't be a wimp.* You cannot contrast 12-point type with 14-point type; most of the time they will simply conflict. You cannot contrast 65-point type with 72-point type. If you're going to contrast two typographic elements through their size, *then do it.* Make it obvious—don't let people think it's a mistake.

HEY, SHE'S CALLING YOU A LITTLE

 **WIMP**

Decide on the typographic element that you want seen as a focus. Emphasize it with contrasts.

A N O T H E R

 **newsletter**

Volume 1 ■ Number 1   January ■ 2010

Often other typographic elements have to be there, but aren't really that important to the general reading public. Make them small. Who cares what the volume number is? If someone does care, it can still be read. It's okay not to set it in 12-point type!

typefaces
Folio Light **and Extra Bold**
ITC American Typewriter Medium **and Bold**

A contrast of size does not always mean you must make the type large—it just means there should be a contrast. For instance, when you see a small line of type alone on a large newspaper page, you are compelled to read it, right? An important part of what compels you is the contrast of very small type on that large page.

If you came across this full page in a newspaper, would you read that small type in the middle? Contrast does that.

Sometimes the contrast of big over little can be overwhelming; it can overpower the smaller type. Use that to your advantage. Who wants to notice the word "incorporated" anyway? Although it's small, it's certainly not invisible so it's there for those who need it.

typefaces

Wade Sans Light
DivaDoodles
Brioso Pro
Memphis Extra Bold and Light

Over and over again I have recommended not to use all caps. You probably use all caps sometimes to make the type larger, yes? Ironically, when type is set in all caps, it takes up a lot more space than the lowercase, so you have to make the point size smaller. If you make the text lowercase, you can actually set it in a much larger point size, plus it's more readable.

MERMAID TAVERN

Bread and Friday Streets
Cheapside • London

This title is in 20-point type. That's the largest size
I can use in this space with all caps.

Mermaid Tavern

Bread and Friday Streets
Cheapside • London

typefaces
Silica Bold
Wendy Medium

By making the title lowercase, I could enlarge it to 28-point
type, plus still have room to make it heavier.

Use a contrast of size in unusual and provocative ways. Many of our typographic symbols, such as numbers, ampersands, or quotation marks, are very beautiful when set extremely large. Use them as decorative elements in a headline or a pull quote, or as repetitive elements throughout a publication.

The Sound & the Fury

An unusual contrast of size can become a graphic element in itself—handy if you are limited in the images that are available for a project.

typefaces
Zanzibar Regular
(Zanzibar Regular)

Travel Tips

 Take twice as much money as you think you'll need.

Take half as much clothing as you think you'll need.

Don't even bother taking all the addresses of the people who expect you to write.

typefaces
Bodoni Poster
Bauer Bodoni Roman

If you use an item in an unusual size, see if you can repeat that concept elsewhere in the publication to create an attractive and useful repetition.

Weight

In which category of type does this face belong?

The weight of a typeface refers to the thickness of the strokes. Most type families are designed in a variety of weights: regular, bold, perhaps extra bold, semibold, or light. When combining weights, remember the rule: *don't be a wimp.* Don't contrast the regular weight with a semibold—go for the stronger bold. If you are combining type from two different families, one face will usually be bolder than the other—so emphasize it.

Most of the typefaces that come standard with your personal computer are missing a very strong bold in the family. I heartily encourage you to invest in at least one very strong, black face. Look through online type catalogs to find one. A contrast of weight is one of the easiest and most effective ways to add visual interest to a page without redesigning a thing, but you will never be able to get that beautiful, strong contrast unless you have a typeface with big, solid strokes.

Formata Light
Formata Regular
Formata Medium
Formata Bold

These are examples of the various weights that usually come within a family. Notice there is not much contrast of weight between the light and the next weight (variously called regular, medium, or book).

Silica Extra Light
Silica Regular
Silica Bold
Silica Black

Garamond Light
Garamond Book
Garamond Bold
Garamond Ultra

Nor is there a strong contrast between the semibold weights and the bolds. If you are going to contrast with weight, don't be a wimp. If the contrast is not strong, it will look like a mistake.

ANOTHER NEWSLETTER

Headline

Lorem ipsum dolor sit amet, consectetur adips cing elit, diam nonnumy eiusmod tempor incidunt ut lobore et dolore nagna aliquam erat volupat. At enim ad minimim veniami quis nostrud exercitation ullamcorper suscripit laboris nisi ut alquip exea commodo consequat.

Another Headline

Duis autem el eum irure dolor in reprehenderit in voluptate velit esse mol-eratie son conswquat, vel illum dolore en guiat nulla pariatur. At vero esos et accusam et justo odio dis-nissim qui blandit praesent lupatum delenit aigue duos dolor et.

Molestais exceptur sint occaecat cupidat non provident, simil tempor.

Sirt in culpa qui officia deserunt aliquan erat volupat. Lorem ipsum dolor sit amet, consec tetur adipscing elit, diam nonnumy eiusmod tem por incidunt ut lobore

First subhead

Et dolore nagna aliquam erat volupat. At enim ad minimim veni ami quis nostrud exer citation laboris nisi ut al quip ex ea commodo consequat.

Duis autem el eum irure dolor in rep rehend erit in voluptate velit esse moles taie son conswquat, vel illum dolore en guiat nulla pariatur. At vero esos et accusam et justo odio disnissim qui blan dit praesent lupatum del enit aigue duos dolor et molestais exceptur sint el eum irure dolor in repre-

Another Newsletter

Headline

Lorem ipsum dolor sit amet, consectetur adips cing elit, diam nonnumy eiusmod tempor incidunt ut lobore et dolore nagna aliquam erat volupat. At enim ad minimim veniami quis nostrud exercitation ullamcorper suscripit laboris nisi ut alquip exea commodo consequat.

Another Headline

Duis autem el eum irure dolor in reprehenderit in voluptate velit esse mol-eratie son conswquat, vel illum dolore en guiat nulla pariatur. At vero esos et accusam et justo odio dis-nissim qui blandit praesent lupatum delenit aigue duos dolor et.

Molestais exceptur sint occaecat cupidat non provident, simil tempor.

Sirt in culpa qui officia deserunt aliquan erat volupat. Lorem ipsum dolor sit amet, consec tetur adipscing elit, diam nonnumy eiusmod tem por incidunt ut lobore

First subhead

Et dolore nagna aliquam erat volupat. At enim ad minimim veni ami quis nostrud exer citation ullamcorper sus cripit laboris nisi ut al quip ex ea commodo consequat.

Duis autem el eum irure dolor in rep rehend erit in voluptate velit esse moles taie son conswquat, vel illum dolore en guiat nulla pariatur. At vero esos et accusam et justo odio disnissim qui blan dit praesent lupatum del enit aigue duos dolor et molestais exceptur sint

Remember these examples in the first part of the book? On the left, I used the fonts that come with the computer; the headlines are Helvetica (Arial) Bold, the body copy is Times Roman Regular.

On the right, the body copy is still Times Roman Regular, but I used a heavier (stronger weight) typeface for the headlines (Aachen Bold). With just that simple change—a heavier weight for contrast— the page is much more inviting to read. (The title is also heavier and is reversed out of a black box, adding contrast.)

Mermaid Tavern

Bread and Friday Streets
Cheapside • London

Remember this example from the previous page? By setting the company name in lowercase instead of all caps, I could not only make the type size larger, but I could make it heavier as well, thus adding more contrast and visual interest to the card. The heavier weight also gives the card a stronger focus.

Not only does a contrast of weight make a page more attractive to your eyes, it is one of the most effective ways of organizing information. You do this already when you make your newsletter headlines and subheads bolder. So take that idea and push it a little harder. Take a look at the table of contents below; notice how you instantly understand the hierarchy of information when key heads or phrases are very bold. This technique is also useful in an index; it enables the reader to tell at a glance whether an index entry is a first-level or a second-level entry, thus eliminating the confusion that often arises when you're trying to look up something alphabetically. Look at the index in this book (or in any of my books).

Contents

Contents

By making the chapter headings bolder, the important information is available at a glance, and there is also a stronger attraction for the eye. Plus it sets up a **repetition** (one of the four main principles of design, remember?). I also added a tiny bit of space **above** each bold heading so the headings would be grouped more clearly with their subheadings (principle of **proximity,** remember?).

typefaces
Warnock Pro Regular
Ronnia Bold

If you have a very gray page and no room to add graphics or to pull out quotes and set them as graphics, try setting key phrases in a strong bold. They will pull the reader into the page. (If you use a bold sans serif within serif body copy, you will probably have to make the bold sans serif a point size smaller to make it appear to be the same size as the serif body copy.)

Wants pawn term dare worsted ladle gull hoe lift wetter murder inner ladle cordage honor itch offer lodge, dock, florist. Disk ladle gull orphan worry putty ladle rat cluck wetter ladle rat hut, an fur disk raisin pimple colder Ladle Rat Rotten Hut.

Wan moaning Ladle Rat Rotten Hut's murder colder inset.

Ladle Rat Rotten Hut, heresy ladle bsking winsome burden barter an shirker cockles. Tick disk ladle basking tutor cordage offer groin-murder hoe lifts honor udder sit offer florist. Shaker lake! Dun stopper laundry wrote! Dun stopper peck floors! Dun daily-doily in ner

florist, an yonder nor sorghum-stenches, dun stopper torque wet no strainers!

Hoe-cake, murder, resplendent Ladle Rat Rotten Hut, and stuttered oft oft. Honor wrote tutor cordage offer groin-murder, Ladle Rat Rotten Hut mitten anomalous woof. Wail, wail, wail, set disk wicket woof, Evanescent Ladle Rat Rotten Hut! Wares are putty ladle gull goring wizard cued ladle basking?

Armor goring tumor oiled groin-murder's, reprisal ladle gull. Grammar's seeking bet. Armor ticking arson burden barter an shirker cockles.

O hoe! Heifer gnats woke, setter wicket woof, butter

taught tomb shelf, Oil tickle shirt court tutor cordage offer groin-murder. Oil ketchup wetter letter, and den—O bore!

Soda wicket woof tucker shirt court, an whinny retched a cordage offer groin-murder, picked inner windrow, an sore debtor pore oil worming worse lion inner bet.

Inner flesh, disk abdominal woof lipped honor bet, paunched honor pore oil worming, any garbled erupt. Den disk ratchet ammonol pot honor groin-murder's nut cup an gnat-gun, any curdled ope inner bet, paunched honor pore oil worming, any garbled erupt. Inner ladle wile, Ladle Rat Rotten Hut a raft

Wants pawn term dare worsted ladle gull hoe lift wetter murder inner ladle cordage honor itch offer lodge, dock, florist. **Disk ladle gull orphan worry putty ladle rat cluck** wetter ladle rat hut, an fur disk raisin pimple colder Ladle Rat Rotten Hut.

Wan moaning Ladle Rat Rotten Hut's murder colder inset.

Ladle Rat Rotten Hut, heresy ladle bsking winsome burden barter an shirker cockles. Tick disk ladle basking tutor cordage offer groin-murder hoe lifts honor udder sit offer florist. Shaker lake! Dun stopper peck floors!

Dun daily-doily in ner florist, an yonder nor sorghum-stenches, dun stopper torque wet no strainers!

Hoe-cake, murder, resplendent Ladle Rat Rotten Hut, and stuttered oft oft. Honor wrote tutor cordage offer groin-murder, **Ladle Rat Rotten Hut mitten anomalous woof.** Wail, wail, wail, set disk wicket woof, Evanescent Ladle Rat Rotten Hut! Wares are putty ladle gull goring wizard cued ladle basking?

Armor goring tumor oiled groin-murder's, reprisal ladle gull. Grammar's seeking bet. Armor ticking arson burden barter an shirker cockles.

O hoe! Heifer gnats woke, setter

wicket woof, butter taught tomb shelf, **Oil tickle shirt court tutor cordage offer groin-murder.** Oil ketchup wetter letter, and den—O bore!

Soda wicket woof tucker shirt court, an whinny retched a cordage offer groin-murder, picked inner windrow, an sore debtor pore oil worming worse lion inner bet.

Inner flesh, disk abdominal woof lipped honor bet, paunched honor pore oil worming, any garbled erupt. **Den disk ratchet ammonol pot honor groin-murder's nut cup an gnat-gun,** any curdled ope inner bet, paunched honor pore oil worming, any garbled erupt. Inner

A completely gray page may discourage a casual reader from perusing the story. With the contrast of bold type, the reader can scan key points and is more likely to delve into the information.

(Sometimes, of course, what a reader wants is a plain gray page. For instance, when you're reading a book, you don't want any fancy type tricks to interrupt your eyes—you just want the type to be invisible. And some magazines and journals prefer the stuffy and formal look of a gray page because their audience feels it imports a more serious impression. There is a place for everything. Just make sure the look you are creating is conscious.)

typefaces
Arno Pro Regular
Bailey Sans Extra Bold

Structure

In which category of type does this face belong?

The structure of a typeface refers to how it is built. Imagine that you were to build a typeface out of material you have in your garage. Some faces are built very monoweight, with almost no discernible weight shift in the strokes, as if you had built them out of tubing (like most sans serifs). Others are built with great emphasis on the thick/thin transitions, like picket fences (the moderns). And others are built in-between. If you are combining type from two different families, *use two families with different structures.*

Remember wading through all that stuff earlier in this section about the different categories of type? Well, this is where it comes in handy. Each of the categories is founded on similar *structures.* So you are well on your way to a type solution if you choose two or more faces from two or more categories.

Ode	Ode	Ode
Ode	**Ode**	**Ode**
Ode	Ode	Ode
Ode	Ode	Ode

Little Quiz: Can you name each of the typeface categories represented here (one category per line)?

If not, re-read that section because this simple concept is very important.

Structure refers to how a letter is built, and as you can see in these examples, the structure within each category is quite distinctive.

Robin's Rule: Never put two typefaces from the same category on the same page. There's no way you can get around their similarities. And besides, you have so many other choices—why make life difficult?

Did you read *The Mac is not a typewriter* or *The PC is not a typewriter*? (If you haven't, you should.) In that book I state you should never put two sans serif typefaces on the same page, and you should never put two serif typefaces on the same page—*until you have had some typographic training.* Well, this is your typographic training—you are now qualified and licensed to put two sans serifs or two serifs on the same page.

The law is, though, that you must pull two faces from two different categories of type. That is, you can use two serifs as long as one is an oldstyle and the other is a modern or a slab serif. Even then you must be careful and you must emphasize the contrasts, but it *is* perfectly possible to make it work.

Along the same line, avoid setting two oldstyles on the same page—they have too many similarities and are guaranteed to conflict no matter what you do. Avoid setting two moderns, or two slabs, for the same reason. Avoid using two scripts on the same page.

You can't let
the seeds
stop you
from enjoying
the watermelon.

There are five different typefaces in this one little quote. They don't look too bad together because of one thing: they each have a different structure; **they are each from a different category of type.**

typefaces
Formata Bold (sans serif)
Bauer Bodoni Roman (modern)
Blackoak (slab serif)
Goudy Oldstyle (oldstyle)
Shelley Volante (script)

At first, different typefaces seem as indistinguishable as tigers in the zoo. So if you are new to the idea that one font looks different from another, an easy way to choose contrasting structures is to pick one serif font and one sans serif font. Serif fonts generally have a thick/thin contrast in their structures; sans serifs generally are monoweight. Combining serif with sans serif is a time-tested combination with an infinite variety of possibilities. But as you can see in the example below-left, the contrast of structure alone is not strong enough; you need to emphasize the difference by combining it with other contrasts, such as size or weight.

monoweight
20 pt — **sans serif**
thick/thin — vs. serif
20 pt

sans serif vs. — monoweight
serif 8 pt
thick/thin
50 pt

You can see that the contrast of structure alone is not enough to contrast type effectively.

But when you add the element of size—voilà! Contrast!

Oiled Mudder Harbored

Oiled Mudder Harbored
Wen tutor cardboard
Toe garter pore darker born.
Bud wenchy gut dare
Door cardboard worse bar
An soda pore dark hat known.

Oiled Mudder Harbored

Oiled Mudder Harbored
Wen tutor cardboard
Toe garter pore darker born.
Bud wenchy gut dare
Door cardboard worse bar
An soda pore dark hat known.

As the example above shows, the combination of typefaces with two different structures is not enough. It's still weak—the differences must be emphasized.

See how much better this looks! Adding weight to the title highlights the difference in the structure of the two typefaces—and strengthens the contrast between the two.

typefaces
ITC Garamond Light
Folio Light
Warnock Pro Light
Antique Olive Roman and Black

Setting two sans serifs on one page is always difficult because there is only one structure—monoweight. If you are extraordinarily clever, you might be able to pull off setting two sans serifs if you use one of the rare ones with a thick/thin transition in its strokes, but I don't recommend even trying it. Rather than try to combine two sans serifs, build contrast in other ways using different members of the same sans serif family. The sans serif families usually have nice collections of light weights to very heavy weights, and often include a compressed or extended version (see pages 182–185 about contrast of direction).

Look—two serifs together! But notice each face has a different **structure,** one from the modern category (Bodoni) and one from the slab serif (Clarendon). I also added other contrasts—can you name them?

Here are two sans serifs together, but notice I combined a mono-weight sans (Imago) with one of the few sans serifs that has a thick/thin transition in its letterforms (Cotoris), which gives that sans a different structure. I also maximized the contrasts by using Imago in all caps, larger, bold, and roman.

And here are three sans serifs working well together. But these three are from the same family, Universe: Ultra Condensed, Bold, and Extra Black. This is why it's good to own at least one sans serif family that has lots of different family members. Emphasize their contrasts!

Form

In which category of type does this face belong?

The form of a letter refers to its shape. Characters may have the same structure, but different "forms." For instance, a capital letter "G" has the same *structure* as a lowercase letter "g" in the same family. But their actual *forms,* or shapes, are very different from each other. An easy way to think of a contrast of form is to think of caps versus lowercase.

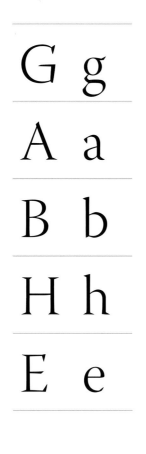

The **forms** of each of these capital letters (Warnock Pro Light Display) are distinctly different from the **forms, or shapes,** of the lowercase letters. So caps versus lowercase is another way to contrast type.

This is something you've probably been doing already, but now, being more conscious of it, you can take greater advantage of its potential for contrast.

In addition to each individual capital letterform being different from its lowercase form, the form of the entire all-cap word is also different. This is what makes all caps so difficult to read. We recognize words not only by their letters, but by their forms, the shapes of the entire words. All words that are set in capital letters have a similar rectangular form, as shown below, and we are forced to read the words letter by letter.

You're probably tired of hearing me recommend not using all caps. I don't mean *never* use all caps. All caps are not *impossible* to read, obviously. Just be conscious of their reduced legibility and readability. Sometimes you can argue that the design "look" of your piece justifies the use of all caps, and that's okay! You must also accept, however, that the words are not as easy to read. If you can consciously state that the lower readability is worth the design look, then go ahead and use all caps.

Every word in all caps has the same form: rectangular.

> The best remedy for a bruised heart is not, as so many seem to think, repose upon a manly bosom. Much more efficacious are honest work, physical activity, and the sudden acquisition of
>
> # WEALTH.
>
> *Dorothy L. Sayers*

Caps versus lowercase (contrast of form) usually needs strengthening with other contrasts. Size is the only other contrast added in this example.

Another clear contrast of form is roman versus italic. Roman, in any typeface, simply means that the type stands straight up and down, as opposed to italic or script, where the type is slanted and/or flowing. Setting a word or phrase in italic to gently emphasize it is a familiar concept that you already use regularly.

G g nerdette

G g nerdette

The first line is roman type; the second line is italic. They are both Brioso Pro; their **structures** are exactly the same, but their **forms (shapes)** are different.

Be far flung away

Be far flung away

Particularly notice that "true-drawn" italic (first line) is not simply slanted roman (second line). The true-drawn italic letterforms have actually been redrawn into different shapes. Look carefully at the differences between the e, f, a, g, and y (both lines use the same font).

Be far flung away

Be far flung away

Sans serifs faces usually (not always) have "oblique" versions, which look like the letters are just tilted. Most sans serif roman and oblique forms are not so very different from each other.

"Yes, oh, *yes,*" she chirped.

"Yes, oh, *yes,*" she chirped.

Which of these two sentences contains a word in fake italic?

Since all scripts and italics have a slanted and/or flowing form, it is important to remember to never combine two different italic fonts, or two different scripts, or an italic with a script. Doing so will invariably create a conflict—there are too many similarities. Fortunately, it's not difficult to find great fonts to combine with scripts or italics.

Work Hard
There is no shortcut.

So what do you think about these two typefaces together? Is something wrong? Does it make you twitch? One of the problems with this combination is that both faces have the same form—they both have a cursive, flowing form. One of the fonts has to change. To what? (Think about it.)

Yes—one face has to change to some sort of roman. While we're changing it, we might as well make the **structure** of the new typeface very different also, instead of one with a thick/thin contrast. And we can make it heavier as well.

Work Hard
there is no shortcut

typefaces
Charme
Goudy Oldstyle Italic
Aachen Bold

Direction

In which category of type does this face belong?

An obvious interpretation of type "direction" is type on a slant. Since this is so obvious, the only thing I want to say is don't do it. Well, you might want to do it sometimes, but only do it if you can state in words why this type must be on a slant, why it enhances the aesthetics or communication of the piece. For instance, perhaps you can say, "This notice about the boat race really should go at an angle up to the right because that particular angle creates a positive, forward energy on the page." Or, "The repetition of this angled type creates a staccato effect which emphasizes the energy of the Bartok composition we are announcing." But please, never fill the corners with angled type.

Type slanting upward to the right creates a positive energy. Type slanting downward creates a negative energy. Occasionally you can use these connotations to your advantage.

Sometimes a strong re-direction of type creates a dramatic impact or a unique format—which is a good justification for its use.

the shakespeare papers

Amusing, Tantalizing, and Educative

Lorem ipsum dolor sit amet, consectetur adips cing elit, diam nonnumy eiusmod tempor incidunt ut lobore et dolore nagna aliquam erat volupat. At enim ad minimim veniami quis nos trud ex ercitation ullamcorper sus cripit laboris nisi ut alquip exea commodo consequat.

Unexpected

Duis autem el eum irure dolor in reprehenderit in volu ptate velit esse mol eratie son conswquat, vel illum dolore en guiat nulla pariatur. At vero esos et accusam et justo odio disnissim qui blandit pra esent lupatum delenit ai gue duos dolor in. Molestais

exceptur sint occaecat cupidat non pro vident, simil tempor. Sirt in culpa qui officia des erunt aliquan erat volupat. Lorem ipsum dolor sit amet, consec tetur adip scing elit, diam no numy eiusmod tem por incidunt ut lobore.

Intriguing and Controversial

Et dolore nagna aliquam erat volupat. At enim ad minimim veni ami quis nostrud exer citation ulla mcorper sus cripit laboris nisi ut al quip ex ea commodo consequat.

Duis autem el eum irure dolor in rep rehend erit in proles to maheminit and smit off their heads forthwith.

VOLUPTATE VELIT ESSE moles taie son conswquat, vel illum dolore en guiat nulla pariatur. At veros esot et accusam et justo odio disnissim qui blan dit praesent lupatum del enit aigue duos dolor et mol estais exceptur sint. El eum irure dolor in rep rehend erit in voluptate. At enim ad minimim veniami quis nostrud ex ercitation ullamcorper sus cripit laboris nisi ut alquip exea commodo consequat. Et dolore nagna aliquam erat volupat. At enim ad minimim veni ami quis nostrud exer citation ulla mcorper sus cripit laboris nisi ut al quip ex ea commodo consequat. Vero esos et accusam et justo odio disnissim qui blan dit praesent.

typefaces
Fountain Pen
Formata Light **and Bold**
Brioso Pro Caption

But there is another form of "direction." Every element of type has a direction, even though it may run straight across the page. A *line* of type has a horizontal direction. A tall, thin *column* of type has a vertical direction. It is these more sophisticated directional movements of type that are fun and interesting to contrast. For instance, a double-page spread with a bold headline running across the two pages and the body copy in a series of tall, thin columns creates an interesting contrast of direction.

Experience

teaches

you to

recognize

a mistake—

when

you've

made it

again.

If you have a layout that has the potential for a contrast of direction, emphasize it. Perhaps use an extended typeface in the horizontal direction, and a tall typeface in the vertical direction. Emphasize the vertical by adding extra linespace, if appropriate, and narrower columns than you perhaps originally planned on.

typefaces
Sneakers UltraWide
Coquette Regular
Adobe Wood Type Ornaments Two

You can involve other parts of your layout in the contrast of type direction, such as graphics or lines, to emphasize or contrast the direction.

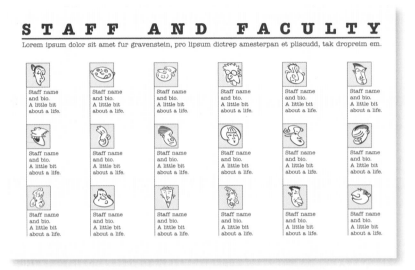

Long horizontals and tall, thin columns can be combined in an endless variety of elegant layouts. Alignment is a key factor here—strong visual alignments will emphasize and strengthen the contrasts of direction.

typefaces
ITC American Typewriter
Medium **and Bold**
MiniPics HeadBuddies:

In this example, the direction of the text provides a counter-balance to a horizontal image.

typefaces
Industria Solid
Cotoris Bold

In the example below, there is a nice, strong contrast of direction. But what other contrasts have also been employed to strengthen the piece? There are three different typefaces in that arrangement—*why* do they work together?

Also notice the texture that is created from the structures of the various typefaces, their linespacing, their letterspacing, their weight, their size, their form. If the letters were all raised and you could run your fingers over them, each contrast of type would also give you a contrast of texture—you can "feel" this texture visually. This is a subtle, yet important, part of type. Various textures will occur automatically as you employ other contrasts, but it's good to be conscious of texture and its effect.

MARY SIDNEY
COUNTESS OF PEMBROKE

IF IT'S BEEN
SAID IN
ENGLISH,
MARY
SAID IT
BETTER.

Ay me, to whom shall I my case complain that may compassion my impatient grief? Or where shall I unfold my inward pain, that my enriven heart may find relief?

To heavens? Ah, they alas the authors were, and workers of my unremedied woe: for they foresee what to us happens here, and they foresaw, yet suffered this be so.

To men? Ah, they alas like wretched be, and subject to the heavens ordinance: Bound to abide what ever they decree, their best redress is their best sufferance.

Then to my self will I my sorrow mourn, since none alive like sorrowful remains, and to my self my plaints shall back return, to pay their usury with doubled pains.

Spend a few minutes to put into words why these three typefaces work together.

If you choose a modern in all caps for the headline, what would be a logical choice for body text?

If you had, instead, chosen a modern typeface for the short quote, what would then be a logical choice for the headline?

typefaces

Bodoni Poster Compressed
Eurostile Bold Extended 2
ITC American Typewriter Medium

Color

In which category of type does this face belong?

Color is another term, like direction, with obvious interpretations. When you're talking about actual color, remember to keep in mind that warm colors (reds, oranges) come forward and command our attention. Our eyes are very attracted to warm colors, so it takes very little red to create a contrast. Cool colors (blues, greens), on the other hand, recede from our eyes. You can get away with larger areas of a cool color; in fact, you *need* more of a cool color to create an effective contrast.

Notice that even though the name "Scarlett" is much smaller, it competes with the larger word because of the warm color.

Now the larger name in the warm color overpowers the smaller name. You usually want to avoid this—or take advantage of it.

Notice how the light blue "Scarlett" almost disappears.

To contrast with a cool color effectively, you generally need to use more of it.

typefaces
Shelley Volante Scripte
Goudy Oldstyle

But typographers have always referred to **black-and-white type** on a page as having **color.** It's easy to create contrast with "colorful" colors; it takes a more sophisticated eye to see and take advantage of the color contrasts in black-and-white.

In the quote below, you can easily see different "colors" in the black and white text.

"Color" is created by such variances as the weight of the letterforms, the structure, the form, the space inside the letters, the space between the letters, the space between the lines, the size of the type, or the size of the x-height. Even within one typeface, you can create different colors.

Just as the voice adds emphasis
to important words, so can type:
it shouts or whispers
by variation of size.

Just as the pitch of the voice adds
interest to the words, so can type:
it modulates by lightness
or darkness.

Just as the voice adds color to the
words by inflection, so can type:
it defines elegance,
dignity, toughness
by choice of face.

Jan V. White

Squint your eyes and look at this. Get used to considering the different values of blocks of text as having "color."

typefaces
Cochin Medium *and Italic*
Eurostile Bold Extended 2

A light, airy typeface with lots of letterspacing and linespacing creates a very light color (and texture). A bold sans serif, tightly packed, creates a dark color (with a different texture). This is a particularly useful contrast to employ on those text-heavy pages where there are no graphics.

A gray, text-only page can be very dull to look at and uninviting to read. It can also create confusion: in the example below, are these two stories related to each other?

Ladle Rat Rotten Hut

Wants pawn term dare worsted ladle gull hoe lift wetter murder inner ladle cordage honor itch offer lodge, dock, florist. Disk ladle gull orphan worry Putty ladle rat cluck wetter ladle rat hut, an fur disk raisin pimple colder Ladle Rat Rotten Hut.

Wan moaning Ladle Rat Rotten Hut's murder colder inset. "Ladle Rat Rotten Hut, heresy ladle basking winsome burden barter an shirker cockles. Tick disk ladle basking tutor cordage offer groin-murder hoe lifts honor udder site offer florist. Shaker lake! Dun stopper laundry wrote! Dun stopper peck floors! Dun daily-doily inner florist, an yonder nor sorghum-stenches, dun stopper torque wet strainers!"

"Hoe-cake, murder," resplendent Ladle Rat Rotten Hut, an tickle ladle basking an stuttered oft. Honor wrote tutor cordage offer groin-murder, Ladle Rat Rotten Hut mitten anomalous woof.

"Wail, wail, wail!" set disk wicket woof, "Evanescent Ladle Rat Rotten Hut! Wares are putty ladle gull goring wizard ladle basking?"

"Armor goring tumor groin-murder's," reprisal ladle gull. "Grammar's seeking bet. Armor ticking arson burden barter an shirker cockles."

"O hoe! Heifer gnats woke," setter wicket woof, butter taught tomb shelf, "Oil tickle shirt court tutor cordage offer groin-murder. Oil ketchup wetter letter, an den—O bore!"

Soda wicket woof tucker shirt court, an whinny retched a cordage offer groin-murder, picked inner windrow, an sore debtor pore oil worming worse lion inner bet. Inner flesh, disk abdominal woof lipped honor bet, paunched honor pore oil worming, an garbled erupt. Den disk ratchet ammonol pot honor groin-murder's nut cup an gnat-gun, any curdled ope inner bet.

Inner ladle wile, Ladle Rat Rotten Hut a raft attar cordage, an ranker dough ball. "Comb ink, sweat hard," setter wicket woof, disgracing is verse. Ladle Rat Rotten Hut entity bet rum, an stud buyer groin-murder's bet.

"O Grammar!" crater ladle gull historically, "Water bag icer gut! A nervous sausage bag ice!"

"Battered lucky chew whiff, sweat hard," setter bloat-Thursday woof, wetter wicket small honors phase.

"O, Grammar, water bag noise! A nervous sore suture anomalous prognosis!"

"Battered small your whiff, doling," whiskered dole woof, ants mouse worse waddling.

"O Grammar, water bag mouser gut! A nervous sore suture bag mouse!"

Daze worry on-forger-nut ladle gull's lest warts. Oil offer sodden, caking offer carvers an sprinkling otter bet, disk hoard-hoarded woof lipped own pore Ladle Rat Rotten Hut an garbled erupt.

Mural: Yonder nor sorghum stenches shut ladle gulls stopper torque wet strainers.

—H. Chace
Anguish Languish

Old Singleton

. . . Singleton stood at the door with his face to the light and his back to the darkness. And alone in the dim emptiness of the sleeping forecastle he appeared bigger, colossal, very old; old as Father Time himself, who should have come there into this place as quiet as a sepulcher to contemplate with patient eyes the short victory of sleep, the consoler. Yet he was only a child of time, a lonely relic of a devoured and forgotten generation. He stood, still strong, as ever unthinking; a ready man with a vast empty past and with no future, with his childlike impulses and his man's passions already dead within his tattooed breast.

—Joseph Conrad

This might be a typical page in a newsletter or other publication. The monotonous gray does not attract your eye; there's no enticement to dive in and read.

typefaces

Warnock Pro Regular *and Italic*

If you add some "color" to your heads and subheads with a stronger weight, or perhaps set a quote, passage, or short story in an obviously different "color," then readers are more likely to stop on the page and actually read it. And that's our point, right?

Besides making the page more inviting to read, this change in color also helps organize the information. In the example below, it is now clearer that there are two separate stories on the page.

Ladle Rat Rotten Hut

Wants pawn term dare worsted ladle gull hoe lift wetter murder inner ladle cordage honor itch offer lodge, dock, florist. Disk ladle gull orphan worry Putty ladle rat cluck wetter ladle rat hut, an fur disk raisin pimple colder Ladle Rat Rotten Hut.

Wan moaning Ladle Rat Rotten Hut's murder colder inset. "Ladle Rat Rotten Hut, heresy ladle basking winsome burden barter an shirker cockles. Tick disk ladle basking tutor cordage offer groin-murder hoe lifts honor udder site offer florist. Shaker lake! Dun stopper laundry wrote! Dun stopper peck floors! Dun daily-doily inner florist, an yonder nor sorghum-stenches, dun stopper torque wet strainers!"

"Hoe-cake, murder," resplendent Ladle Rat Rotten Hut, an tickle ladle basking an stuttered oft. Honor wrote tutor cordage offer groin-murder, Ladle Rat Rotten Hut mitten anomalous woof.

"Wail, wail, wail!" set disk wicket woof, "Evanescent Ladle Rat Rotten Hut! Wares are putty ladle gull goring wizard ladle basking?"

"Armor goring tumor groin-murder's," reprisal ladle gull. "Grammar's seeking bet. Armor ticking arson burden barter an shirker cockles."

"O hoe! Heifer gnats woke," setter wicket woof, butter taught tomb shelf, "Oil tickle shirt court tutor cordage offer groin-murder. Oil ketchup wetter letter, an den—O bore!"

Soda wicket woof tucker shirt court, an whinny retched a cordage offer groin-murder, picked inner windrow, an sore debtor pore oil worming worse lion inner bet. Inner flesh, disk abdominal woof lipped honor bet, paunched honor pore oil worming, an garbled erupt. Den disk ratchet ammonol pot honor groin-murder's nut cup an gnat-gun, any curdled ope inner bet.

Inner ladle wile, Ladle Rat Rotten Hut a raft attar cordage, an ranker dough ball. "Comb ink, sweat hard," setter wicket woof, disgracing is verse. Ladle Rat Rotten Hut entity bet rum, an stud buyer groin-murder's bet.

"O Grammar!" crater ladle gull historically, "Water bag icer gut! A nervous sausage bag ice!"

"Battered lucky chew whiff, sweat hard," setter bloat-Thursday woof, wetter wicket small honors phase.

"O, Grammar, water bag noise! A nervous sore suture anomalous prognosis!"

"Battered small your whiff, doling," whiskered dole woof, ants mouse worse waddling.

"O Grammar, water bag mouser gut! A nervous sore suture bag mouse!"

Daze worry on-forger-nut ladle gull's lest warts. Oil offer sodden, caking offer carvers an sprinkling otter bet, disk hoard-hoarded woof lipped own pore Ladle Rat Rotten Hut an garbled erupt.

Mural: Yonder nor sorghum stenches shut ladle gulls stopper torque wet strainers.

—H. Chace, *Anguish Languish*

Old Singleton

. . . Singleton stood at the door with his face to the light and his back to the darkness. And alone in the dim emptiness of the sleeping forecastle he appeared bigger, colossal, very old; old as Father Time himself, who should have come there into this place as quiet as a sepulcher to contemplate with patient eyes the short victory of sleep, the consoler. Yet he was only a child of time, a lonely relic of a devoured and forgotten generation. He stood, still strong, as ever unthinking; a ready man with a vast empty past and with no future, with his childlike impulses and his man's passions already dead within his tattooed breast.   —Joseph Conrad

This is the same layout, but with added "color." Also, look again at many of the other examples in this book and you'll often see contrasting typefaces that create variations in color.

typefaces
Aachen Bold
Warnock Pro Caption and Light Italic Caption
Eurostile Extended 2 **and Demi**

Below, notice how you can change the color in one typeface, one size, with minor adjustments. As you can see, these minor adjustments can also affect how many words fit into a space.

Center Alley worse jester pore ladle gull hoe lift wetter stop-murder an toe heft-cisterns. Daze worming war furry wicket an shellfish parsons, spatially dole stop-murder, hoe dint lack Center Alley an, infect, word	9 point Warnock Regular, 10.6 leading.
Center Alley worse jester pore ladle gull hoe lift wetter stop-murder an toe heft-cisterns. Daze worming war furry wicket an shellfish parsons, spatially dole stop-murder, hoe dint lack	9 point Warnock Bold, 10.6 leading. This is exactly the same as the example above, except it is the Bold version.
Center Alley worse jester pore ladle gull hoe lift wetter stop-murder an toe heft-cisterns. Daze worming war furry wicket an shellfish parsons, spatially dole stop-murder, hoe dint lack Center Alley an, infect, word orphan traitor pore gull mar lichen	9 point Warnock Light, 10.6 leading. This is exactly the same as the first example above, except it is the Light version of the font, not the Regular.
Center Alley worse jester pore ladle gull hoe lift wetter stop-murder an toe heft-cisterns. Daze worming war furry wicket an shellfish parsons, spatially dole stop-murder, hoe dint lack	9 point Warnock Light, 13 leading, extra letterspacing. Notice it has a lighter color than the example above (same font) due to the extra space between the lines (the leading) and the letters.
Center Alley worse jester pore ladle gull hoe lift wetter stop-murder an toe heft-cisterns. Daze worming war furry wicket an shellfish parsons, spatially dole stop-murder, hoe dint lack Center	9 point Warnock Light Italic, 13 leading, extra letterspacing. This is exactly the same as the one above, except italic. It has a different color and texture.

Below you see just plain examples of typeface color, without any of the extra little manipulations you can use to change the type's natural color. Most good type books display a wide variety of typefaces in blocks of text so you can see the color and texture on the page. An excellent type specimen book from a type vendor might show you each face in a block of text for color comparisons, or you can make your own on your computer.

Center Alley worse jester pore ladle gull hoe lift wetter stop-murder an toe heft-cisterns. Daze worming war furry wicket an shellfish parsons, spatially dole stop-murder, hoe dint lack Center Alley an, infect, word

American Typewriter, 8/10

Center Alley worse jester pore ladle gull hoe lift wetter stop-murder an toe heft-cisterns. Daze worming war furry wicket an shellfish parsons, spatially dole stop-murder, hoe dint lack Center Alley an, infect, word orphan traitor pore gull mar lichen ammonol dinner hormone bang.

Daze worming war furry wicket an shellfish parsons, spatially dole stop-murder, hoe dint lack Center Alley an, infect, word orphan traitor pore gull mar lichen ammonol dinner hormone bang.

Bernhard Modern, 8/10

Center Alley worse jester pore ladle gull hoe lift wetter stop-murder an toe heft-cisterns. Daze worming war furry wicket an shellfish parsons, spatially dole stop-murder, hoe dint lack Center Alley an, infect, word orphan traitor pore gull mar lichen ammonol dinner hormone bang.

Imago, 8/10

Center Alley worse jester pore ladle gull hoe lift wetter stop-murder an toe heft-cisterns. Daze worming war furry wicket an shellfish parsons, spatially dole stop-murder, hoe dint lack Center Alley an, infect, word orphan traitor pore gull mar lichen ammonol dinner hormone bang.

Memphis Medium, 8/10

Center Alley worse jester pore ladle gull hoe lift wetter stop-murder an toe heft-cisterns. Daze worming war furry wicket an shellfish parsons, spatially dole stop-murder, hoe dint lack Center Alley an, infect, word orphan traitor pore gull mar lichen ammonol dinner hormone bang.

Photina, 8/10

Center Alley worse jester pore ladle gull hoe lift wetter stop-murder an toe heft-cisterns. Daze worming war furry wicket an shellfish parsons, spatially dole stop-murder, hoe dint lack Center Alley

Eurostile Extended, 8/10

Combine the contrasts

Don't be a wimp. Most effective type layouts take advantage of more than one of the contrasting possibilities. For instance, if you are combining two serif faces, each with a different structure, emphasize their differences by contrasting their form also: if one element is in roman letters, all caps, set the other in italic, lowercase. Contrast their size, too, and weight; perhaps even their direction. Take a look at the examples in this section again—each one uses more than one principle of contrast.

For a wide variety of examples and ideas, take a look through any good magazine. Notice that every one of the interesting type layouts depends on the contrasts. Subheads or initial caps emphasize the contrast of size with the contrast of weight; often, there is also a contrast of structure (serif vs. sans serif) and form (caps vs. lowercase) as well.

Try to verbalize what you see. *If you can put the dynamics of the relationship into words, you have power over it.* When you look at a type combination that makes you twitch because you have an instinctive sense that the faces don't work together, analyze it with words.

Before trying to find a better solution, you must find the problem. To find the *problem,* try to name the *similarities*—not the differences. What is it about the two faces that compete with each other? Are they both all caps? Are they both typefaces with a strong thick/thin contrast in their strokes? How effective is their contrast of weight? Size? Structure?

Or perhaps the focus conflicts—is the *larger* type a *light* weight and the *smaller* type a *bold* weight, making them fight with each other because each one is trying to be more important than the other?

Name the problem, then you can create the solution.

Summary

This is a list of the contrasts I discussed. You might want to keep this list visible for when you need a quick bang-on-the-head reminder.

Size Don't be a wimp.

Weight Contrast heavy weights with light weights, not medium weights.

Structure Look at how the letterforms are built—monoweight or thick/thin.

*F*ORM Caps versus lowercase is a contrast of form, as well as roman versus italic or script. Scripts and italics have similar forms—don't combine them.

Direction Think more in terms of horizontal type versus tall, narrow columns of type, rather than type on a slant.

Color Warm colors come forward; cool colors recede. Experiment with the "colors" of black text.

Little Quiz #6: Contrast or conflict

Look carefully at each of the following examples. Decide whether the type combinations **contrast** effectively, or if there is a **conflict** going on. **State why the combination of faces works** (look for the differences), **or state why it doesn't** (look for the similarities). [Ignore the words themselves—don't get wrapped up in whether the typeface is appropriate for its product, because that's another topic altogether. *Just look at the typefaces.*] If this is your book, circle the correct answers.

contrasts

conflicts

FANCY PERFUME

contrasts

conflicts

extremely good DOGFOOD

contrasts

conflicts

MY MOTHER
This is an essay on why my Mom will always be the greatest mother in the world. Until I turn into a teenager.

contrasts

conflicts

FUNNY FARM
Health Insurance

contrasts

conflicts

let's **DANCE** tonight

Little Quiz #7: Dos and don'ts

Rather than give you a list of **do**s and **don't**s, I'm going to let you decide what should and should not be done. Circle the correct answers.

1   Do   Don't   Use two scripts on the same page.

2   Do   Don't   Use two moderns, two sans serifs, two oldstyles, or two slab serifs on the same page.

3   Do   Don't   Add importance to one typographic element by making it bolder, and to another on the same page by making it bigger.

4   Do   Don't   Use a script and an italic on the same page.

5   Do   Don't   If one face is tall and slender, choose another face that is short and thick.

6   Do   Don't   If one face has strong thick/thin transitions, choose a sans serif or a slab serif.

7   Do   Don't   If you use a very fancy decorative face, find another fancy, eye-catching typeface to complement it.

8   Do   Don't   Create a type arrrangement that is extremely interesting, but unreadable.

9   Do   Don't   Remember the four basic principles of design when using any type in any way.

10   Do   Don't   Break the rules, *once you can name them.*

An exercise in combining contrasts

Here is a fun exercise that is easy to do and will help fine-tune your typographic skills. All you need is tracing paper, a pen or pencil (the little colorful plastic-tip markers are great for this), and a magazine or two.

Trace any word in the magazine that appeals to you. Now find another word in the magazine that creates an effective contrast with the one you just traced. In this exercise, the words are completely irrelevant—you are looking just at letterforms. Here is an example of a combination of three faces that I traced out of a news magazine:

The first word I traced was "Hawk." Once I did that, I didn't even have to look at any more sans serifs. "Rebate" has a very different form from "hawk," and I needed something small and light and with a different structure as a third face.

Trace the first word, and then make a conscious, verbal decision as to what you need to combine with that word. For instance, if the first word or phrase is some form of sans serif, you know that whatever you choose next won't be another sans serif, right? What *do* you need? Put your choices into conscious thoughts.

Try a few combinations of several words, then try some other projects, such as a report cover, a short story on one page with an interesting title, a newsletter masthead, a magazine cover, an announcement, and anything else that may be pertinent to you. Try some colored pens, also. Remember, the words don't have to make any sense at all.

The advantage of tracing from magazines is that you have an abundance of different typefaces that you probably don't have on your computer. Is this going to make you lust after more typefaces? Yes.

So, Does it Make Sense?

Is all this making sense to you? Once you see it, it seems so simple, doesn't it? It won't take long before you won't even have to think about the ways to contrast type—you will just automatically reach for the right typeface. That is, if you have the right typeface in your computer. Fonts (typefaces) are so inexpensive right now, and you really only need a few families with which to make all sorts of dynamic combinations—choose one family from each category, making sure the sans serif family you choose contains a heavy black as well as a very light weight.

And then go to it. And have fun!

The process

Where do you begin when you start to design or re-design something?

Start with the focal point. Decide what it is you want readers to see first. Unless you have chosen to create a very concordant design, create your focal point with strong contrasts.

Group your information into logical groups; decide on the relationships between these groups. Display those relationships with the closeness or lack of closeness **(proximity)** of the groups.

As you arrange the type and graphics on the page, **create and maintain strong alignments.** If you see a strong edge, such as a photograph or vertical line, strengthen it with the alignments of other text or objects.

Create a repetition, or find items that can have a repetitive connection. Use a bold typeface or a rule or a dingbat or a spatial arrangement. Take a look at what is already repeated naturally, and see if it would be appropriate to add more strength to it.

Unless you have chosen to create a concordant design, make sure you have **strong contrasts** that will attract a reader's eye. Remember—contrast is *contrast.* If *everything* on the page is big and bold and flashy, then there is no contrast! Whether it is contrasting by being bigger and bolder or by being smaller and lighter, the point is that it is different and so your eye is attracted to it.

An exercise

Open your local newspaper or telephone book yellow pages. Find any advertisement that you know is not well-designed (especially with your newly heightened visual awareness). You won't have any trouble finding several, I'm sure.

Take a piece of tracing paper and trace the outline of the ad (no fair making it bigger). Now, moving that piece of tracing paper around, trace other parts of the ad, but put them where they belong, giving them strong alignments, putting elements into closer proximity where appropriate, making sure the focal point is really a focal point. Change the capital letters into lowercase, make some items bolder, some smaller, some bigger, get rid of obviously useless junk.

Tip: The neater you do this, the more impressive the result. If you just scratch it on, your finished piece won't look any better than the original.

(And that's a trick I taught my graphic design students—whenever you have a client who insists on his own dorky design and doesn't want to think seriously about your more sophisticated work, make your rendering of his design a little messy. Spill some coffee on it, let the edges get raggedy, smear the pencil around, don't line things up, etc. For the designs that you know are much better, do them brilliantly clean and neat, print them onto excellent paper, mount them onto illustration board, cover them with a protective flap, etc. Most of the time the client will think lo and behold your work really does look better than his original concept, and since he is a VIP* (which you are no longer), he won't be able to pinpoint why his doesn't look so good anymore. His impression is that yours looks better. And don't you dare tell anybody I told you this.)

*VIP: visually illiterate person

Okay—redesign this!

Here's a little poster. Not too bad—though it could use a little help. A few simple changes will make a world of difference. Its biggest problem is the lack of a strong alignment, plus there are several different elements competing for the focal point. Use tracing paper to rearrange elements, or sketch a few versions right onto this page.

Url's Training Camp

Get on the Internet and do stuff!

Join Url for a weekend of training in the high desert of Santa Fe.

Workshops in:
Web design and CSS
Keywords
Searching
Blogging and podcasting

Friday, Saturday, Sunday
First weekend in May

Answers
to Quizzes

As a college teacher, all the quizzes, tests, and projects I give are "open book, open mouth." Students can always use their notes, they can use their books, they can talk with each other, they can talk with me. Having taken hundreds of college units myself, from a science major to a design major, I learned that I was much more likely to *retain* the correct information if I *wrote down* the correct information. Rather than guessing and then writing down a wrong answer, the process of finding the correct answer on a test was much more productive. So I encourage you to bounce back and forth between the quiz and the answers, to discuss them with friends, and especially to apply the questions to other designed pages you see around you. "Open eyes" is the key to becoming more visually literate.

Listen to your eyes.

Answers: Quiz #1 (page 86)

Remove the border to open up space. New designers tend to put borders around everything. Stop it! Let it breathe! Don't contain it so tightly!

Proximity

The headings are too far away from their related items: *move them closer.*

There are double Returns above and below the headings: *take out all double Returns, but add a little extra space* **above** *the headings so they are more closely connected to the following material they belong with.*

Separate personal info from résumé items with a little extra space.

Alignment

Text is centered and flush left, and second lines of text return all the way to the left edge: create a strong flush left alignment—all heads align with each other, all bullets align, all text aligns, second lines of text align with first lines.

Repetition

There is already a repetition of the hyphen: *strengthen that repetition by making it a more interesting bullet and using it in front of every appropriate item.*

There is already a repetition in the headings: *strengthen that repetition by making the headings strong and black.*

The strong black impression in the bullets now repeats and reinforces the strong black in the headings.

Contrast

There isn't any: *use a strong, bold face for contrast of heads, including "Résumé" (to be consistent, or repetitive); add contrast with the strong bullets.*

By the way: the numbers in the new version use the "proportional oldstyle" form that is found in many OpenType fonts. If you don't have them, make the numbers a point size or two smaller so they don't call undue attention to themselves.

Answers: Quiz #2 (page 87)

Different typefaces: There are three different sans serifs, one serif face, one script, and one decorative. Choose two of those: perhaps the decorative face that's used in the title, plus a nice serif to imply classic grace.

Different alignments: Oh my gawd. Some elements are flush left, some are centered, some are centered in the middle of empty space, some have no connection or alignment with anything else in the world.

Strong line: The logo could provide a strong line against which to align other elements.

Lack of proximity: Group the information. You know what should be grouped together.

Lack of focal point: Several items are competing for attention. Choose one.

Lack of repetitive elements: The four logos do *not* qualify as repetitive elements—they are randomly placed in each corner merely to fill the empty corners; that is, they were not placed as conscious design elements. But perhaps you can pick up the color of the logo to use as a repetitive item.

Remove the boxes inside the border. Use square corners on the remaining border to reinforce the square corners of the logo and to keep the edges clean.

TAKE OFF THE CAPS LOCK!!!

The example on the next page is only one of many possibilities.

The Shakespeare Papers

Shakespeare by Design

The Shakespeare Papers are bimonthly booklets of amusing, tantalizing, peculiar, educative, unexpected, brilliant, surprising, intriguing, and occasionally controversial tidbits about the Shakespearean plays and sonnets.

Subscription-based:
Only $38 a year for six
collectible issues

7 Sweet Swan Lane
Cygnet City, CA 94536
505.424.7926
TheShakespearePapers.com
cleo@TheShakespearePapers.com

typefaces
Wade Sans Light
Brioso Pro Light
and Bold Italic

Answers: Quiz #3 (page 161)

Oldstyle:	As I remember, Adam
Modern:	High Society
Slab serif:	The enigma continues

Sans serif:	It's your attitude
Script:	Too Sassy for Words
Decorative:	At the Rodeo

Answers: Quiz #4
(page 162)

Giggle:	B
Jiggle:	C
Diggle:	A
Piggle:	A
Higgle:	C
Wiggle:	B

Answers: Quiz #5
(page 163)

Diggle:	C
Riggle:	A
Figgle:	B
Biggle:	D
Miggle:	D
Tiggle:	A

Answers: Quiz #6 (page 194)

Fancy Perfume: **Conflict.** There are too many similarities: they are both all caps; they are both about the same size; they are both "frufru" typefaces (kind of fancy); they are similar in weight.

Dogfood: **Contrast.** There is a strong contrast of size, color, form (both caps vs. lowercase and roman vs. italic), weight, and structure (although neither typeface has a definite thick/thin contrast in their strokes, the two faces are definitely built out of very different materials).

My Mother: **Conflict.** Although there is a contrast of form in the caps vs. lowercase, there are too many other similarities that conflict. The two faces are the same size, very similar weight, the same structure, and the same roman form. This is a twitcher.

Funny Farm: **Conflict.** There is potential here, but the differences need to be strengthened. There is a contrast of form in the caps vs. lower-case, and also in the extended face vs. the regular face. There is a slight contrast of structure in that one face has a gentle thick/thin transition and the other has monoweight, extended letters. Can you put your finger on the biggest problem? (Think a minute.) What is the focus here? "Health Insurance" is trying to be the focus by being larger, but it uses a light weight face. "Funny Farm" is trying to be the focus, even though it's smaller, by using all caps and bold. You have to decide which one is the boss and emphasize one of the concepts, either "Funny Farm" or "Health Insurance."

Let's Dance: **Contrast.** Even though they are exactly the same size and from the same family (the Formata family), the other contrasts are strong: weight, form (roman vs. italic and caps vs. lowercase), structure (from the weight contrasts), color (though both are black, the weight of "dance" gives it a darker color).

Answers: Quiz #7 (page 195)

1. **Don't.** Two scripts will conflict with each other because they usually have the same form.

2. **Don't.** Typefaces from the same category have the same structure.

3. **Don't.** They will fight with each other. Decide what is the most important and emphasize that item.

4. **Don't.** Most scripts and italics have the same form—slanted and flowing.

5. **Do.** You instantly have a strong contrast of structure and color.

6. **Do.** You instantly have a contrast of structure and color.

7. **Don't.** Two fancy faces will usually conflict because their fancy features both compete for attention.

8. **Don't.** Your purpose in putting type on a page is usually to communicate. Never forget that.

9. **Do.**

10. **Do.** The basic law of breaking the rules is to know what the rules are in the first place. If you can justify breaking the rules—and the result works—go ahead!

Typefaces in this Book

14

There are more than three hundred fonts, or typefaces, in this book. Now, when someone (especially a font vendor) tells you there are "a certain number" of fonts, they usually include all the variations of one font—the regular version is a font, the italic is another, the bold is another, etc. Since you are (or were) a new designer, I thought you might be interested in knowing exactly which fonts were used in this book. **Most fonts are shown in 14-point type,** unless otherwise noted. Have fun!

Primary faces

Main body text:	Warnock Pro Light, 10.5/14.25 (which means 10.5-point type with 14.25-point leading).
Chapter titles:	Bauer Bodoni Bold Condensed, 66/60
Chapter numbers:	Bauer Bodoni Roman, 225 point, 10 percent plum
Tiny little type:	Warnock Pro Caption (most of the time)
Main heads:	Silica Regular, 26/22
Captions:	Proxima Nova Alt Light, 9.5/11.5
Cover:	Glasgow

Modern

Bauer Bodoni Roman, *Italic,* **Bold Condensed**

Bodoni Poster, Poster Compressed

Didot Regular, **Bold**

Madrone

Mona Lisa Solid

Onyx Regular

(Berthold) Walbaum Book Regular, **Bold**

Times New Roman Bold

Oldstyle

Arno Pro Regular

New Baskerville Roman

Bernhard Modern

Brioso Pro Light, *Light Italic,* Regular, *Regular Italic,* **Bold,** ***Bold Italic***

Cochin Medium, *Italic,* **Bold,** ***Bold Italic***

ITC Garamond Light, Book, **Bold, Ultra**

Garamond Premier Pro Regular, *Italic*

Golden Cockerel Roman

Goudy Oldstyle, *Italic*

Minister Light, *Light Italic,* **Bold**

Palatino Light, *Italic*

Photina Regular, *Italic*

Times New Roman Regular, *Italic,* **Bold,** ***Bold Italic***

Adobe Jensen Pro Regular

Warnock Pro Light, *Light Italic,* Regular, *Regular Italic,* **Bold,** ***Bold Italic,*** Caption, Light Caption (specifically for small type)

Slab serif

Aachen Bold

American Typewriter Medium, **Bold**

Blackoak

Clarendon Light, Roman, Bold

Memphis Light, Medium, **Bold, Extra Bold**

New Century Schoolbook Roman

Silica Light, Extra Light, Regular, **Bold, Black**

Sans serif

Antique Olive Roman, **Black**

Bailey Sans Book, **Bold, Extra Bold**

Cotoris Regular, *Italic,* Bold

Delta Jaeger Light, **Medium, Bold**

Eurostile Demi, **Bold,** Extended Two, **Bold Extended Two,** Bold Condensed

Folio Light, **Medium, Bold, Extra Bold**

Formata Light, Regular, **Medium,** *Medium Italic,* **Bold,** *Bold Italic,* **Bold Condensed,** Light Condensed

Franklin Gothic Book

Helvetica Regular, **Bold,** *Bold Oblique*

Imago Extra Bold

Myriad Pro Condensed

Officina Sans Book, **Bold**

Optima Roman, *Oblique,* **Bold**

Proxima Nova Regular, **Black**

Proxima Nova Alt Light, Semibold, **Bold, Extra Bold**

Ronnia Regular, *Italic,* **Bold,** *Bold Italic*

Shannon Book, *Book Oblique,* **Extra Bold**

Syntax Roman, **Bold, Black,**

Trade Gothic Light, Medium, *Medium Oblique,* Condensed No. 18, **Bold, Bold Condensed No. 20**

Trebuchet Regular, *Italic*

Universe 39 Thin Ultra Condensed, **65 Bold, 75 Black, 85 Extra Black**

Verdana Regular

Script

Anna Nicole

Arid

Bickham Script Pro
  (24 point)

Carpenter (24 point)

Charme

Cocktail Shaker

Coquette Regular, **Bold**

Emily Austin (24 point)

Fountain Pen

Linoscript (20 point)

Milk Script

Ministry Script

Miss Fajardose (18 point)

Shelley Volante Script

**Snell Roundhand Bold,
  Black**

Spring Light, *Regular*

Tekton Regular, *Oblique*,
  Bold

*Wendy Medium,
  Bold* (24 point)

Viceroy

Ornaments

Birds

Diva Doodles

Gargoonies

MiniPics Lil Folks

MiniPics Head Buddies

Renfield's Lunch

Golden Cockerel Ornaments

Minion Pro (ornaments)

Type Embellishments One

Type Embellishments Two

Type Embellishments Three

Adobe Woodtype Ornaments 2

ITC Zapf Dingbats

Decorative

(all fonts below are 18 point)

Bodoni Classic
Bold Ornate

By George Titling

Canterbury Oldstyle

Blue Island

Coquette Regular,
Bold

Escaldio Gothico

FAJITA MILD

FLYSWIM

frances uncial

GLASGOW

Improv Regular

Industria Solid

Jiggery Pokery

JUNIPER

LITHOS
EXTRA LIGHT

Percolator Expert

Pious Henry

Potzrebie

SCARLETT

Schablone Rough

Schablone
Labelrough
Positive

Schmutz Cleaned

Scriptease

**Sneakers
Ultrawide**

Spumoni

Stoclet Light, **Bold**

Tabitha

Tapioca

THE WALL

Wade Sans Light

Zanzibar

Appendix

OpenType

When you set a typeface in a very large size, very small size, or average size for reading, the letterforms should be shaped a little differently for each size. Very small sizes need to be a wee bit heavier, and very large sizes need to be lighter or else the thin strokes become thick and clunky. But most typefaces on a computer use one standard matrix, say for size 12 point, and just enlarge or reduce it. Warnock Pro, however, is a collection of faces within the family that are specifically designed for the different uses of type. You can see below that the "Caption" font looks heavy at 20 point, but at 8 point it's perfect. The "Display" font looks a little scrawny at 8 point, but those thin strokes are just lovely when set larger. An OpenType Pro font also has the option to use these oldstyle lining figures (234987) or the tabular figures (234987), as well as several other options. If your computer and software are up-to-date, you can access up to 16,000 characters in one OpenType font, and you can use the same font file on both Macs and PCs.

Warnock Pro Caption
at 20 point

Warnock Pro Caption at 8 point

Warnock Pro Display
at 20 point

Warnock Pro Display at 8 point

Here is a Warnock Pro Regular W in gray directly behind the Display font W. You can clearly see the difference in the strokes.

Mini-glossary

The **baseline** is the invisible line on which type sits (see page 164).

Body copy, body text, or sometimes just plain **body** or **text** refers to the main block of text that you read, as opposed to headlines, subheads, titles, etc. Body text is usually set between 9- and 12-point type with 20 percent added between the lines.

A **bullet** is a little marker, typically used in a list instead of numbers, or between words. This is the standard bullet: •.

A **dingbat** is a small, ornamental character, like this: ■❖✓✎❤. You might have the fonts Zapf Dingbats or Wingdings, which are made up of dingbats.

Elements are the separate objects on the page. An element might be a single line of text, or a graphic, or a group of items that are so close together they are perceived as one unit. To know the number of elements on a page, squint your eyes and count the number of times your eye stops, as it notices each separate item.

Extended text refers to the body copy (as above) when there is a lot of it, as in a book or a long report.

Eye flow, or your **eye,** refers to your eyes as if they are an independent body. As a designer, you can control the way someone moves her "eye" around a page (the eye flow), so you need to become more conscious of how *your* eye moves around on the page. Listen to your eyes.

Justified type is when a block of text is lined up on both the left and right edges.

Resolution refers to how well an image appears to be "resolved"; that is, how clear and clean it looks to us. It's a complicated subject, but here is the gist:

Printed pages: Generally, images that will be printed on paper need to be 300 dpi (dots [of ink] per inch). Always check with the press that will print the job to find out what resolution they want. To get a 300 dpi image, use your image editing application (such as Photoshop) to resize the image *to the size it will be when printed,* and make it 300 ppi (pixels per inch).

For print, use **.tif** images, 300 dpi, CMYK color mode.

Screen pages: Images on the screen are 72 ppi (pixels per inch). These will look crummy when printed, but will look perfect on the screen. Use your image editing application (such as Photoshop) to resize the image *to the size it will appear on the screen.* This means if you have a thumbnail image linked to a larger image, you need *two* separate files of the same image!

For screen, use **.jpg** images, 72 ppi, RGB color mode.

A **rule** is a line, a drawn line, such as the one under the headline "Mini-glossary," above.

White space is the space on a page that is not occupied by any text or graphics. You might call it "blank" space. Beginners tend to be afraid of white space; professional designers use lots of white space.

Trapped white space is when the white, or blank, space on a page is trapped between elements (such as text or photos), with no space through which to flow.

Resources

Veer.com

MyFonts.com

iStockPhoto.com

Before & After Magazine;
BAMagazine.com

Layers Magazine;
LayersMagazine.com

InDesign PDF Magazine;
InDesignMag.com

Index

About this book

I updated, designed, composed, and indexed this book directly in Adobe InDesign on a Mac.

The main fonts are Warnock Pro Light and Regular for the body copy (an incredible OpenType font from Adobe; see the note on page 210), Silica Regular for the headlines, and Proxima Nova Alt for the callouts. The cover font is Glasgow, originally designed by Epiphany Design Studio. The other three hundred+ fonts are listed inside.

About this author

I live and work on several acres in the high desert just outside of Santa Fe, New Mexico. I see the sunrise every morning and the sunset every evening. My kids have grown and gone and I'm writing books about things other than computers and traveling to interesting places in the world and life continues to be a grand adventure.

Some of the other books I've written

The Non-Designer's Type Book

The Non-Designer's Web Book (with John Tollett)

Robin Williams Design Workshop (with John Tollett)

A Blip in the Continuum (celebrating ugly typography, with illustrations by John Tollett)

And a bunch of Mac books:

The Mac is not a typewriter, second edition

Robin Williams Mac OS X Book (every os versions)

The Little Mac Book, Leopard edition (and others)

Cool Mac Apps (John Tollett; I helped)

And my favorite book (of mine):

Sweet Swan of Avon: Did a Woman Write Shakespeare?

John drew the above portrait in pen-and-ink in Venice, inspired by a Picasso exhibit of pen-and-ink portraits.

The Non-Designer's Type Book

Second Edition

Insights and techniques
for creating professional-level type

Robin Williams

Peachpit Press
Berkeley ✽ California

The Non-Designer's Type Book, second edition
Robin Williams

Copyright © 2006 by Robin Williams
Cover illustration and cover design: John Tollett
Interior design and production: Robin Williams
Update assistance: Barbara Sikora
Editing: Nancy Davis

Peachpit Press
1249 Eighth Street
Berkeley, California 94710
800.283.9444
510.524.2178 phone
510.524.2221 fax

Find us on the web at www.peachpit.com
To report errors, please send a note to errata@peachpit.com

Peachpit Press is a division of Pearson Education
The appendix article "Listen to Your Eyes" was printed in
Layers, The How-To Magazine for Everything Adobe, July/
August 2005. Reprinted with permission.

The chapter "Telltale Signs of Desktop Publishing" was
originally printed in slightly altered form in *Adobe Magazine,*
July/August 1995 under the title "Thirteen Telltale Signs."
©1995 Adobe Systems, Inc., all rights reserved.

To Allan Haley
with grateful appreciation
for inspiring, educating,
and befriending me.

I advise the layperson
to spread India ink
on an uncarved board,
lay paper on top of it,
and print it.
He will get a black print,
but the result is not
the blackness of ink,
it is the blackness of prints.

Now the object
is to give this print
greater life and greater power
by carving its surface.
Whatever I carve
I compare with an uncarved print
and ask myself,
"Which has more beauty,
more strength,
more depth,
more magnitude,
more movement,
more tranquility?"

If there is anything here
that is inferior to an uncarved block,
then I have not created my print.
I have lost to the block.

Shiko Munakata

Contents

The trumpet don't make the music
  and the computer don't make the type.
    You can put a cat in the oven
      but that don't make it a biscuit.

Introduction

With the advent of computers on the desktop in the late twentieth century, type and typography reached new heights of popularity. With this increased awareness has come increased sophistication and the need for the average person to understand how to create beautiful, professional typography that emphasizes the message, typography that is pleasing to the reader, and that invites readers in and keeps them there.

If you have read and followed the guidelines in *The Mac is not a typewriter* or *The PC is not a typewriter,* you are already creating type on a more professional level than you were before. Most of the techniques in this book can only be accomplished in a page layout application such as Adobe InDesign, Adobe PageMaker, or QuarkXPress. This book takes you several steps beyond those basic guidelines that you might have used in a word processor, into more subtle details that make the difference between good and sophisticated. You already recognize the difference—I'm sure you can glance at the two samples on the following page and instantly give an opinion as to which one is of higher quality. But can you name exactly what is creating that difference? Some differences are easily identified, others are more subtle. All are important.

If you're creating web pages, you'll find that many of the most important typographic techniques cannot be accomplished in the plain text on a web page. Type on the web will grow more sophisticated in the future, but for now many of the special techniques can only be applied to web pages as graphic pieces of type; that is, you create the headlines or fancy type in a graphics application, then put that graphic onto the web page. When you make that graphic text, you should of course apply every professional technique available.

Some of the guidelines in this book are too time-consuming for many everyday jobs, and I don't want you to think that unless you follow every suggestion here, your type will be inferior. But a key to creating great type is knowing what the options are in the first place. Once you know them, you can make choices as to when it might be appropriate to forgo some of the finer features.

So spend a couple of moments with the next few pages, make yourself conscious of the details, and see how many differences you can name before you look at the list. Then onward through the rest of the book, gleefully!

· ·

Training your eye

Glance quickly at the two quotations set below, and be conscious of your instant reaction as to which one has a more sophisticated appearance. Then look more closely at the one on the left, and see how many details you can pinpoint that contribute to its unprofessional appearance. Then look carefully at the quotation on the right, and see how many differences you can spot. Each of those differences helps to create the cleaner and more sophisticated appeal of the second quotation setting.

"HUMAN SOCIETY, the world, man in his entirety is in the alphabet. The alphabet is a source…first comes the house of man and its construction, then the human body, its build and deformities; then justice, music, the church; war, harvest, geometry; the mountain, nomadic life and secluded life, astronomy, toil and rest; the horse and the snake; the hammer and the urn which--turned over and struck--makes a bell; trees, rivers, roads; and finally destiny and God.

That is what the alphabet signifies."

--*Victor Hugo*, 1802-1885

"*H*UMAN SOCIETY, the world, man in his entirety is in the alphabet. The alphabet is a source . . . first comes the house of man and its construction, then the human body, its build and deformities; then justice, music, the church; war, harvest, geometry; the mountain, nomadic life and secluded life, astronomy, toil and rest; the horse and the snake; the hammer and the urn which—turned over and struck—makes a bell; trees, rivers, roads; and finally destiny and God.

"That is what the alphabet signifies."

~*Victor Hugo*, 1802–1885

Wrong	Better
The 12-point type is large and clunky.	The 10-point type is easier to read because you can see entire phrases, plus it has a more sophisticated look. (p. 193)
The line length is too short to justify the size of the text, creating uneven word spacing and too many hyphenated words.	Setting the type flush left instead of justified ensures that there is even spacing between the words. (pp. 38, 123)
The quote marks are ditto marks, not true quotation marks. And the first "quote" mark makes the text appear to indent in the first line.	The quotation marks are true quote marks, and the first one is hung into the margin, eliminating the appearance of an indent. (pp. 53, 57)
The computer ellipsis (…) is too tight.	The ellipsis is set with thin spaces and periods for more elegant spacing. (pp. 66–67)
Double-hyphens are used instead of em dashes.	Em dashes are used instead of double hyphens. (p. 68)
The paragraph space is created by hitting two Returns, making much too much space between paragraphs.	The space between paragraphs is only half a line space, maintaining a closer connection between paragraphs. (p. 118)
There are two-letter hyphenations. And the last paragraph has the worst sort of widow (a hyphenated last word).	Hyphenations have been eliminated. (p. 148)
There is a hyphen between the dates instead of an en dash.	Oldstyle figures are used for the dates, separated by an en dash. The baseline shift of the en dash was adjusted. (p. 72)
The small caps are computer generated, creating a discrepancy between the stroke weights of the small caps and those of the other letters and the capital.	The small caps in the first line are true-drawn. (p. 91)
The byline (Victor Hugo) is italic, so the comma after his name should also be italic, not roman. (p. 67)	In the byline, an ornament has been used instead of a dash. (pp. 163–164)
*Technically, the phrase does not need quotation marks around it, but I wanted to display them. When more than one paragraph is quoted, the proper convention is to place quotation marks at the **beginning** of each paragraph, but only at the **end** of the **last** paragraph.*	Swash characters were used for the first letters of Victor Hugo's name. These are not only a subtle visual pleasure, but also prevent the italic V from bumping into the dot on the lowercase i. (p. 151–154)
	Auto pair kerning has been used. Manual kerning has been used, where necessary. (pp. 107–111) Where appropriate, ligatures have been used. (pp. 95–96)

BOLDNESS HAS GENIUS,

POWER,

AND MAGIC IN IT.

■ Goethe

15

Review

This book is meant to follow *The Mac is not a typewriter* or *The PC is not a typewriter.* Rather than repeat everything I wrote in those first books, I must assume you have read it and are following those basic typographic principles. But just in case you think you're ready for this book without having read the other, I am including here a brief review. If you answer no (**N**) to any of these points, please take a few moments to read *The Mac/PC is not a typewriter.*

Y N　I type *one* space after periods, commas, colons, semicolons, exclamation points, question marks, parentheses, and any other punctuation.

Y N　I *always* use true quotation marks (""), *never* dumb ol' ditto marks (" ").

Y N　I *always* use true apostrophes (' not '), and I *always* put them in the right places.

Y N　I know the differences between hyphens, en dashes, and em dashes; when to use each; and how to type them.

Y N　I know how to use Special Characters on my Macintosh or the Character Map on my PC to access special characters such as ©, ™, ¢, ®, £, or €.

Y N　I know how to place accent marks over the appropriate letters, as in résumé.

Y N　I know to *never* underline text.

Y N　I *rarely* use all caps, and when I do it is certainly not under the mistaken assumption that all caps are easier to read.

Y N　I *always* avoid leaving widows and orphans on the page.

In this book I elaborate on some of the information that's presented in *The Mac/PC is not a typewriter,* but the material in this volume is very different from that in the previous books. If necessary, run down to your library, find *The Mac/PC is not a typewriter,* and take twenty minutes to get the gist of it. Especially if you're still typing two spaces after periods.

Robin

Anatomy of type

Before we begin, let's look at a few characters up close so when you read specific typographic terms throughout the rest of the book, you'll know what I'm talking about.

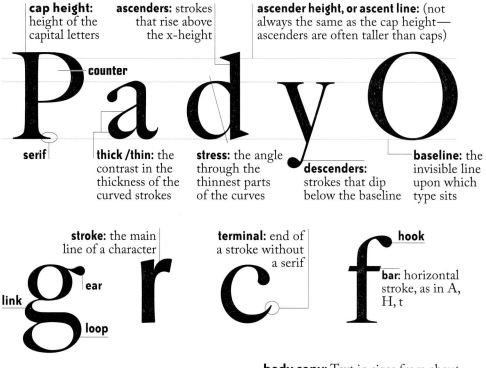

cap height: height of the capital letters

ascenders: strokes that rise above the x-height

ascender height, or ascent line: (not always the same as the cap height—ascenders are often taller than caps)

counter

serif

thick /thin: the contrast in the thickness of the curved strokes

stress: the angle through the thinnest parts of the curves

descenders: strokes that dip below the baseline

baseline: the invisible line upon which type sits

stroke: the main line of a character

terminal: end of a stroke without a serif

hook

link

ear

loop

bar: horizontal stroke, as in A, H, t

SERIF
SANS

Serif type has "serifs," as circled above. "Sans" is French for "without," so "sans serif" type has no serifs.

a*a* *ff* g*g* h*h*
aa ff gg hh

Notice how the serif letter **a** changes from a "two-story" **a** into a "one-story" ***a*** when it is italic, but the sans serif does not. That is typical of how the design of most serifs and sans serifs change when italic (but not all).

body copy: Text in sizes from about 8- to 12-point, set in paragraphs, as shown here (this is 10-point type).

display type: Text in sizes above 14 point, as in headlines or advertising titles. Shown above is 90-point display type.

roman: Type that does not slant. This type you're reading is roman.

italic: A style of type where the letters slant to the right. Most serif faces have true italic versions—the letters have been redesigned. See the comparisons (to the left) of the roman and italic versions of the same typeface.

oblique: The type is just slanted. This is typical of most sans serif "italic" faces (but not all).

· ·

The x-height

The x-height of a typeface is the size of the body of the characters as epito-mized by the letter x, since x is the only letter that reaches out to all four corners of the space.

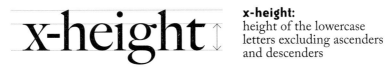

x-height:
height of the lowercase
letters excluding ascenders
and descenders

It is the x-height that creates the impression of the font's size. You see, the point size of the type as you know it, let's say 24 point, originally referred to the size of the little piece of metal on which the letter was created. Within that 24-point space, the designer could do anything he wanted—he could make tall ascenders, a large x-height, a small x-height, short descenders. He didn't even have to take up the whole 24-point space. So when we say a typeface is a certain point size, we are really only getting an approximation of the actual number of points from the top of the character's ascenders to the bottom of its descenders. And even if the actual measurement from top to bottom is the same in several typefaces, the x-height varies widely. Since most of what you see of a typeface is the x-height, it is that which gives a face its visual impact.

Every one of the fonts shown below is set in 24-point type. You can see how radically the x-height changes the impression, even though most of the capital letters are relatively the same size. Be conscious of the x-height in the fonts you use—you will make some typographic decisions, such as linespacing, point size for body copy, and readability enhancement based on the x-height of the typeface.

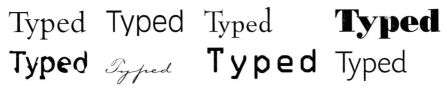

These are all 24-point type.

· ·

Points and picas

When you're working with type, you need to work in points and picas. It's just like using inches and feet, but the sizes are smaller—there are 12 inches in a foot; there are 12 points in a pica. But like I said, points and picas are much smaller—6 picas in 1 inch (which makes 72 points, then, in one inch).

Even if you've never formally worked with points before, you have a pretty good idea about how big 10-point type is as opposed to 24-point type because you choose and use point sizes of type on your computer all the time. So don't get nervous, just be conscious about those tiny sizes and try to use them more often. When your software, for instance, gives you a choice of using points or inches or lines, try using points. Once you start doing it, you'll probably find that it is actually easier to use points. I have a much clearer idea of how much space will be between the paragraphs if I ask for 6 points than if I ask for .083 inches. And I get confused about whether .083 inches is more or less than .072 inches, but I know darn well that 10 points is more than 8 points. Try dividing an 11-inch page into thirds. Ha! But change the measurement to picas, and the page is 66 picas, which is much easier to divide into thirds.

In general, we measure type sizes in points, and the space between lines or paragraphs in points. When measuring distances, such as the length of a line or the depth of a block of text, we use picas. Combining the two measurements is just like combining feet and inches: just as we write 6′2″ (6 feet, 2 inches), we write 3p4 (3 picas, 4 points).

Just so you know, traditionally (before desktop publishing) 72 points did not equal *exactly* 1 inch (it was a tiny smidgeon off). But when the Macintosh was originally created with a screen resolution of exactly 72 pixels per inch, our measurements for points became, on the Mac and then later on the PC, exactly 72 points per inch. Some software will let you override this standard, computerized amount and change it back to the traditional amount, but it's just about never necessary to do that.

A Brief History of Type

In which we briefly explore
the history of the world and
how it affects typography,
and how this in turn affects
your typographic choices.
Don't skip this chapter—
many references will be made
to the categories of type
as described herein.

Type is one of the most
eloquent means of expression
in every epoch of style.
Next to architecture,
it gives the most characteristic portrait
of a period and the most severe testimony
of a nation's intellectual status.

❧ Peter Behrens

Centuries of Type

The number of digitized typefaces is astounding, numbering well past 100,000 at the moment. It can be an overwhelming experience to decide which ones to buy, or even which ones to use.

However, if you group typefaces that have similar characteristics into a small number of categories, it makes the selection process much more manageable—it's easier to choose the typefaces you need to buy for your library by choosing a few from each category, and it's easier to decide which combination of faces to use on the page by making sure you grab no more than one from each category. And the process of grouping fonts makes you notice their more subtle features, makes you become more intimately involved.

It makes about as much sense to group several thousand faces into seven categories as it does to group human personalities into several character "types." There are always typefaces (or humans) with little quirks that prevent them from being conveniently pigeonholed, but there are generally enough shared characteristics in type to make it worth the effort.

I'm going to talk about seven different categories: oldstyle, modern, slab serif, sans serif, fringe/distressed, script, and decorative. The first five groups follow a historical perspective—there are interesting parallels between type development and developments in other areas of civilization such as architecture, archeology, philosophy, even economics. This doesn't mean that every typeface in a category was developed at that point in history. Goudy Oldstyle, designed by Frederic Goudy in 1915, is a classic example of the oldstyle category which began developing around 1500. The printer Aldus Manutius is credited with cutting the first oldstyle type in 1495; in fact, Aldus was such an important character that I have reprinted a story about him at the end of this chapter.

. . . .

Oldstyle

The characteristics of the oldstyle typefaces originally developed out of the traditional handlettering form, following the way the scribes held the pens and drew letters. When moveable type was developed in the mid 1400s, the letterforms that were carved out of metal resembled what everyone was familiar with—letters formed with a broad-tipped pen held at an angle. At that point in history, the only printed material was books. Big books. Books that sat on lecterns and were read aloud from. Since the only project for a printing press was to create books (there were no business cards or bread wrappers yet), the first typefaces were eminently *readable* because that was their only job.

Oldstyle typefaces tend to have a warm, graceful appearance and are the best choice for setting readable, lengthy bodies of text. Classic oldstyles are among the most "invisible," meaning that the character forms don't interrupt the communication; usually there are no design characteristics that trip your eye. The main body text you're reading right now is set in a classic oldstyle called Caslon (Adobe Caslon Pro).

Oldstyle typefaces always have serifs. The serifs on the lowercase letters slant and are "bracketed," meaning the serifs connect to the main strokes with a curve. The strokes make a gentle transition from thick to thin, as the broad pen made naturally. And if you draw a line through the thinnest parts of the rounded forms of a letter, the line is diagonal—this is called the "stress"; oldstyle faces have a diagonal stress.

Caslon   Minion   *Oldstyle typefaces*

Bembo   Times   *Note the diagonal stress*

Palatino Garamond

· ·

Modern

Times changed. The world changed. Type changed. Typefaces in the modern style were developed at a time when people were beginning to view the world differently. America ushered in democracy, France ushered out monarchy, the Industrial Revolution was underway, and political and social theorists were establishing a more rational, mechanical view of the universe and its inhabitants. Baroque, rococo, and oldstyle faces were rendered obsolete. Modern type reflected strict emphasis on structure and form, and the last vestige of type's handwritten origins disappeared.

Modern typefaces have a sparkle and an elegance, but they also tend to have a severe and cold appearance. They are not very *readable;* that is, they are not often the best choice for *lengthy* or small text, as the strong thick/thin contrast creates an effect called "dazzling" that is hard on the eyes.

Modern faces have serifs, but the serifs on all characters are horizontal and very thin, with little or no bracketing (there is no curve where the serif meets the stroke). The strokes that create the letterforms change radically from thick to thin. The stress is now absolutely vertical.

Onyx Didot   *Modern typefaces*

Bodoni *Note the vertical stress*

Bodoni Poster

· ·

Slab serif

Well, the Industrial Revolution really got going, and one of the results was a new field of business: advertising. Until then, of course, there were very few products to advertise. At first type designers tried to fatten up the thick strokes of the moderns, but the excessively strong combination of very fat strokes with very thin strokes made the text almost impossible to read. So they fattened up the entire letterform.

Slab serif typefaces also have serifs, and the serifs are horizontal, but they're thick. Fat. Slabs. The strokes that create the letterforms may make a very slight transition from thick to thin, or there may be no transition at all in some faces. The stress, when there is any, is vertical. Slab serif typefaces have a more regimented and strong appearance than do oldstyles.

I'll bet you were wondering why so many slab serif fonts are not named after their designers. Many of the *oldstyle* faces are named for their designers, such as Goudy and Baskerville and Garamond, but many *slab serifs* are named with Egyptian references such as Scarab, Memphis, Nile, and Glypha. It's indirectly because of Napoleon. One of his engineers found the Rosetta Stone, which turned out to be the key that unlocked the ancient hieroglyphics. This created a worldwide interest in Egyptian archeology and a mania for anything Egyptian. Type foundries noticed that if they named their typeface with an Egyptian reference, it sold better. To this day this category of type is sometimes called "Egyptian," even though there is no correlation between the style and the country except a fad. Slab serifs are also called "Clarendons" because the Clarendon typeface is the quintessential example of this category, as shown below.

Clarendon   *Slab serif typefaces*

Memphis

New Century Schoolbook

Candida, **Candida Bold**

· ·

Sans serif

In 1816 William Caslon IV created a "two-line Egyptian" typeface in which he took off all the serifs because he hated slab serifs. This face was not a big hit. It wasn't until the Bauhaus school of design was formed in 1919 that sans serifs (typefaces without serifs; "sans" is French for "without") began to be popular. Under the Bauhaus motto of "form follows function," typefaces were stripped down to their bare essentials, to their simplest, most functional forms, epitomized in the font Futura. This new school of design influenced the world.

Sans serifs, of course, have no serifs at all. Also, the strokes that create the letterforms have almost no visible transition from thick to thin (there are a very few exceptions, such as the typeface Optima). Sans serifs tend to have very large x-heights and so present quite a presence on the page.

Futura: form follows function

Today Sans

Sans serif typefaces

Formata Trade Gothic

. . . .

Grunge or distressed type

With the advent of the Macintosh computers and desktop publishing, type design—for the first time on earth—was put into the hands of the masses. Even more important, I believe, is that a mass *interest* in type was sparked— many people who never noticed typefaces before were suddenly wondering about the fonts on billboards and bread wrappers. With the power to create personal typefaces and to manipulate their layout on the screen, all the rules of traditional design and typography can be demolished. Who knows where this typographic anarchy will lead, but it is certainly fun and exciting to watch (and to use!).

Fringe typefaces (also variously called distressed, grunge, garage, deconstructive, edge, lawless, or just plain ugly) are typically distorted, schizophrenic, deliberately trashed, often difficult to read. But they are certainly identifiable and different from any other typefaces in history, and many are exquisitely beautiful in their ugliness. And they are incredibly fun to use. You might want to check out an old book of mine called *A Blip in the continuum*, illustrated by John Tollett, that is simply a celebration of ugly type.

GLADYS

Fringe typefaces—aren't they amazing? I love them.

Marie Luise

Bad Copy

Amoebia Rain

fragile

Dirty One

THE WALL

Rapture

schablone

Canadian Photographer

Scripts

Script and decorative typefaces have popped up in just about every period of typographic history. Script faces, of course, emulate handlettering in many varieties—blackletter (as in many of the Bibles handlettered by scribes), calligraphic (as in wedding invitations), drafting (as in architects' drawings), cartoon, and so on. No one has trouble identifying typefaces in this category.

Lamar Pen *Script typefaces*

Dorchester Script *Dear Sarah*

Cocktail Shaker *Nuptial*

Emmascript *Scriptorama*

Decorative

Decoratives are quite noticeable as well—the fonts made of ballet shoes or rope or Japanese pagodas or eraser dust. Decorative faces are not meant for anything else except to be decorative, which is far from an idle occupation. They can add punch to a publication, create a definite "look," or emphasize the content. If overused, they can destroy a design.

Baileywick *Decorative typefaces*

PLANET Serif   ChildA DOS

BILL'S FAT FREDDY

Blue Island   Mister Frisky

Aldus Manutius

AL   DVS

Have you ever wondered why roman type is called roman and italic type is called italic? Well, you can stop losing sleep over it.

Strange as it seems, in fifteenth-century Italy, land of the Romans, very few publications were printed with Roman letters—almost all scholarly or religious works were set in Greek. There weren't many other sorts of books anyway, except scholarly or religious works. Not many romance novels or horror stories.

When the man Aldus Manutius entered the publishing business with his company called the Dolphin Press, the printing industry was less than fifty years old. But there were already more than a thousand presses operating across Europe, and literally millions of books had been printed. Aldus was proud and protective of his Greek fonts, but a bit sloppy and diffident about his Roman fonts. In fact, most of them were not very well designed, and he used them only for jobs sponsored by wealthy clients or academic friends. In 1496, though, Aldus published an essay for Pietro Bembo, an Italian scholar and friend. The Bembo typeface, with its lighter weight, more pronounced weight stress, and more delicate serifs, was an instant success. Claude Garamond picked it up in France and spread its influence throughout the rest of Europe. This "Aldine roman" typeface, Bembo, affected type design for hundreds of years. (The body copy you are reading right now is set in Bembo.)

Aldus himself produced well over 1,200 different book titles in his 25 years as a publisher. Over 90 percent of the books he produced were Greek classics. Aldus was a well-patronized scholar before he entered the printing and publishing trade, so the classics were close to his heart. The market for his books was made up of the educated, the worldly, and the wealthy. Aldus created small books, or octavos, intended for busy people, for nobility traveling across Europe on errands of state, and for members of the "educational revolution" who were studying in the growing number of universities. Thus Aldus was the first creator of small, portable, "paperback" books.

The official writing style of the learned and professional scribes of southern Italy in the late 1400s was a relaxed, oblique, and flourishy script called *cancellaresca*. To make his books more appealing to the higher-class market, Aldus took this exclusive writing style and developed a typeface out of it. It was a hit. What a marketeer.

Aldus had his new type style copyrighted. He was trying to protect not just the one font—he wanted a monopoly on the cursive sort of style. He got it; he even got a papal decree to protect his rights. But as we all know, that doesn't mean no one will steal it. People did. At least the other Italians called the style "Aldino"; the rest of Europe called it "italic," since it came from Italy. The first italic Aldus ever cut (well, actually Francesco Griffo cut it) was produced in 1501 in Venice.

These innovations of Aldus Manutius place him in history as perhaps the most important printer of the Renaissance, next to Gutenberg himself. Popularizing the italic typeface, albeit inadvertently, had a profound influence on typeface development for generations. Prior to Aldus's beautiful octavos, the only small, portable books were prayer books; all other works were massive volumes that sat on lecterns for reading out loud. With the development of his italic type, more text could be set on a page, thus saving paper and space and making books more affordable. Education became more accessible, and the world changed. Again.

The function of reada-
   bility
   is often taken too liter
----ally
anD over-eMphasized.
         at the
   cost of individuality.

                Paul Rand

Readability and Legibility

In which we come to
understand what makes
type readable or legible,
and how to improve the
readability or legibility
of typefaces in various
situations.

THERE ARE THOSE WHO CONTEND that culture alone dictates our reading preferences, and that readability is based not upon the intrinsic forms of the characters, but upon what we are *accustomed* to reading. Often cited as "proof" of this is the German preference for blackletter that continued centuries after the rest of the world had moved on to more sensible typefaces. Without proposing any scientific studies, I venture to suggest that just because someone *prefers* a particular typeface does not mean it is more *readable*. Your grandmother, I am sure, preferred that you send her a handwritten letter; in fact, she was probably offended if you wrote her a letter on a typewriter. Even though your typewritten letter would have been easier to read than your handwriting, Grandma was not basing her preference upon readability, but upon other, more emotional responses. And I would propose that the German preference for blackletter was not because the letterforms were easier for them to read than what the rest of the world was reading, but that they had some other bonding with the blackletter forms.

Robin

Dear Grandma,
I wish you would let me use my computer to write to you. These darn letters take me two weeks to prepare. C'mon, this blackletter style is so old fashioned. Let me use one of my new and cool faces, like C h i c k e n ! It's easier to read than this silly font!

Love,
Sonny Boy

The Art of Readability

Readability and legibility are two elements of printed text that typographers strive to maximize. **Readability** refers to whether an *extended* amount of text—such as an article, book, or annual report—is easy to read. **Legibility** (discussed in the next chapter) refers to whether a *short burst of text*— such as a headline, catalog listing, or stop sign—is instantly recognizable.

What makes a typeface readable?

There are several factors that determine whether text is readable. Most typefaces are either high or low on the readability scale simply due to the way they are designed. But a typesetter or designer can make any readable face unreadable, and conversely she can improve the readability of any face. It is your job to be conscious of both.

What makes a typeface intrinsically readable? Mainly it is a matter of a moderation of features, an invisibility. That is, whenever a feature of a typeface becomes noticeable, that face becomes slightly less readable. If a typeface has a very distinctive lowercase g, so distinctive that it makes you stop and say, "wow, look at that g," then it is lower on the readability scale.

Any part of the type that calls attention to itself—thick strokes, very thin strokes, a strong contrast between the thick and thin strokes of a letterform, very tall and narrow forms, short and squatty forms, slanted characters, fancy serifs, swashes, or other extreme features—lowers the readability of the face because then you notice the letterforms rather than the message.

· ·

The most readable

The typefaces that make the most readable text are the classic oldstyle serif faces (remember those from Chapter 1?), either remakes of the original ones or new faces built on oldstyle characteristics. These typefaces were originally designed for long documents, since that's all there was in print at that time (late fifteenth to early seventeenth century). There were no brochures, advertising, business cards, packaging, freeway signs—there were only books. Big books. (In fact, it was Aldus Manutius, whose face made it into the 20th century on software packaging, who printed the first portable books in 1495.)

Other factors

Besides the distinguishing features of the typeface, there are other factors that can make text more or less readable, as described on the following pages. Once you are conscious of these factors, you can work with them to make even the least readable face more usable.

This is Belwe Light. Does your eye trip over the lowercase g or v or y? If your eye stumbles over the look of the type, it's not good for extended text.

This is Bernhard Modern, a very beautiful face, but too distinctive for extended readability. Great for brochures or other places where there is not an extended amount of text.

These faces have strong, noticeable features which make them quite distinctive. They are thus attractive for many uses, but there is too much distraction built into the faces to make them easy to read in extended text.

This is Minion Regular, a lovely font that was created specifically for lots of reading.

This is Garamond Pro Regular, also a lovely font that was created specifically for lots of reading.

Oldstyle typefaces have moderate features: there is moderation in the serifs, in the weight of the strokes, in the contrast between the thick and thin parts of the strokes, and in the x-height. I'll bet you can hardly tell these typefaces apart, right? It is this moderation, this lack of calling attention to the typeface itself, that makes oldstyles "invisible," which is ideal for communicating without an attitude.

· ·

Serif vs. sans serif

There are arguments about exactly why, but extensive studies do show that today in our society it is easier to read an extended amount of text when it is set in a serif typeface. Perhaps it is the serifs themselves that lead the eye from one character to the next, linking the letters into words. Perhaps it is the subtle thick-thin contrast in the strokes, which most sans serifs do not have. Perhaps it is the moderate ratio of x-height to cap height (the body of the letter in relation to the height of the capital letters or the ascenders), since sans serif letterforms tend to have larger x-heights.

Whatever the reason may be, accept the truth of it and use the knowledge in your typography.

Garamond Regular, 11-point type

She had not gone much farther before she came in sight of the house of the March Hare; she thought it must be the right house, because the chimneys were shaped like ears and the roof was thatched with fur. It was so large a house, that she did not like to go nearer till she had nibbled some more of the left-hand bit of mushroom, and raised herself to about two feet high: even then she walked up towards it rather timidly, saying to herself, "Suppose it should be raving mad after all! I almost wish I'd gone to see the Hatter instead!"

Lewis Carroll, *Alice in Wonderland*

Formata Regular, 10-point type

She had not gone much farther before she came in sight of the house of the March Hare; she thought it must be the right house, because the chimneys were shaped like ears and the roof was thatched with fur. It was so large a house, that she did not like to go nearer till she had nibbled some more of the left-hand bit of mushroom, and raised herself to about two feet high: even then she walked up towards it rather timidly, saying to herself, "Suppose it should be raving mad after all! I almost wish I'd gone to see the Hatter instead!"

Lewis Carroll, *Alice in Wonderland*

Which of these feels easier to read? If you really want to use sans serif in your body copy, shorten the line length, add a little extra linespace, and use a smaller size type than for a serif.

Caps vs. lowercase

Text set in all capital letters (all caps) is more difficult to read. We don't read letter by letter—we read in phrases. When you see a word, you don't sound it out letter by letter, do you? No, you glance at the word, recognize it, and move on. A significant factor in our recognition of whole words at a time is the *shape* of the word. But when words are set in all caps, every word has a rectangular shape and we have to go back to reading the letters.

Now, although all caps are definitely more difficult to read, especially when there is a lot of text, sometimes you *want* the rectangular shapes of all caps. If that is an appropriate solution for your piece, do it freely. Just keep in mind that you are making a choice to exchange better readability for a design choice—sometimes it's worth it.

Temper this decision with the purpose of your piece. If you really need strength in readability, as in extended text (or in the case of all caps, more than ten words), or if you want people to be able to browse quickly as in catalog headings, a parts list, the phone book, a list of names and addresses, headlines, a table of contents, then don't use all caps!

Momma Poppa Sister Brother

MOMMA POPPA SISTER BROTHER

You can see how the shapes of the words in lowercase are so different from each other, helping us identify them. In all caps, all words have the same shape.

Is this word Momma, Poppa, Sister, or Brother?

Does this shape represent the word cat, dog, or garbage?

· ·

Letter spacing
and word spacing

Again, since we read in phrases, uneven letter and word spacing disturbs our natural reading pattern; our eyes have to make constant adjustments between words. Spacing that is consistently too close or too far apart also disturbs our reading. There is no perfect rule that will fix the spacing for every typeface and every project—you must simply learn to see more clearly and then *trust your eyes.* If it looks like the words are too close together, they are. If it looks like the letters are too far apart, they are. Once you recognize appropriate and inappropriate spacing, you have the responsibility to learn exactly how your particular software controls the letter and word spacing. Ha! Read that manual.

Many script faces have connecting letters that need slightly *tighter* letter spacing so their letters will actually connect, but they also often need *extra* word spacing because the tails of the letters bump into the spaces between the words. Again, I cannot emphasize enough that you need to know how to control the spacing in your page layout application! (Most word processors do not have features to fine-tune the letter spacing.)

You are guaranteed to get poor word spacing if you justify text in a narrow column, so don't do it. How do you know if it's too narrow? See the next page.

It isn't what I do, but how I do it.

It isn't what I say, but how I say it.

And how I look when I do it and say it.

Mae West

So which one of the lines above is too tight? Which one has too much word space? Which one looks okay? See how good you are at this already? Trust your eyes.

· ·

Line length and justification

If a line is too long, we have trouble finding the beginning of the next line. If a line is too short, it breaks up those phrases we recognize. If you try to justify your type on a short line, you will get awkward word spacing and rivers. So how do you know what's a decent line length?

There are several rules of thumb to determine this measure. Some people suggest no more than nine to ten words on a line as a maximum, or no more than 2.5 times the alphabet, which is 65 characters. The rule I find easiest to remember for an optimum line length (the minimum line length for justifying) is this:

> Double the point size of your type, and use a line length no longer than that in picas.

Say what? Well, let's say your type size is 9 point—your line length should be 18 picas. If your type is 24 point, your line length should be 48 picas.

All you have to remember is that there are 6 picas in one inch: thus 18 picas is 3 inches; 48 picas is 8 inches. (Did you read page 18 about points and picas?)

Don't justify any text if your line length is shorter than this minimum! If you're using a classic, readable oldstyle and you really want it justified but you find that the word spacing varies too much even on this line length, make the line a few picas longer and perhaps add a tiny bit more linespace.

Figure out your optimum line length and then analyze your typeface. Shorten the line length of *non-justified* text for these reasons:

- If the typeface has a very large x-height or a very small x-height.
- If the typeface is a sans serif.
- If you are reversing the type out of a background or solid color.
- If the typeface is script, decorative, or at least rather odd.
- If you are presenting type where it is difficult to read, such as on a presentation slide or on a web page.

Linespacing (leading)

Linespacing is, obviously, the space between the lines. You have total control over how much space appears. Linespacing that is too tight decreases readability because it makes it difficult for the reader to separate the individual words and phrases, and it also makes it more difficult for the reader's eyes to find the beginning of the next line.

You will generally need to **increase linespacing** for these reasons:

- If the line length is longer than average.
- If the typeface has a large x-height, as most sans serifs do.
- If you are reversing the type out of a background or solid color.

You can **decrease linespacing** on an average line length if your typeface has a very small x-height since the small x-height creates more space between the lines naturally. But often when using a distinctive typeface with a small x-height, it is nice to reinforce that airy, open feeling by actually adding more linespace. See Chapter 15 on linespacing for more details and specific examples.

My way is and always has been to obey no one and no thing except that reasoning which seemed best to me at the moment when I made my decision. Never judge past action by present morality.

Socrates

The paragraph above is set with the default linespacing (leading) value. Notice it seems a little tight between the lines. Typeface is Formata Light.

My way is and always has been to obey no one and no thing except that reasoning which seemed best to me at the moment when I made my decision. Never judge past action by present morality.

Socrates

Just adding one point of space in the paragraph above helped to open up the text so it is more pleasant to read. Sometimes all you need to add is half a point; sometimes you'll need to add several extra points.

. . . .

Reverse type and light or heavy weights

White type on a dark background (reverse) appears to be smaller than black type on a white background. Compensate for this by using a slightly heavier typeface and slightly larger point size. If you have a Pro version of an OpenType font (see Chapter 30), use the caption weight, which is a little heavier.

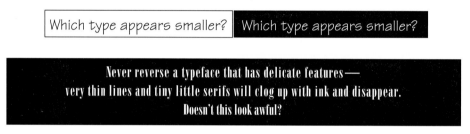

Never reverse a typeface that has delicate features—
very thin lines and tiny little serifs will clog up with ink and disappear.
Doesn't this look awful?

The same guideline applies for text that is dropped out of a graphic image. I know it looks great on the screen, but when ink hits absorbent paper, all kinds of havoc is wreaked upon unsuspecting delicate type. Don't let your work look foolish by ignoring the realities of the reproduction process.

Extra bold type and extra light type are also less readable than a regular weight face. If you use them, be sure to compensate—you may need extra letterspace, extra linespace, a bit larger or smaller point size. Your eyes will tell you what is necessary.

On **web pages,** avoid colored text on a dark background. If you must, enlarge the size of the type a wee bit, and don't use bold or italic except in small doses.

Italic or script

Italics and scripts are more difficult to read in general because of their tight spacing, their curves and slants, their approximations to handwritten letterforms. Don't ever use them for extended text or no one will read your work. Maximize their readability:

- *Pay close attention to their letter and word spacing.*
- *Increase their linespacing if necessary.*
- *Make the line length shorter than average.*
- *Don't reverse them unless they are set in a relatively large size.*

Do you find this section less readable, even in this small amount of copy? Yes, these things are true—I am not just making them up.

· ·

Moderation is the key

I'm sure you see the pattern by now—moderation in every facet of typography is the key to eminent readability. Now, this does not mean that you have to be dull and boring and moderate at all times! It just means that you need to be conscious and make conscious choices.

- ❧ Perhaps you want to use a very distinctive face in a brochure. If the face itself is not intrinsically readable, then make up for it in other areas of readability—an appropriate line length and word spacing, avoid all caps, etc. Make sure that all other text is eminently readable, and then you can get away with areas of fancy type.

- ❧ If you want to use a sans serif in body copy, use a shorter line length and a little extra space between the lines.

- ❧ If you want to reverse text, make it a bit bolder and larger, and don't use a fine-featured typeface that has tiny little serifs or thin lines that will disappear.

- ❧ Save extra bold and italic and extra light for accents.

- ❧ If your typeface has an extra-large x-height, use more linespacing. If it has very tall ascenders, you can use less linespacing.

- ❧ If you're setting a book, manual, magazine, or other lengthy text, including a lot of text on a web page, use the most readable face in all its moderation. Save the distinctive faces for chapter titles, headlines, subheads, poetry, etc.

THROUGH TYPOGRAPHIC
MEANS, the designer
now
preSents, in one image,
both the mes-
sage and the
pictorial idea.
Sometimes,
this "playing"
with type has
resulted in th-
e loss of a cer-
tain amount of
legibility. Re-
searchers con-
sider this a
deplorable
state of
af-fairs,
but on th-
e other
hand, the ex-
citement cre-
ated by a no-
vel im-
age someti-
mes more than
compensates

for the slight
DIFFICULTY
in readabil-
ity.

Herb Lubalin

The Art of Legibility

Readability, as discussed in the previous chapter, refers to whether an extended amount of text—such as an article, book, or annual report—is easy to read. **Legibility** refers to whether a short burst of text—such as a headline, catalog listing, or stop sign—is instantly recognizable.

There have been extensive studies on type to determine which factors influence different aspects of reading, such as reading speed, retention of information, recognition of letterforms, etc. Interestingly, these studies show that in our culture and in our era, serif typefaces are easier to read when there is a lot of text, but sans serif letterforms are more instantly recognizable when there is a small amount of text. Sans serif characters tend to be direct and clear, with no serifs to add unnecessary tidbits to the shapes. When we read a large body of text, however, those same serifs help to guide us along the lines.

We don't read letter by letter; we see the entire word or the phrase and it goes straight to our brains. When text is less than perfectly legible, we have to take extra time to read it. Sometimes this is only a split second, sometimes it's a more significant struggle, but it can make a big difference in whether the information is absorbed or tossed aside.

Text needs to be most legible (as opposed to readable) in situations where people are scanning pages, reading signs, or skimming through catalogs or lists—wherever they need to instantly recognize words without having to spend extra seconds to read them. For instance, in a newsletter, the headlines should just pop right off the page into the reader's brain. In a parts list, the reader should be able to slide down the page, absorbing the names of parts. In a table of contents, a reader should be able to scan the contents. Street signs, "Warning," "Danger," and all freeway signs should be instantly recognizable.

. . . .

What are you saying?

Always be conscious of the words themselves. Some words, such as "Sale," can probably be set in just about anything and people will get it. But if you have an unusual name, don't set it on your business card in a typeface that is difficult to read! If words are long or foreign and extremely important, be especially careful to choose a typeface with great legibility.

What makes type legible?

Not all sans serif typefaces are eminently legible. One of the keys to legibility is the clarity of the letterforms, or how easy it is to distinguish one character from another. For instance, the typeface Hobo eliminates the descenders (see below); this is useful in certain applications, but it is not what we are accustomed to and thus this feature decreases its legibility.

I don't make jokes. I just watch the government and report the facts.
Will Rogers

Legibility depends on the instant recognition of letterforms.
When characters have odd shapes, we don't recognize them instantly.

· ·

Large or small x-height

An exceptionally large x-height decreases legibility. Some faces have such large x-heights that an "n" is hardly different from an "h."

And a very small x-height also decreases legibility. The body of the character is disproportionate to the cap height, and our eyes find this to be distracting —besides the fact that the letters appear too small.

I dote on his very absence.   William Shakespeare

Notice there is not much difference between the "n" and the "h," nor between the "i" and the "l" in "William." Typeface is Antique Olive Roman.

Hercules himself could not beat out his brains, for he had none. William Shakespeare

Although this typeface is pretty and very distinctive, it is not the most legible. Typeface is Bernhard Modern.

· ·

Weight and proportion

❧ **Extra-heavy or extra-thin weights are less legible. A good solid bold, however, as long as it is not extra-heavy or condensed, can enhance legibility by giving a substantial contrast to the rest of the text. For instance, headlines are great in bold because the contrast of their weight attracts attention against the background of gray, readable text. But how do you like reading even this short paragraph in an extra-bold face (Antique Olive Compact)?**

❧ A monospaced font (such as Courier) creates inconsistent letter and word spacing, which makes it less legible (and less readable) because our eyes have to keep adjusting to the differences in spacing. Some faces are so poorly spaced that words can be misread at a glance.

❧ Using the computer to compress the typeface distorts its proportions and makes it less legible. If you want a compressed face, buy a specially designed font. See Chapter 12 for details and more examples on this topic.

All caps or
mixing caps and lowercase

❧ Mixing Lowercase And Caps In The Same Sentence Makes Type Less Legible *And* Less Readable. Your Eyes And Brain Have To Figure Out What's Going On Because We Are Not Accustomed To Reading This Way. This Is Called Title Case And Is Meant For Titles, Not Sentences or Captions.

Killing time takes practice. Karen Elizabeth Gordon

This typeface, Peignot, is interesting but not particularly legibile. Or readable. It mixes caps and lowercase in the middle of words, confusing our pea brains.

❧ WORDS SET IN ALL CAPS ARE THE LEAST LEGIBLE OF ALL, NO MATTER WHICH TYPEFACE YOU USE. MANY PEOPLE THINK IF YOU SET TYPE IN ALL CAPS IT IS BIGGER AND THEREFORE EASIER TO READ. Wrong. We recognize words by their shapes as well as by their letters. Set in all caps, all words have the same shape. Have you heard this before?

INDEPENDENCE AVE.	Independence Ave.
CONSTITUTION AVE.	Constitution Ave.
MASSACHUSETTS AVE.	Massachusetts Ave.

In Washington, D.C., the streets have long names. The street signs are set in all caps, squished to fit into the standard green shape. Consequently, you must get very close to a sign to tell what it says. If the street names were in upper- and lowercase, you would be able to tell Independence Avenue from Constitution Avenue long before you could actually read the letters.

. . . .

The most legible type

To make your text the most legible, use:

- A plain sans serif with an average x-height.
- A regular or medium weight (sometimes bold when appropriate).
- Lowercase letters (plus capitals where they belong).
- Not condensed or expanded or oblique (slanted).
- A little extra letter spacing in small point sizes (below 10 point); less letter spacing in large sizes (above 14 or 18 point).

Which of the following type samples is the most legibile?

1. Few forgive without a fuss.   Hobo

2. *Few forgive without a fuss.*   Dear Sarah

3. Few forgive without a fuss.   Antique Olive Bold

4. FEW FORGIVE WITHOUT A FUss.   THE WALL

5. Few forgive without a fuss.   Peignot

6. Few forgive without a fuss.   Formata

7. Few forgive without a fuss.   Bernhard Regular

. . . .

Temper the rules with choice!

Now, please remember that these guidelines do not mean you should never use certain typefaces or formatting! It just means you must look carefully at your typeface and make a conscious choice—if your piece requires a high level of legibility, watch for the danger signs. If your job is one that people can take a tiny bit longer to absorb or if the words are not unusual, then feel free to play with features that are not at the top of the legibility list. Use that beautiful face with the tall ascenders and small x-height for a sign, or that lovely, graceful script for a special title, or that extra-bold face for web page headlines. People can *read* it, of course. Know the guidelines, be conscious of your typeface and your purpose of communication, and make clear decisions based on knowledge.

And don't forget Herb Lubalin's theory, as presented on page 42. Lighten up and smile.

**No passion in the world
is equal to the passion
to alter someone else's draft.**

H. G. Wells

Punctuation

In which we explore
quotation marks
and prime marks,
hanging punctuation,
optical alignment of characters,
punctuation style,
and baseline shift
for hyphens, dashes,
and parentheses.

I OFTEN QUOTE MYSELF.

IT ADDS SPICE TO MY CONVERSATION.

GEORGE BERNARD SHAW

Quotation Marks— or not?

If you are choosing to read this book, you are probably already conscious of the difference between typewriter quote marks (" ") and true quotation marks (" "), often called "curly quotes" or "smart quotes." But let's make sure you are also using single and double prime marks where appropriate, and leaving the ditto marks in their place.

First, a review of quotation marks and apostrophes

Most software has a checkbox called something like smart quotes, true quotes, typographer's quotes, or a similar phrase, like one of these:

☑ "Smart quotes"

☑ Use Typographer's Quotes

Replace
☑ "Straight quotes' with "smart quotes"

If you check that box, the software will automatically insert true quotation marks when you type the " key on the keyboard. You will also get a true apostrophe when you type the ' key on the keyboard, as displayed below:

"No, don't do this."   "Yes, isn't this better?"

But be careful—if you trust the computer to always put the correct mark in the correct place, you will find people snickering at your work. For instance, when the automatic feature is on you will get quotation marks where you need inch and foot marks, like so: Bridge Clearance 12'6". Or when you have a quotation mark that appears right after a dash—"like this"—the quote mark goes the wrong way!

You need to know the key combinations to type the correct single and double quotes, both opening and closing, for those times when your software doesn't do it correctly. See the charts in Appendix C.

Don't embarrass yourself

Follow these basic rules so your work doesn't look dumb:

- Quotation marks at the beginning of a word or sentence are *opening quote marks* and curl *toward* the text (").

  Quotation marks at the end of a word or sentence are *closing quote marks* and curl *toward* the text (").

  These are often called "sixes and nines" because the opening marks are shaped like sixes and the closing marks are shaped like nines.

- An apostrophe belongs where a letter is missing, as in **cookies 'n' cream** or **rock 'n' roll.**

  Notice your computer automatically inserts a ***backwards*** apostrophe at the beginning of a word! For instance, your computer will do this: **cookies 'n' cream.** This is WRONG! And dumb!

  Know the keyboard shortcut to insert the correct mark:

To type this:	Mac	Windows
opening single quote '	Option Shift]	Alt 0145

- The word **it's** with an apostrophe means *it is* or *it has.* **Always.** Really and truly **always.**

  The word **its** *without* an apostrophe is the possessive form of the word, as in *hers, his, theirs,* or *its.* Notice none of those possessive words contains an apostrophe. *Don't put an apostrophe in **its** unless you mean **it is** or **it has!***

- When talking about decades, such as **in the '90s,** there is an apostrophe where the other numbers are missing.

  Make sure you set an apostrophe and not an opening single quote! The phrase should not look like this: **in the '90s,** which is what you will get if you let the computer type it for you.

  Also notice there is no apostrophe before the s (not **in the '90's**) because generally you are referring to a plural number of years, not a possessive number.

. . . .

Single and double prime marks

Another problem with letting your computer automatically type the quotation marks for you is that you end up with quotation marks and apostrophes when you really need inch and foot marks.

Wrong: **Ryan stands 6' 2" tall.**   Right: **Ryan stands 6′ 2″ tall.**

Now, you might think that you should be typing those ugly typewriter apostrophes and quotation marks for inch and foot marks. Wrong, dear. In excellent typography, feet and inches are represented by single and double *prime marks,* which are at a slight angle, as shown below.

These are typewriter quote marks: **" '**

These are double and single prime marks: **″ ′**

If you have the Symbol font on your computer (which you probably do), you can use the prime marks in it:

To type this:		Mac	Windows
single prime mark	′	Option 4	Alt 0162
double prime	″	Option Comma	Alt 0178

However, it's very possible that the prime marks in the Symbol font do not match the weight of your characters. Until every font has prime marks built in, you might often have to use the italic version of your typewriter apostrophes or quotations marks, as shown below.

Using the Symbol font might look inconsistent: **Kiki stands 5′ 8″ tall.**

Use italic typewriter marks: **Kiki stands 5′ 8″ tall.**

Technically, prime marks are not meant specifically as inch and foot marks, but as markers of divisions of equal parts. For instance, you would also use the single prime mark to show the minutes or degrees of an angle or a turn, as in 12° 8′ (read 12 degrees and 8 minutes).

Ditto marks

So what good *are* those typewriter quote marks on your keyboard? Well, go ahead and use them in email because it's too much trouble to take the time to set real quotation marks. And until every browser and email client used on the web can interpret the code correctly, we have to be patient with typewriter apostrophes and quote marks in most HTML code. You can use these as ditto marks, should you ever need to set ditto marks to show that an item is repeated, as shown below (although some people do prefer to use double prime marks as ditto marks).

Superman	128 Power Street	Metropolis	USA	
Lois Lane	327 Reporter Way	"	"	*ditto marks*

A helpful chart

In case you are still confused, here is a handy little chart that sums up the wrongs and the rights. Find the phrase that matches what you want to say and follow its example.

Wrong	Why it's wrong	Right
Food at it's best	The phrase does *not* say, "Food at it is best."	Food at its best
In it's shell	The phrase does *not* say, "In it is shell."	In its shell
Where its at	The phrase is supposed to say, "Where it is at."	Where it's at
Hall 'o' Fame House "O" Glass	The "f" is missing from "of." There is nothing missing in front of the letter "o."	Hall o' Fame House o' Glass
Gone fishi'n	The "g" is missing.	Gone fishin'
Rock 'n' Roll Rock 'n Roll Rock n' Roll Rock 'n Roll	Both the "a" and the "d" are missing from "and." So an *apostrophe* belongs where each letter is missing—an *apostrophe,* not an opening single quote mark!	Rock 'n' Roll Rock 'n' Roll Rock 'n' Roll Rock 'n' Roll
In the 60's (decade)	This is not possessive, it is plural. The "19" is missing from "1960."	In the '60s

Hang that Punctuation

Using real quotation marks and apostrophes is a good sign that you've progressed beyond typewriter mentality. Now that you're using the correct punctuation, the next step is to hang it (where appropriate).

What does it mean to "hang the punctuation"? Well, take a look at the quotations below. In the left one, would you agree that the first line appears to be indented? Obviously, it is the empty space below the quotation mark that creates that illusion. Take a look at the same quotation on the right. Now the left edge of that text has a strong, clean alignment, and the punctuation is "hanging" outside that edge. That clean edge is what you want; it is a sign of being conscious of your typography.

"What you do speaks so loudly that I cannot hear what you say."

Ralph Waldo Emerson

"What you do speaks so loudly that I cannot hear what you say."

Ralph Waldo Emerson

You can easily see, in the example on the left, what a visual gap the quotation mark creates. Hanging the punctuation off the edge of the text maintains the strong, clean alignment. Typeface is Bailey Sans Bold.

· ·

When to hang it

Punctuation should always be hung when type is set aside from the main body of text or when set large, as in a quotation, pull quote, headline, poster, etc. If the type is set flush right, the periods or commas at the ends of the lines should also be hung if they interrupt the right edge of the type. (Except in very fine typography, punctuation in body text is usually not hung because of the trouble it takes and because the interruption in the line is not as significant when the type is small.)

"I'm laughing
at the thought
of you laughing,
and that's how laughing
never stops in this world."

Zorba the Greek

"I'm laughing
at the thought
of you laughing,
and that's how laughing
never stops in this world."

Zorba the Greek

I'm sure you agree that both of these pieces of type need the punctuation hung.

"I'm laughing
at the thought
of you laughing,
and that's how laughing
never stops in this world."

Zorba the Greek

"I'm laughing
at the thought
of you laughing,
and that's how laughing
never stops in this world."

Zorba the Greek

Oooh, look at those nice clean edges. The strength of that edge gives strength to the page. Typeface is Bailey Sans Bold.

. . . .

Optical alignment

The point of hanging the punctuation is to keep a strong left or right edge. Often this means aligning the edge with a stem (vertical stroke) rather than with a bar (horizontal stroke), as in the letter "T." Align the second line of type with whatever is the strongest edge of the initial character you see—remember, your eye is always right! *If it doesn't look aligned, it isn't.* You might have to align with the bottom point of the capital "V," or just inside the outside curve of an "O." Whichever part of the letter is the closest or most obvious visual connection, align with it. This is called "optical alignment" because you are not aligning by a ruler, but by your eye.

**"You believe easily
that which you
hope for earnestly."**

Terence

Even though the top edge of the letter "Y" is aligned with the second line of type, it still appears to be indented. That's because our eyes see the vertical stem of the "Y," rather than the top angle, much more closely related to the "t." Typeface is Today Sans Medium.

**"You believe easily
that which you
hope for earnestly."**

Terence

Above, the stem of the "Y" is visually aligned with the "t." This is an optical alignment rather than a measured alignment.

. . . .

Just how do you hang it?

At first, hanging the punctuation might seem like a silly task. But as your typographic consciousness is raised, I guarantee you will also begin to see it as a sign of professional type. There are several methods of doing this, depending on the project and the software.

Software features

InDesign can hang the punctuation with the click of a button. From the Type menu, choose the "Story" palette. Put a check in the box, "Optical Margin Alignment." Enter the point size of your type. This will hang punctuation even in the middle of a paragraph, when it's flush left, flush right, or justified. This applies to the entire *story* and can slow down the redraw and composition, so only use it when necessary.

QuarkXPress can hang the punctuation of left-aligned type. For repeated instances of hanging indents, use the "Formats" command in the Style menu. For a single instance you can use the key command for "Indent Here," which is Command/Control \ (backslash).

Use an indent

If you have to hang the punctuation by hand, one of the easiest ways is to use an indent, as shown below. This works when the quote is a paragraph on its own and is flush left. If you use this setup regularly in your publication, make a style sheet for it.

**"It's as large as life
and twice as natural,"
said Alice.**

*Set your indents so the first line marker
is flush left, and the left indent marker is
aligned along the stem of the first letter.*

Reverse the punctuation

This next trick is kind of a kludge (which means a dorky solution), but it works: select the punctuation and paste it in front of (or at the end of, if flush right) each of the other lines. Select the punctuation you have pasted in and then choose the "reverse" style from your font formatting menu to make the characters invisible. (In a word processing application, you might not have the option to make type reverse; perhaps you can color it white.)

The reason I suggest you paste the punctuation instead of simply typing it is that very often when type is set fairly large (above 14 point), you need to reduce

. . . .

the size of the punctuation so it doesn't appear unnecessarily important. By pasting the punctuation, you ensure that all your reverse spaces are the same size, even if you changed the type sizes.

"Run mad as often as you choose, but do not faint."	**"Run mad as." often as you." choose," but do not." faint."**	**"Run mad as often as you choose, but do not faint."**
Jane Austen in *Mansfield Park*	Jane Austen.," in *Mansfield Park.*	Jane Austen in *Mansfield Park*
A. *The punctuation needs to hang.*	**B.** *Paste in copies of the punctuation.*	**C.** *Reverse the punctuation you don't need.*

Use hard spaces

A "hard space" is an empty space that is different from the regular space that you type with the Spacebar. A hard space doesn't "break" like a regular word space does—a non-breaking, hard space connects two words as if they were one word. For instance, to prevent the name "Ms. Scarlett" from breaking into "Ms." at the end of one line and "Scarlett" at the beginning of the next line, you would type a hard space between "Ms." and "Scarlett," and then the phrase "Ms. Scarlett" would never break into two words

You can indent on the left or right with hard (non-breaking) spaces, if your software allows it (try it and see). Almost all applications can set a standard hard, non-breaking space in place of the regular blank space, and some, like Adobe InDesign, can set em, en, and thin spaces (see the charts in Appendix C). Use these blank spaces to indent lines of type so you have a strong flush alignment. If the space you set is too large, select that blank space and reduce the size of it.

"I knew who I was when I woke up this morning, but I must have changed several times since then," said Alice.

"I knew who I was when I woke up this morning, but I must have changed several times since then," said Alice.

In this example, I typed an en space in front of the first word of every line (except the first one) to align them with the first letter in the paragraph.

. . . .

Kern outside the text block or box

If for some reason you must do it by hand, try this in your page layout application: Insert a hard space *in front of* the first quotation mark. Then kern until the
quotation mark hangs outside the text block or box. In QuarkXPress, the mark
may seem to disappear, but it will print just fine.

"But look, the morn, in russet
mantle clad, walks o'er the dew
of yon high eastward hill."
Horatio

*Notice the quotation mark is
hanging outside of the text block.*

To type this:	Mac in general	Windows
non-breaking space	Option Spacebar	Alt 0160
	Mac InDesign	**Windows InDesign**
	Command Option X	Control Alt X

In InDesign, you can also select the space and use the contextual menu
(right-click; on a Mac, Control-click); choose "Insert White Space,"
then "Nonbreaking Space."

Punctuation Style

All of us now circumvent the professional typesetter and create beautiful publications on our own desktops. We've heard all about the typesetting standards of setting one space after periods, and how to access em dashes and en dashes and true quotation marks and apostrophes. Although most of us know how to *create* these alternate characters, there still seems to be considerable confusion over *when* to use them. The punctuation in your publication affects the professional appearance of your work just as powerfully as the characters themselves. (It's interesting that when the "rules" of design are broken it is called "creative," but when the established rules of punctuation are broken it is called "uneducated." Creative punctuation is not a well-accepted idea.)

So following are some guidelines to help give your desktop-designed work a more professional edge. If you have other questions, read *The Chicago Manual of Style,* William Strunk's wonderful little book, *The Elements of Style,* or check the back of your dictionary—most dictionaries include a basic manual of style.

It is often the very small details that set mediocre work apart from outstanding work. To push a publication to the professional edge, make sure you carry your style all the way through, even to such mundane principles as punctuation.

Quotation Marks

Of course you are using proper quotation marks (" ") and not typewriter marks ("). American standards decree that periods and commas be placed inside quotation marks, *always.* Like it or not, that's the way it is in America; some other countries do it differently.*

"Oh Bear," said Christopher Robin, "How I do love you."
"So do I," said Pooh.

Colons and **semicolons** are always placed *outside* the quotation marks, and they are both followed by one space.

This is how to pronounce "forte": fort.

Most people mispronounce "victuals"; it is properly pronounced "vittles."

Exclamation points and **question marks** follow logic: If the mark belongs to the quoted matter, it goes inside. Otherwise it is set outside.

She said, "I love to crack crawdads!"

Did she say, "I love to crack crawdads"?

She asked me, "Don't you love to crack crawdads?"

My son warned me, "Mom, I met a girl who loves to crack crawdads"!

Note: The delightful book that you may have seen called **Eats, Shoots and Leaves is from Britain where they use quotation marks differently (essentially, their rule is similar to our rule, above, about exclamation points and question marks). In the American version, the publishers did not adjust the book for American usage; consequently, every quotation mark in that book is **WRONG** according to our standards. It's rather odd that a book bitterly complaining that people don't follow the correct standards did not standardize the book for its market here.*

. . . .

Parentheses

If the text inside the parentheses is just an aside within or at the end of a sentence (like this one), then the punctuation goes after and *outside* the closing parenthesis.

If the text inside the parentheses is a complete sentence that starts with a capital letter and ends with a period (or other final mark), then the punctuation belongs *inside* the parentheses. (This is an example.)

There are no extra spaces surrounding parentheses, other than the normal word space before and after. There is no extra space between the closing parenthesis and any punctuation that might follow.

Meet me under the magnolia at twilight (without the wig), and we will waddle down the trail together.

Notice the comma is directly after the parenthesis, and there is just the regular word space after the comma.

Also see Chapter 7 for information on when you might need to shift the baseline position (up or down) of the parentheses.

· ·

Apostrophes

In contractions and informal writing, the apostrophe belongs where the letter is missing. Remember that simple principle and you will never go wrong. I repeat myself on this because it is so important; the misuse of the apostrophe is rampant and really annoying.

In case you missed it: One of the two most common mistakes in typography is with the word **and** between words such as **Mom 'n' Pop** or **peaches 'n' cream.** Set the apostrophe where the letters are missing! If a letter or number is missing at the beginning of a word, *don't turn the apostrophe around so it looks like an opening single quote.* It *should* be an apostrophe.

To know where the apostrophe belongs in **possessive words,** turn the phrase around. The apostrophe belongs *after* the word in the turned phrase. For instance, "all the horses oats." Is it all the oats that belong to the *horse* (which would then be *horse's oats*) or all the oats that belong to the *horses* (which would then be *horses' oats*)? Notice the apostrophe is set *after* the word you used in the turned-around phrase.

Its or It's

The other most prevalent mistake is the word **its .** Do you put an apostrophe in *hers,* or *his,* or *theirs,* or *yours?* No. The word **its,** when possessive, is in the same category as hers, his, and yours—*there is no apostrophe!* **It's** with an apostrophe always, always, always reads **it is** (or *it has*). **Always.**

Ellipsis

The ellipsis character (the three dots: …) is used to indicate where text has been omitted from the original material. There is a character on your keyboard for this.

To type this:	**Mac**	**Windows**
ellipsis …	Option Semicolon	Alt 1033

But this character is too tight for professional typographic standards. You can type a space between periods, but then it might break at the end of a line and you would have one or two periods at the beginning of the next line. Preferably, type a thin or en space before and after each period in an ellipsis (see the chart at the end of the book). If you can't type thin or en spaces kern the three periods open. If you have an ellipsis at the end of a sentence, type a period after the ellipsis.

Wrong: **It's so...silly.**   Right: **It's so . . . silly.**

Type style

The style of the punctuation should match the style of the word it follows. For instance, if a word followed by a comma is **bold,** then the comma itself should also be bold. You may have a semicolon following *italic words;* the semicolon should be italic. Follow the same principle for any style change.

Parentheses, though, do not pick up the style unless everything within the parentheses is the same style. That is, if all the text in the parentheses is italic, then the parentheses are both italic. But if only the last word is italic, the parentheses are set in the regular style of the rest of the text. The same goes for bold or any other style change. Like so:

She's willing (and able) and she'll be ready in a while.

She's willing (and I do believe she's ***able***), but not ready.

She's willing *(but not able)* and will be ready in a while.

Don't worry if you think it looks a little odd to have a big fat bold period or comma in the middle of your **paragraph,** like so. This is one of those things you get used to and then the wrong way begins to look glaringly wrong. It's like knowing that the pronunciation of the word **forte** (as in "Pickle-making is my forte") is really "fort," not "fortay." The word "fortay" means "loud, forcefully," as in music notation. At first it sounds wrong to say "fort," and you must have conviction to pronounce it properly among others who assume you are wrong, since most people pronounce it incorrectly. But once you accept that "fort" is the correct pronunciation, "fortay" is wrong (unless you choose to use a dictionary that has succumbed to popular pronunciation rather than correctness, which is what happens to our language). (Oh well.)

· ·

Em dashes

Text within parentheses is like whispering; text within commas is an average statement; text within em dashes is more emphatic. The example below illustrates this concept.

Use em dashes to set off a phrase that has a lot of commas in it—like this, and thus, and so—to avoid confusing the reader.

Or mark an abrupt change in thought or sentence structure—I learned this yesterday—with an em dash.

Em dashes are set with no space before or after the dash. This bothers many people, though, because the dash tends to bump into the letters. So add a tiny bit of space on either side by kerning (see Chapter 14 on Kerning). But if you insert an entire word space before and after the dash, you exacerbate the interruption in the flow of text.

The origins of printing are almost as obscure as the origins of writing, and for much the same reason — its inventors never used their new medium to record the process.
Sean Morrison

When there is a space on either side of an em dash, it creates a disturbing gap in the text and calls too much attention to itself. Typeface is Memphis Light.

The origins of printing are almost as obscure as the origins of writing, and for much the same reason—its inventors never used their new medium to record the process.
Sean Morrison

Kern a little bit of space on either side of the em dash, if necessary, just enough so it doesn't bump into the letters.

To type this:	Mac	Windows
em dash —	Option Shift Hyphen	Alt 0151

· ·

En dashes

The most common use of an en dash is to indicate a duration. Read the sentence; if you substitute the word "to" for the dash, then the proper mark is an en dash. Actually, in a real sentence I would spell out the word "to," but you will often find occasions outside of sentences where an en dash is the appropriate mark.

> **All children ages 3–10 are welcome to attend
> the crawdad party from 6–8 p.m. every Monday
> from September–November.**

En dashes are commonly used with a little extra space on either side, especially when indicating a duration. Either add a little space with your kerning function, or insert a thin space on either side—*do not* type a whole word space with the Spacebar on either end of the en dash.

Also use an en dash instead of a hyphen in a compound adjective when one of the items is two words or a hyphenated word.

> **She took the New York–London plane to be at the opening
> of the post–Vietnam War presentation.**

> **The Internet cafe was filled with the over–sixty-five crowd.**

To type this:	Mac	Windows
en dash –	Option Hyphen	Alt 0150

Hyphens

Just because you know how to use em and en dashes, don't ignore hyphens! Em and en dashes do not replace hyphens—they simply replace *the incorrect uses of the hyphen.* If you are breaking a word at the end of a line, or if you are using a compound adjective as in "blue-green eyes," of course type a hyphen!

The following situation is difficult to describe, so I am going to illustrate it instead. When you have something like this:

> **Martha was both a first-place and second-place winner in the gravedigging contest.**

"First-place" and "second-place" are adjectives composed of two words, making them "compound." You probably want to combine those compound adjectives into something like this:

> **Martha was both a first- and second-place winner in the gravedigging contest.**

Does it bug you that the word "first" has a hyphen after it? Well, too bad because that is the correct way to set the text. The hyphen indicates that this word is also connected with the rest of the adjective. Once you understand and accept the correctness of it, you can have a little uppity attitude when you see others set it wrong. Gently teach them.

Shift that Baseline

Ahhh, so you have surely by now read *The Mac is not a typewriter* or *The PC is not a typewriter*, as well as the previous chapters in this book, and you have been diligently typing one space after periods, using real apostrophes and quotation marks, putting the apostrophes in the right places, and creating true fractions. Right? Now that you're feeling sassy, it's time to move on to a more sophisticated matter: baseline shift.

First, let's clarify the term **baseline.** The baseline is the invisible line upon which all the characters sit, as shown below. Some characters, such as j, p, g, and y, have strokes that hang below the baseline; these strokes are called the "descenders." The term "baseline shift" refers to moving characters up or down in relation to that baseline.

I have a frog in my pocket, darling.

The grey line indicates the baseline of the text. Most characters are designed to sit directly on the baseline; descenders hang below.

Once you are familiar with the baseline shift technique, you will find uses for it more often than you might think!

. . . .

Parentheses and hyphens

I'll bet it drives you nuts that the hyphens in phone numbers seem set too low. And the parentheses around the area codes bump into the numbers, which probably makes you crazy. You see, parentheses and hyphens are designed to be used with lowercase letters because that is where they appear most of the time. So when these characters are used with all caps or numbers, they appear to be low in relation to the taller size of the caps or numbers. But, thank goodness, this can be fixed.

Below, I shifted the hyphen and the parentheses up a little higher until they appeared to be centered—doesn't it look much better, more consistent, in better balance? There is no scientific formula for the exact placement—*your eye is the judge.* If it looks centered, it is. If it looks too low, it is. If it looks too high, it is. Listen to your eyes.

(707) 123-4567

The parentheses bump into the tops of the numbers, but hang below the bottoms. Also notice how low the hyphen sits.

(707) 123-4567

To make parentheses and hyphens appear to be in the correct position when you're working with caps or lining numbers, raise them up a little.

A. The Cul-de-Sac reopens (dinner only)

B. THE CUL-DE-SAC REOPENS (DINNER ONLY)

C. THE CUL-DE-SAC REOPENS (DINNER ONLY)

*Parentheses and hyphens are designed for lowercase letters, since that is where they are used most often (**A**). If you use all caps (**B**), the hyphens and parentheses are too low. Raise them higher off the baseline to make them appear centered (**C**).*

Dingbats as bullets

Another occasion to take advantage of the baseline shift feature is when using dingbats or ornaments. Suppose you have a list of items and you really want to use a fancy dingbat from the Zapf Dingbats or Wingdings font, instead of using the boring ol' round bullet (or—heaven forbid—a hyphen). But the dingbat character is usually too big. When you reduce its size, though, the dingbat is too low because the character is still sitting on the baseline. So select the character and shift it higher up above the baseline.

Pick any three adjectives that describe yourself:

- Ruffatory
- Doaffie
- Byblow
- Regnant
- Backgone
- Illy-willy
- Fustian
- Dorty
- Fuzzled

A. *Choose a dingbat instead of the dumb ol' bullet or hyphen.*

Pick any three adjectives that describe yourself:

✤ Ruffatory
➞ Doaffie
✳ Byblow
❤ Regnant
❖ Backgone
❑ Illy-willy
❀ Fustian
✪ Dorty
▼ Fuzzled

B. *You have lots of dingbats to choose from, but they are usually too big. (Choose one dingbat.)*

Pick any three adjectives that describe yourself:

▾ Ruffatory
▾ Doaffie
▾ Byblow
▾ Regnant
▾ Backgone
▾ Illy-willy
▾ Fustian
▾ Dorty
▾ Fuzzled

C. *You can decrease the point size of the bullet, but then it sits too low.*

Pick any three adjectives that describe yourself:

▾ Ruffatory
▾ Doaffie
▾ Byblow
▾ Regnant
▾ Backgone
▾ Illy-willy
▾ Fustian
▾ Dorty
▾ Fuzzled

D. *Raise the small dingbat higher off the baseline.*

. . . .

Initial caps

You can also create a quick initial cap with baseline shift. Change the size and font and perhaps color of the first letter. If it disrupts the line spacing, select the entire paragraph and apply a fixed amount of leading (just type in a number—don't use "auto"; see Chapter 15). Then select the first letter and apply the baseline shift downward—making sure the baseline of the letter aligns on one of the baselines of the paragraph! (See Chapter 24 for lots of suggestions for initial caps.)

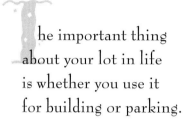

The important thing about your lot in life is whether you use it for building or parking.

In this paragraph, I selected the "T" and changed its typeface and size. I used the technique in Chapter 5 (hard space and kerning) to hang the "T" so it aligned with the rest of the text. I used the baseline shift feature to drop the bottom of the "T" down to the second line. I kerned the "h" in toward the "T."

Typeface is Bernhard Modern with the cap T in Scarlet.

Decorative words

You can also create interesting special effects with words, as shown below. Some of the letters have been shifted up, then kerned into the caps. The "W" has been shifted down slightly. The word "That" has been shifted up and kerned close, also.

This arrangement was created with baseline shifts and kerning. Typeface is Cocktail Shaker.

· ·

Corrections

Sometimes, especially in decorative type or logos, the characters are not exactly where you want them. So use your baseline shift to adjust their positions. Remember one of the Rules of Life: You are never stuck with anything. Get busy. Get creative.

This is the way the text set as I simply typed it. I wanted the apostrophe lower and the Z to come down a bit to balance the word.

That's better, and that was easy.

Typefaces are Las Bonitas Bold and Schmelvetica.

. . . .

How do you do it?

To baseline shift, check your manual. All page layout applications can shift the baseline, as well as many word processors. The *amount* of baseline shift is determined by your preferences, which you can change. Here are a couple of keyboard shortcuts for Adobe InDesign and QuarkXPress.

First select the character(s). Then:

- **Mac InDesign**:

  to move up   Shift Option ↑ (UpArrow)

  to move down   Shift Option ↓ (DownArrow)

  Add the Command key to increase by 5 times the increment set in your preferences.

- **Windows InDesign**:

  to move up   Shift Alt ↑ (UpArrow)

  to move down   Shift Alt ↓ (DownArrow)

  Add the Control key to increase by 5 times the increment set in your preferences.

- **Mac QuarkXPress**:

  to move up   Command Option Shift +

  to move down   Command Option Shift -

  (Use the + and - from the keyboard, not the numeric keypad).

- **Windows QuarkXPress**:

  to move up   Control Alt Shift)

  to move down   Control Alt Shift (

Expert Type

In which we look at
OpenType, true-drawn
small caps, compressed
and expanded characters,
as well as ligatures and
oldstyle figures (numbers).

We also explore
expert sets and
discuss display type.

I would 'twere bedtime, Hal, and all well.

Falstaff

OpenType & Expert Sets

What I love most about the recent revolution in electronic design and communication is the explosion in the awareness of typography. People who, ten years ago, didn't know there was more than one typeface in the world now scrutinize menus and advertisements and posters, wondering what font is on the page.

It also never ceases to amaze me how quickly we become inured to the magic, how quickly we find that what we have isn't enough, how quickly we want more and better and bigger. It's hard to imagine that we could want more than the standard set of 256 characters in a typical font, which is many more than we had on typewriters. But we do, and that's just the way it is. And that's why several of the major font vendors created **expert sets,** which are additions to basic font sets designed for when we get to that point of wanting more and better, such as oldstyle figures, true small caps, fractions, swashes, display versions, superior and inferior characters, and extra ligatures.

And that's one reason why Adobe and Microsoft jointly created **OpenType,** which takes advantage of the double-byte of the latest operating systems, both Mac and Windows, to let us have fonts that can contain more than 65,000 glyphs (variations of characters).

In this chapter I'll explain what OpenType and expert set fonts are and why you might want to use them. In the following chapters I elaborate on when and why to use each of the expert typographic features.

What's in an OpenType or expert set font?

This chapter is an introduction to what you might find in OpenType or expert set fonts. The following chapters elaborate on the various typographic features, such as those listed below, that you'll find in these special fonts.

Small Caps

Almost any program can turn selected lowercase letters into SMALL CAPS, where a capital is still a capital and the other letters become capital letters about the height of lowercase letters. The problem, though, is that the computer simply reduces the size of the existing capital letters. This creates a proportion distortion between the cap and the small cap, where the capital letter appears much heavier than the corresponding smaller capitals, as shown on page 90. In many OpenType and expert set fonts, the small caps are not just small capitals, but are letterforms that have been totally redesigned to visually match the large cap in the same point size. See Chapter 9.

Oldstyle figures

Regular numerals (figures), such as 45,872, appear too large when set within body text. Numerals used to be designed like lowercase letters, with ascenders and descenders, like so: 45,872. Many OpenType fonts and expert sets include these oldstyle figures, which blend smoothly with the body copy. Oldstyle figures are also particularly beautiful when set in extra-large sizes. Once you start using them it's hard to go back to the other characters. See Chapter 10.

Display type or titling caps

Traditionally, small letterforms and large letterforms in a well-designed typeface differ not just in their height, but in their thick/thin stroke differences, the proportion of the x-height to the cap height of the character, the space between the letters, and the open space in the "counters" (the holes in letters like e, g, or c). But on the computer when you use a large point size, say 128 point, of a regular font, the computer just takes the 12 point size and enlarges it to 128 point. The letterforms start looking a little clunky.

Some expert fonts offer display type (which includes lowercase) or titling capitals. The characters in display typefaces have been specially designed for larger sizes, those above 24 point. The difference isn't readily noticeable at 24 point, but becomes quite significant on headline or poster-sized type. See Chapter 13. OpenType fonts sometimes include not only a display version of the typeface, but separately designed versions for captions and subheads. See page 84.

. . . .

Ligatures

In addition to the standard ligatures *fi* and *fl* (Mac only) expert sets usually offer many more combinations, such as an Rp for rupees or *&* for special effects in words like a&tion. See Chapter 11. OpenType fonts might include dozens of great ligatures; see page 85.

Swash characters

The more elaborate expert sets offer alternate swash characters that can add a nice touch to your work. *Remember*, swash characters are like cheesecake—it's easy to overdose. And be sensible where you place them. The swash is meant to end a phrase or tuck under adjacent letters, not to create an unsightly gap. *See Chapter 23.* Swash characters are often built into the italic version of an OpenType font.

Em dashes

Convention decrees that we set em dashes with no space on either side—like so. But those long dashes often bump right into the letters and have to be manually letterfit. Many people insist on using a space on either side of the em dash, which exacerbates the interruption in the reading and creates an even larger gap in the overall look of the type. Some expert sets contain a wonderful character that solves this problem—a ¾-em dash with a thin space built into both sides. You have to look for it, unfortunately.

Ornaments

There are often pretty little ornaments ( ) in expert sets and OpenType fonts that offer elegant alternatives to dingbats. See Chapter 26.

OpenType in particular

There is so much to tell you about OpenType fonts. Please see pages 84–86.

· ·

The details are delightful

The subtle distinctions that OpenType and expert sets offer would have passed fairly unnoticed in the general public years ago. But the level of type sophistication has increased so dramatically across an incredible variety of professions, so the subtle distinctions in type are now being noticed and appreciated. Even though the changes are what some may call minor, the overall professional effect comes through clearly.

This life is but a Penelope's web, where we are always doing and undoing; a sea open to all winds, which sometime within, sometime without never cease to torment us; a weary journey through extreme heats and colds, over high mountains, steep rocks, and thievish deserts. And so we term it in weaving at this web, in rowing at this oar, in passing this miserable way.

A Discourse of Life and Death translated by Mary Sidney Herbert, 1592
original in French by Philipe de Mornay

This is a simple example of the difference the specialty fonts in an expert set can make in a piece of type. To the left is plain ol' Times Roman, 12/14.5, justified.

*T*HIS LIFE IS BUT A PENELOPE'S WEB, where we are always doing and undoing; a sea open to all winds, which sometime within, sometime without never cease to torment us; a weary journey through extreme heats and colds, over high mountains, steep rocks, and thievish deserts. *A*nd so we term it in weaving at this web, in rowing at this oar, in passing this miserable way.

A DISCOURSE OF LIFE AND DEATH
translated by Mary Sidney Herbert ❦ 1592
original in French by Philipe de Mornay

This is Brioso Pro Regular, 10.5/15, with small caps, display swash italic, regular swash italic, and oldstyle proportional numerals. The bylines use Brioso Pro Caption, also with small caps, an ornament, italic, and oldstyle numerals.

Expert set fonts

You can buy expert sets at most of the font web sites (see a partial list in Appendix B). Because a regular font can only hold up to 256 characters, an expert set is actually a collection of fonts in the same family. That is, in an expert package you will get the regular font, plus you might get a font that contains just the small caps, another that contains oldstyle figures, superscripts, and subscripts. And yet another for italic swash. A complete expert set package might contain up to thirty different fonts in the one family! Each font will show up in your font list separately (see pages 87–88).

An expert set font might be labeled "Expert," "OSF," "SC," "Small Caps," or some other descriptive term. Be sure to check the specifications and the samples for the font before you invest in it.

This is the Adobe Caslon Expert family with all the individual fonts for the regular character set and each of the expert additions.

Before you run out and buy a bunch of expert sets, carefully read about OpenType. OpenType is eventually going to replace expert sets. If you're using InDesign, skip expert sets and move right into OpenType. If you're using QuarkXPress, any version earlier than 7.0, you're stuck with expert sets.

OpenType fonts

OpenType is a font format from Adobe and Microsoft. It's based on Unicode, which uses a double-byte encoding system. You don't need to know the technical points of it—all you need to know is that by using this encoding, a font can now contain more than 65,000 glyphs instead of the basic 256 we've been limited to all this time.

A **glyph** is an individual symbol for a character. For instance, the lowercase letter "z" is a character. But you might have a capital Z, a small cap z, a swash Z, and an accented Ź. Each of these is considered a glyph, even though they are all the same character.

An OpenType font can include **entire character sets** for true-drawn small caps, fractions, swashes, ligatures—all explained in the following chapters.

With the possibility of more than 65,000 glyphs in one font, it's also possible for one font to include **multiple language characters.** For instance, an Adobe OpenType Pro font typically includes Cyrillic characters for Russian and other Slavic languages, a full range of accented characters to support European languages such as Polish and Turkish, and even Greek characters. μ'αγαπάς;

OpenType fonts are **cross-platform** — you buy one font file and it works on Mac, Linux, Unix, and Windows platforms. This is a tremendous help when files are moving between one operating system and another.

An OpenType font might include several **optical size variations.** As explained in more detail on page 80, fonts really should be redesigned for different sizes, not just enlarged or reduced on the computer screen. An OpenType font might provide you with a redesigned version of the typeface specifically to be used in small sizes, called the **caption** font for 6- to 8-point text; a **regular** version for 9- to 13-point text; a **subhead** version for 14- to 24-point; and a **display** version for 25- to 72-point or larger. In the examples below, you can see the different weights and thick-thin proportions in each of the variations, depending on the point size at which it's designed to be used—smaller type needs to be a little heavier with a little more letterspacing; larger type needs thinner thins and less letterspacing.

Warnock Pro Caption, 18 point
Warnock Pro Regular, 18 point
Warnock Pro Subhead, 18 point
Warnock Pro Display, 18 point

· ·

OpenType fonts are smart

When you use OpenType in an application that knows what to do with it, you'll find that OpenType fonts are "smart." That is, they automatically substitute characters that are more appropriate in particular typographic situations.

For instance, when you set type in all caps, OpenType adds the appropriate amount of baseline shift so characters such as hyphens and parenthesis fit better (see Chapter 7).

In a script face, glyphs might change depending on whether the character is at the beginning, in the middle, or at the end of a word. In a handwriting font, OpenType can automatically use different glyphs for the same characters so the set text more closely resembles handwriting.

❶ *This* **e** *is designed for use in the middle of a word. The connector on the left side usually attaches to the previous letter.*

❷ *This* **e,** *without a connector, is great when* **e** *is the first letter of a word or directly after a capital letter to which it will not connect.*

❸ *This* **e** *is obviously perfect for the last letter.*

❹ *This* **e** *is great as the first character in a word that appears on its own line (so the swash won't bump into the previous word).*

❺ *Ministry Script also has a huge number of ligatures.*

The OpenType face used for the chapter openers in this book is Ministry Script from Umbrella (shown in the examples above), available at Veer.com. Flip through the chapters and take a look at the huge variety of glyphs, including ligatures, available in this font. Below is the font Zapfino, which is included with Mac OS X. The different ligatures and glyphs for the letter "f" appear automatically; you can see OpenType change its mind as you type. Notice also the lovely ligature for the "Th."

This fish flies free

. . . .

Check before you buy

Not all OpenType fonts include extra characters! Many have just had a facelift and are now in the OpenType format, but the great things you see in this chapter are not included. The Adobe OpenType fonts that are feature-rich have the word "Pro" in their names. When buying a font, look for features such as "automatic characters substitution" or "opticals." On a web site like Veer.com, the specs clearly tell you what you can expect in any OpenType font. Veer also provides PDFs that explain more about OpenType and how to use it; you can download the PDF from any page that displays an OpenType font.

Two types of OpenType fonts

There are two types of OpenType fonts. One is PostScript-based, such as those in the Adobe Type Library. They have an .otf extension in the font file name. The other type is TrueType-based and has a .ttf extension.

You can install and use any flavor of OpenType font along with PostScript Type 1 and TrueType fonts.

ACaslonPro-Regular.otf

Nadeem.ttf

Sorry, but . . .

As I write this, only Adobe applications use OpenType efficiently and effectively. QuarkXPress cannot take advantage of the OpenType options beyond the regular 256 characters until version 7.0.

Realities of using OpenType and expert sets

The deterrent to using expert sets in everyday work is that they are actually different fonts that contain only the special characters. If you type an address, for instance, you have to switch from your regular font to the expert font for the numbers, then back to the regular font again. To use the ¾-em dash you must change fonts for that one character. Every time you add a swash character you must change fonts. In many expert sets, the small caps font has no matching large caps at all, so every word that contains a regular cap in addition to small caps requires two font changes. To simplify matters you can often use search-and-replace. Or you might want to set up a macro or quick-key for switching.

Another problem with the expert sets is that the vendors don't always provide much information on the characters that are available, where they might be useful, what some of those strange symbols are good for, or how to access all of them. Some of the sets have hidden characters that are difficult to discover, such as those that take four keys to produce (such as, on the Mac: Option Y, let go, then Shift N).

Font utilities

To find and use the special characters, you'll need an extra little font utility. On a PC, use the Character Map that you find in your Start menu.

On a Mac, use the Character Palette or the Keyboard Viewer: Open System Preferences, choose "International," click the "Input Menu" tab, check "Character Palette" and "Keyboard Viewer." Also check the box at the bottom, "Show input menu in menu bar." Now in your menu bar you'll see an American flag; from that menu you can choose either of these utilities.

In InDesign on a Mac or a PC, use the Glyphs palette found in the Type menu, shown on the following page.

If you are adept at working with a large number of fonts, you probably already use a font management utility like Suitcase, Font Agent Pro, or Font Reserve. It's practically a requirement to use one of these utilities with the larger expert collections, like Adobe's Minion (22 fonts) or Linotype's Centennial (17 fonts).

The Caslon face like the one you're reading totals 26 separate fonts in the expert set version. These families include such treats as more weights, swashes, display type, titling caps, caption fonts, super- and subscript numbers in proportion to the font, and ornaments. However, I am actually using the Adobe OpenType version of Caslon Pro so I have more options for all the special characters, all in one typeface with several different optical weights. It's much easier!

· ·

Adobe InDesign makes using OpenType a breeze. Below you see my font menu for an OpenType font called Warnock Pro. You can see the menu itself tells me it's an OpenType font by the little "O" icon next to its name. Once I have selected the optical size and style I want to use, I can use the Glyphs palette (farther below) to select specific characters.

InDesign's font menu is great. It displays the font's format, a sample of it, and organizes the family very nicely.

The Glyphs palette displays every character in a font.

When you see a tiny triangle in the corner of a glyph's box, you know there are alternate glyphs for that character. Click on the triangle to see the alternates, as shown above. Double-click a glyph to make it appear on the page where the insertion point is flashing or where text is selected.

Small Caps

THERE ARE A NUMBER OF TECHNIQUES that designers and typographers use to make type more beautiful and pleasant—one technique is the use of small caps. Small caps are capital letters that are approximately the size of lowercase letters. Small caps are often used simply for their design effect, but they have several very practical uses in fine typography. Sometimes an article or chapter opening begins with the first line (or part of the first line) in small caps, as in this paragraph. This is a simple, elegant way to lead the reader into the text.

Where to use small caps

If you set acronyms in regular all caps, their visual presence is unnecessarily overwhelming. One standard and practical way to use small caps is in acronyms such as FBI, NRC, CBS, or SIMM.

Traditionally, "A.M." and "P.M." are set with small caps. If you were taught to type on a typewriter (or if you were taught by someone who learned on a typewriter), you were probably told to set these abbreviations in all caps because there were no small caps on typewriters. But now that you have the capability, you can and should set them properly.

> Harriet, an FBI agent, turned on CNN to get the dirt
> on the CIA before going to bed at 9:30 P.M.

> Harriet, an FBI agent, turned on CNN to get the dirt
> on the CIA before going to bed at 9:30 P.M.

The capital letters in the middle of the sentence call too much attention to themselves. Notice how the small caps blend in with the text. The capital letters for P.M. are much too large—the abbreviation is not that important.

· ·

Creating small caps on your computer

Most programs have a command in the Format or Font menu to change selected lowercase letters to small caps. If not, type the text in all caps and then reduce the selected letters to about 70 percent of the point size of the rest of the type (this is what the computer shortcut does).

These two methods are okay if you are going to use small caps just once in a while on fairly low-level jobs. But if you are producing fine typography, you really need to invest in a typeface that has specially designed small caps. When you simply reduce the point size of the type (the same thing the computer does when you use a menu command), all the proportions are reduced and the thickness of the strokes of the smaller letters no longer matches the thickness of the regular caps or other letters in the same sentence.

THERE IS NO REST FOR THE WICKED.

The weight of the computer-drawn small caps is thinner than the weight of the regular initial (first letter) caps. Typeface is Eurostile Condensed.

If you need to use a face that does not have a matching set for small caps, try using the semibold face (if there is one) for the small caps, since when you reduce their size their line thickness will shrink. Or you can try changing the default size of the small caps—if your application sets small caps at 70 percent, try changing that to 82 percent to match the stroke thickness better.

Unfortunately, in QuarkXPress and InDesign the small cap size you set in the preferences applies to your entire document—to every font, every size, every style, every weight, whether it's a large, bold headline or a small, italic caption. This is very poor typographic handling. The more global a typographic preference is, the less useful it is.

In PageMaker, you can change the small cap size per character, and you can add it to your style sheets.

. . . .

True-drawn small caps

There are quite a few font families that include "true-drawn" small caps, which are letterforms that have been totally redesigned as small caps specifically to match the proportions and thicknesses of the matching uppercase. OpenType fonts, which can contain thousands of characters, often include true-drawn small caps. In an application that knows what to do with OpenType, such as InDesign, using the keyboard shortcut to change text to small caps actually chooses the optically correct small cap characters.

Other font families with small caps may be called "expert" sets or perhaps "small cap" sets (see Chapter 8). The result creates an undisturbing, smooth, uniform tone throughout the text.

THERE IS NO REST
FOR THE WICKED.

THE WICKED ARE VERY WEARY.

True-drawn small caps are specially drawn to match the weight of the capital letters in the same face. If you use an OpenType font that includes small caps, you can use the keyboard shortcut to make the text small caps and OpenType will make sure to use the true-drawn characters.

Typefaces are Formata Expert, a PostScript font, and Adobe Caslon Pro, an OpenType font.

. . . .

Readability and legibility of small caps

Pull quotes and captions are sometimes set with small caps, but keep in mind that small caps are no easier to read than all caps. Since every word in all caps is a rectangle, our eyes have to resort to reading letter by letter. This does not mean you should *never* use all caps or small caps—just be aware of this limitation and use them when you can justify the loss in readability and legibility. The more text there is in all caps or small caps, the less likely it is that people will read it.

TO LIVE CONTENT WITH SMALL MEANS; TO SEEK ELEGANCE RATHER THAN LUXURY, AND REFINEMENT RATHER THAN FASHION; TO BE WORTHY, NOT RESPECTABLE, AND WEALTHY, NOT RICH; TO STUDY HARD, THINK QUIETLY, TALK GENTLY, AND ACT FRANKLY; TO LISTEN TO STARS AND BIRDS, TO BABES AND SAGES, WITH OPEN HEART; TO BEAR ALL CHEERFULLY, DO ALL BRAVELY, AWAIT OCCASIONS, HURRY NEVER. ❧ IN A WORD, TO LET THE SPIRITUAL, UNBIDDEN AND UNCONSCIOUS, GROW UP THROUGH THE COMMON. ❧ THIS IS TO BE MY SYMPHONY.
WILLIAM HENRY CHANNING

Do you find that, even though the text is interesting, you have to struggle to stay with it? Small caps are no easier to read than all caps.

Oldstyle Figures

In typography, numbers (or numerals) are called **figures.** Most typefaces use plain old regular numerals, or figures. These regular numerals (also called "lining figures") are similar to all caps in that they appear to be too large when set within body text. But figures used to be designed like lowercase letters, with ascenders and descenders, which blend smoothly and beautifully with body copy. These "oldstyle figures" are also particularly beautiful when set in large sizes. Once you start using them it's hard to go back to the regular lining number.

Notice how large and clunky these figures appear:

Dear John, please call me at 438-9762 at 3:00 to discuss marriage.
Or write to me at Route 916, zip code 87508.

Notice how beautifully these figures blend into the text:

Dear John, please call me at 438-9762 at 3:00 to discuss marriage.
Or write to me at Route 916, zip code 87508.

· ·

Monospaced figures

Regular, or lining, figures are not proportionally spaced as letters are; they are monospaced. That is, every regular number takes up the same amount of space: the number one occupies as much space as the number seven. This is necessary because we often need to make columns of numbers and the numbers need to align in the columns.

Rats	473	*If the numbers were not monospaced,*
Ravens	1,892	*we would have great difficulty*
Robots	19.5	*aligning them in columns.*

But when you use regular, lining figures in body text, the monospacing creates awkward letter spacing and usually requires kerning. Look carefully at the letter spacing in the numbers below:

Call Rosalind at 1.916.911.7546.

Proportionally spaced figures

In most (not all) expert fonts, the oldstyle figures are proportionally spaced, meaning they each take up only as much space as is appropriate for the number—the number one takes up less space than a nine because it's skinnier. This is particularly wonderful for text use because the numbers fit together so well, but don't use proportionally spaced oldstyle figures in columns to be summed or they won't line up! When you buy an expert set and start using oldstyle figures, first make a quick check to see if yours are proportionally spaced or monospaced: just type several rows in columns and see if you can draw a clean line between each column.

1234567
4598021
9768635

1234567
4598021
9768635

Because the numbers on the far-left are monospaced, they align neatly in columns. The numbers on the right are proportionally spaced, so they do not align in columns.

OpenType fonts often include these figure options:

Proportional oldstyle:	1234567890	*for within text; lovely*
Tabular oldstyle:	1234567890	*for oldstyle figures in columns*
Proportional lining:	1234567890	*lining figures in proportional spaces*
Tabular lining:	1234567890	*lining figures in columns*

Ligatures

Ligatures are single typographic characters that are combinations of two or more characters. For instance, there are common ligatures for the "fi" and "fl" combination:

fickle flames   fickle flames

Can you see the problems in the example on the left?
Can you see the solutions in the example on the right?

Ligatures are created either to solve a typographic problem, such as the hook of an "f" bumping into the dot of an "i," or sometimes simply for an elegant look. Almost every Macintosh font contains at least the fi and fl ligature (see the following page), and you will find quite a range of ligatures in OpenType and expert sets. Fonts for Windows machines do not contain even the fi and fl ligature—if you want to use them, you will have to use an OpenType font or a special expert set.

How many ligatures can you find in the following paragraph?

However, a good laugh is a mighty good thing, and rather too scarce a good thing; the more's the pity. So, if any one man, in his own proper person, afford stuff for a good joke to anybody, let him not be backward, but let him cheerfully allow himself to spend and to be spent in that way, and the man that has anything bountifully laughable about him, be sure there is more in that man than you perhaps think for.

❧ *Herman Melville,* Moby Dick

These are the ligatures available in the font Zapf Renaissance Italic Swash, which is designed to be set with the font Zapf Renaissance Italic, (both of which are shown to the left):

*ff ſp fi · ff th Th
fl ſl ffl ffi ſ*

· ·

Setting ligatures

You can always set the fi and fl ligatures in any application in any font on the Mac. If you want other ligatures or if you use a PC, you will have to invest in an OpenType font or an expert font set. To set these ligatures in any Mac font:

| fi | Option Shift 5 |
| fl | Option Shift 6 |

InDesign: Select the text, then from the little menu in the Character palette, choose "Ligatures." Use this in the appropriate style sheets. Ligatures will not cause spell-check problems and will separate when kerned.

QuarkXPress: From the QuarkXPress menu, choose "Preferences," then "Character." Check the "Ligatures" box. Unfortunately, this applies to the entire document regardless of point size or font, which makes it almost useless for professional typography. (The "Break Above" amount is a kerning value so if you letterspace your type beyond that amount, the ligature will automatically separate back into the two characters.)

The dotless i

Generally, ligatures are not used in display type (type in large sizes, above 24-point). If you have a problem with the hook of the "f" bumping into the dot of the "i," try using the dotless i character: ı (type Option Shift B, Mac only). Or use the Glyphs palette in InDesign to find and insert the dotless i.

Flying fish found in pocket!

Notice the problem in the "fi" combination.

Flying fish found in pocket!

The dotless i solves this problem so neatly.

This dotless i character also comes in handy any other time the dot gets in the way, as might happen if you use italic swash caps.

Victor Hugo   Victor Hugo

Oooh, doesn't that dot bumping into the V bother you? Now you can fix it.

Condensed and Extended Type

Type families often have more members than the basic Regular, Italic, Bold, and Bold Italic—a larger family might have Condensed, Bold Condensed, Extra Condensed, Extended, Black Extended, etc. Some typefaces are single-member families and are designed specifically as one very condensed or very extended look.

Condensed type is type that looks like it has been *compressed*, or squished, horizontally, but not vertically. **Extended** type seems to have been *expanded*, or stretched horizontally. You can use condensed or extended type for practical typographic solutions or simply for playful effects.

This is Eurostile Plain, a great face.

This is Eurostile Condensed, another great face.

This is Eurostile Extended, also great.

Condensed faces often have a "tall," elegant look.

Extended faces usually appear squatty, yet appealing.
They often have a high-tech, assertive look.

· ·

Condensed text faces

Condensed text faces are handy when space is at a premium. You've probably noticed that some typefaces take up a lot more room than others. Compare the space occupied by the copy set in the two faces below, Garamond and Times. Times was created for the *London Times* specifically to save space yet still be eminently readable. You can tell even in this small sample that a large body of text in Times would fill significantly less space than the same size type in Garamond, even though Times appears to be larger (because of its x-height; see page 17 for details about the x-height).

They have a wonderful therapeutic effect upon me, these catastrophes which I proofread . . . . When the world blows up and the final edition has gone to press the proofreaders will quietly gather up all commas, semicolons, hyphens, asterisks, brackets, parentheses, periods, exclamation marks, etc., and put them in a little box over the editorial chair. *Comme ça tout est régle.*

Henry Miller, *Tropic of Cancer*

They have a wonderful therapeutic effect upon me, these catastrophes which I proofread . . . . When the world blows up and the final edition has gone to press the proofreaders will quietly gather up all commas, semicolons, hyphens, asterisks, brackets, parentheses, periods, exclamation marks, etc., and put them in a little box over the editorial chair. *Comme ça tout est régle.*

Henry Miller, *Tropic of Cancer*

The face on the left is Garamond; on the right is Times. Both are set 9/12.

. . . .

Computer-drawn vs. true-drawn

You can compress and expand type through most software applications with the click of a button. This is okay for an occasional emergency, but the computer distorts the type by simply squishing it. If you need a compressed face so you can, for instance, get more words into your newsletter, please don't let the computer squish the type—invest in a "true-drawn" condensed face. True-drawn faces have been redesigned with different proportions, stroke thicknesses, counter spaces, and other fine features so as to retain the integrity of the typeface and maintain readability. Below are examples of what the computer does to the letterforms as opposed to what the designer does.

Franklin Gothic, condensed
Franklin Gothic Condensed

In the first example, the computer simply squished the letterforms. The second example is a redesigned face. Notice the differences in the weight, the thin/thick strokes, the counters (spaces inside the letters), the letter spacing, the height of the lowercase letters in relation to the caps, the terminals of the "e" and "s" where open space has been designed into the condensed version, and other subtle differences between the computerized version and the redesigned face.

As for me, I am tormented with an everlasting itch for things remote. I love to sail forbidden seas and land on barbarous coasts.

Herman Melville, *Moby Dick*

A well-designed condensed text face maintains maximum readability within the compressed proportions. This is an example of a true-drawn Garamond text face called Garamond Light Condensed.

. . . .

Break the rules

Occasionally you may want to create some dynamic display of type and you need a condensed or extended version, but it doesn't exist or it isn't enough. It's okay to break the rules, but break them with gusto! Make it look like you *meant* to distort the type. If it's not obvious, the sophisticated reader (of whom there are more and more) will think you just didn't know what you were doing. Don't be a wimp!

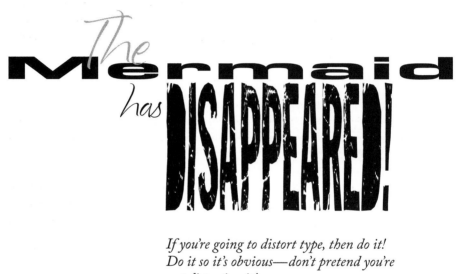

If you're going to distort type, then do it! Do it so it's obvious—don't pretend you're not distorting it!

Typefaces are Dulcimer (script), Eurostile Bold Extended Two, and Bad Copy.

Display Type

Display type refers to type that is large, that is on display, as opposed to body text, which is what you read in paragraphs at smaller point sizes (9 to 12 point). Some people might refer to headlines as display type, but generally it refers to type at least 24 points or above. Decorative typefaces are also called display faces, because you would typically use them only at large sizes for special occasions.

Now, the definitions above are generic definitions. There is also an actual classification of type design called "display type." These faces have been specifically redesigned for larger sizes.

Long ago, when type was carved by hand out of metal, the designer changed subtle features as the sizes got larger: the thin strokes got thinner, the serifs were more delicate, the counters (the space inside the letters) were different, the places where parts of the letters joined were thinner, the letter spacing was tighter, sometimes the ratio of x-height to cap height was different.

The computer, however, makes no distinction between sizes of type. It takes one size, say 12 point, and makes it larger or smaller as you wish. Thus when you use 6-point type, it is simply half of 12-point. This means the strokes are half as heavy, the space between the characters is half as much, etc. When you set 36-point type, it is simply three times as large as 12—the thin strokes are three times thicker, there is more space between the characters, etc. This creates a heavy, clunky look at large sizes. The solution to this problem is to use a specially designed display face.

· ·

Display vs. text

It is easy to see the differences in the two faces below. Both are the typeface Warnock Pro, an OpenType font, but the word on the left is set with Warnock Pro Regular; the word on the right is set with Warnock Pro Regular Display (all examples are set in 80-point type). The instant impression, even if a person is typographically illiterate, is that the display face is finer and more elegant, less chunky and clunky. That's because the letterforms and spacing attributes in the display face have been designed specifically for larger type sizes—they have not been simply enlarged.

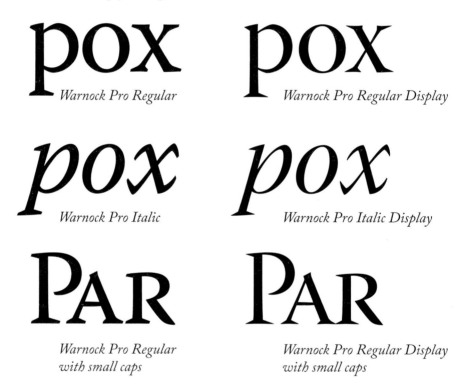

pox
Warnock Pro Regular

pox
Warnock Pro Regular Display

pox
Warnock Pro Italic

pox
Warnock Pro Italic Display

PAR
*Warnock Pro Regular
with small caps*

PAR
*Warnock Pro Regular Display
with small caps*

Take notice of exactly what makes these faces different, which details create the more elegant look of the display face. Look carefully at the serifs, the thick/thin contrasts in the strokes, the places where the parts of the characters join together, the letter spacing, the crispness of the terminals. Which would you choose to use in a billboard or large poster?

Display faces usually come in families of at least Regular, Italic, Bold, and Bold Italic, all designed for large type sizes.

. . . .

Display type and body text

If you have a display face, don't use it in body text! If the computer takes a display face and reduces it, those delicate thins and serifs will be so weak in the smaller size that they'll fall apart when it prints. Remember, if the face was designed at 36-point and you print it at 9, the computer will just reduce everything in the entire face to a quarter of the original. Even if it prints well because you use a high-quality press, it will be less readable than the regular font at the smaller size.

Several of Adobe's OpenType fonts include optical size variations to make it possible to use a font designed for the size of type you are setting. "Opticals" include variations for captions (6–8 point), regular type (9–13 point), subheads (14–24 point) and display type (25–72 point). See Chapter 8.

Below is Brioso Pro Regular, an OpenType font from Adobe set at 65-point. It's not really meant for large sizes—it looks rather heavy.

Serendipity

But Brioso Regular is *meant* for body text. It holds up quite well at this size you are reading right now. Even at 9-point, the strokes are even and full, and the proportions are ideally suited for readable text.

Below is Brioso Pro Display, set at 65-point. The features of this font are more delicately designed than the regular Brioso face so it presents a more elegant presence on the page at the larger size.

Serendipity

But Brioso Pro Display is not as readable or graceful at this small, 9-point size you are reading right now. The proportion of the x-height is too large, the thins are too thin, the letter spacing is too tight, the delicate features are lost or wimpy.

you
can do
a good ad
without
good
typography,
but you can't
do a
great ad
without
good
typography.
hERB LuBALiN

Spacing

In which we discuss
the importance of
and uses for
pair kerning,
auto kerning,
range kerning,
track kerning,
manual kerning,
word spacing,
and letter spacing,
as well as
linespacing (leading)
and paragraph spacing.

The truth is

that typography is an ART
in which Violent Revolutions can scarcely,
in the nature of things,
hope to be successful.
A type of Revolutionary Novelty
may be extremely beautiful in itself;
but for the creatures of habit that we are,
its very Novelty
tends to make it illegiblE.

Aldous Huxley
Typography for the Twentieth-Century Reader

Kerning

In page layout applications, such as Adobe InDesign, QuarkXPress, or Adobe PageMaker, you have an incredible amount of control over the spacing between letters, words, and lines. But to take advantage of this control, you must know what the features refer to. Later in this section I address the space between lines (linespacing, or leading) and the space between paragraphs. This chapter focuses on manipulating the space between the letters: kerning, pair kerning, auto kerning, manual kerning, range kerning, tracking, and letter spacing.

Kerning

Kerning is the process of adjusting the space between individual letters; it is a fine-tuning process. The desirable end result is visually consistent letter spacing because consistent spacing strengthens the readability of the text. Whether that means you increase space between tight letters or decrease space between loose letters, the spacing must be consistent. You don't want the reader's eye to stumble over awkward letterfitting. To a discerning eye, your kerning is symbolic of your attitude and experience toward type.

Canteloupe

This word is not kerned at all. The letters are loose, quite separate from each other.

Canteloupe

This word has been kerned so the letters fit snugly and consistently together without being overly tight.

· ·

Kerning metal type

Until the 1970s, type was set in metal. Some machines set entire lines of type on metal slugs, but many machines followed the older style of using individual pieces. Regardless of the particular method, every character had its own separate metal space. If each letter is on its own piece of lead, then the letters can only get so close to each other—it's simply not physically possible to move them closer without taking a knife and shearing off some of the lead, thereby making that character useless for further typesetting. In lines of metal type, you couldn't even do that much. In those days, designers had to cut apart the proof sheets of type and move the printed letters around to adjust their spacing, then glue them down. If you look at an old magazine, you can instantly tell it's old, right? One of the visual clues that tells you it's old is the loose letter spacing, looser than you are accustomed to reading now that type is being set electronically.

Letter spacing

Letter spacing is not really kerning, but refers to a general and arbitrary adjustment of the space between characters in a large piece of text, whereas kerning is a form of individual letter spacing. You might want to add more letter space to open the look of a typeface, or to create a dramatic headline that stretches across the page. You might want to decrease the letter spacing of a script face so the connectors reach the following letters. Notice the very open (too open) letter spacing of this paragraph. It's rather annoying in this case, isn't it?

Whew. This is better. The letter spacing values that any good page layout application applies to a typeface are based on the values the designer built into the font. These are explained on the following pages.

Word processing applications generally don't use the kerning pairs (see the next page) to fit the letterforms together nicely. This is the biggest reason why you can always glance at a printed page from a word processer and instantly tell it came from a word processor and not a page layout application.

. . . .

Kerning pairs

Most well-made fonts have "kerning pairs" built into them. That is, as designers create fonts, they build in tighter spacing between certain *pairs* of letters that are known to cause inconsistent gaps, such as Ta, To, Yo, we, and many others. Not all fonts have kerning pairs built in, and some have poorly adjusted pairs. Some fonts have 200–300 kerning pairs, others have over a thousand. Just because a font has an extraordinary number of kerning pairs does not mean it's better. In fact, when there are many thousands of pairs it can take longer to display the text on the screen, and it will also take longer to print.

Auto kerning

Page layout applications usually have a checkbox that allows you to tell your program to automatically take advantage of the kerning pairs, if you are using a font that contains them. In most programs you can also specify a point size above which the kerning pairs are automatically used. It's neither necessary nor desirable to auto kern small sizes of type (less than about 7 or 8 point) because when type is set small it should actually have *more* space between characters, not less.

Adobe InDesign utilizes two methods of auto kerning. **Metrics kerning,** the default method, uses the font's built-in kerning pairs which are built into the font metrics. **Optical kerning** takes the shapes of each letter pair into consideration and adds or removes space based on the letter shapes. Optical kerning is the best option when you are combining characters from different typefaces (as in the third example, below), which obviously wouldn't have kerning pairs built in because they come from two different fonts.

Well Told Vermin Take woe

InDesign unkerned type

Well Told Vermin Take woe

InDesign metrics kerning

Well Told Vermin Take woe

InDesign optical kerning

You can clearly see the difference in the letterspacing— look at the ends of the lines. In type this large you will always have to do some manual kerning because auto kerning is just a start.

· ·

Manual kerning

Kerning is a totally visual skill. The computer does the best it can with what it has to work with, but the end result, especially for larger type sizes, depends entirely on your eyes and your judgment. So even if your application has used auto pair-kerning, you must usually kern the larger type manually, selecting the space between two letters and adjusting it to match the visual space between the others.

Every page layout application and many illustration programs have keyboard shortcuts for kerning type on the screen. Sometimes you must insert a numeric value into a dialog box to add or remove the space, and some applications use both methods. Whatever it is, find out and use it.

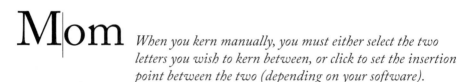 *When you kern manually, you must either select the two letters you wish to kern between, or click to set the insertion point between the two (depending on your software).*

Range kerning

Sometimes you start the fine-tuning process by selecting a "range" of text—a group of consecutive letters—and applying kerning values. This method, called range kerning, adds or removes *the same amount of space between every pair of letters*, regardless of their natural letterfit. If you range kern large type (14-point or over), you will probably need to finish the process by manually kerning certain combinations.

 *When you select a range of text (as shown to the left) and apply a kerning value or use keyboard shortcuts to kern, you are taking out the same amount of space between every pair of letters. This is the first step in the process—you will still need to manually kern the characters for a perfect letterfit.*

. . . .

Tracking

Tracking is a more complex issue, but only Adobe PageMaker uses true tracking. True tracking increases or reduces the letter spacing *according to the point size of the type.* If you use InDesign or QuarkXPress, you can skip the next three paragraphs.

Remember when we talked about display type, and how the original metal letters were redesigned for large and small sizes, and that the spacing values were different for large and small type? Small type requires extra letter spacing; large type, as in headlines, requires less letter spacing the larger it gets.

In PageMaker, if you choose Normal tracking for very *small* type, it *adds* letter space; if you choose Normal tracking for *large* type, PageMaker *subtracts* space. It takes all the built-in pair kerns into consideration as well, so you get as close to optimum letter spacing as possible before having to manually fine-tune.

You might want to add PageMaker's tracking to your headline style sheet so all your heads have a start on proper letter spacing (you may still need to manually kern pairs of letters). You might want to track all your caption style sheets that use very small type so they have the tiny bit of extra space they need. Because PageMaker's tracking is so thorough and complex, it's not a good idea to track large blocks of body copy—most body copy (9- to 12-point type) will not need tracking anyway. Reserve its power for large and small type.

The "tracking" in InDesign and QuarkXPress is simply *range kerning*—it adds or subtracts a fixed amount of space between all letters selected *regardless* of point size or kerning pairs already in use. The tracking value is *added* to any kern pairs or metrics/optical kerning that has been applied.

Find out exactly what your software does when you choose the tracking command. Whether it is true tracking or simply range kerning, understand what it does and use it when appropriate.

Kerning definitions

These are brief definitions of the variety of terms related to kerning.

What it is	What it means	When to use it
Letter spacing	Adding or decreasing the same amount of space between all the letters. Letter spacing is applied to a range of text; kerning is applied to individual pairs.	Usually used to change the spacing of a large amount of text to open the face or tighten it, depending on the natural characteristics of the typeface and its purpose on the page.
Kerning	General term for adjusting the space between letters.	Kern to create a visually consistent look.
Pair kerning	The special kerning built into certain combinations of letters when the typeface was designed. You can use special programs to add more kerning pairs to your fonts.	This is built into your font—don't worry about it.
Auto kerning	When an application is capable of automatically finding and using the pair kerns built into the font.	You can turn auto kerning on or off in your application. Leave it on.
Metrics kerning	An auto-kerning method that automatically uses the kern pairs built into the font.	When you are pretty confident that a typeface has kerning pairs built into it.
Optical kerning	An auto-kerning method that adjusts the fit of the letters depending on their shapes.	When combining characters from different fonts or using a typeface that does not include pair kerns.
Manual kerning	Adjusting the fit of two characters by "hand" (with the computer).	Use this for the final fine-tuning.
Tracking (range kerning)	Selecting a range of text and applying an overall kerning value to all the pairs of letters.	Use this to tighten a range of text in preparation for manual fine-tuning.
Tracking (point-size specific)	PageMaker only. Means by which the computer adjusts the letter spacing, depending on the point size of the type and the auto kern pairs.	Use this for large or very small type as a start for better letter spacing. For large type, you will still have to manually fine-tune the type.

Linespacing (leading)

Linespacing is the space between the lines of type. When type was set in metal (which wasn't that long ago), compositors would insert thin strips of lead (yes, the metal called lead) between the lines of metal characters, which is why the space is called "ledding," not "leeding." Leading is measured in *points*, just like type. The measuring system works like this:

You take the point size of your type, say **12** point.
You take a (metaphorical) thin strip of lead, say **2** points.

12-point type —You add the **12** points of the type size
+2 points of lead | to the **2** points of lead, and you then say
=14 points of total that you have a leading value of **14** points.
space, called leading

This is written as **12/14** and is
pronounced "twelve on fourteen."

The phrase **12/14** used to mean that text should be set at 12 point
and the typesetter should then drop down 14 points
to the next baseline,
but now it simply means that there are 14 points of space
surrounding the line of type,
and various applications apply that space differently,
above and below the baseline.

Traditionally, an average leading is 20 percent
of the point size of the type.
Thus for 10-point type,
the average leading is 2 points,
added to the 10
which makes a 12-point leading value.
For 30-point type, an average leading is 6 points,
which makes a 36-point leading value.

So now if you look at a type specification that calls for 10/16, you instantly know there is a lot of space between the lines. If you see type that is set with the same number for the leading value as for the type size, such as 24/24, which is called "set solid," you know there is very little space between the lines.

Not-so-average linespacing

Although 20 percent of the point size of the type is an average linespace, there are many times when you need to change that. Here are details of several clear-cut cases for when you *must* adjust linespacing, other cases when you might *want* to, and a guideline for what to look at to determine the optimum linespacing for your text.

Headlines

If a headline runs two or more lines, you will probably need to decrease the linespace. The average 20 percent is okay for body copy, around sizes 9 to 12, but above that it starts to become excessive, especially when you get into sizes such as 48 and 72. Also in big headlines, take note of whether you have descenders or not and where they fall. If there are no descenders, you really have to decrease the linespace.

The orchestra played egregiously   **The orchestra played egregiously**

Notice, above, how much extra space there appears to be between the lines, especially since there are no descenders in the first line. You can take out quite a bit of space, as shown in the example on the right.

The setting on the left is 18 point type with an automatic leading value of 21.6, which is 20 percent.

The setting on the right is 18-point type with a leading value of 17 (which is actually what's called a "negative" amount of leading).

Typeface is Trade Gothic Bold No. Two.

• •

All caps

When text is all caps, there are no descenders that drop into the linespacing, but every one of the letters reaches up to the full height of the line. Because the words present such compact rectangles, you must be very conscious of the linespacing.

> IN SMALLER SIZES, SUCH AS BODY TEXT (WHY WOULD YOU SET BODY TEXT IN ALL CAPS?), BE CONSCIOUS OF THE CROWDED FEELING THAT SOMETIMES HAPPENS WITH ALL CAPS—BE LOOSE WITH LINESPACING.

> THE PARAGRAPH ABOVE IS SET WITH AUTO LEADING, WHICH IS 120 PERCENT OF THE POINT SIZE OF THE TYPE. IN THIS PARAGRAPH I ADDED A FEW EXTRA POINTS OF LINESPACE TO LOOSEN AND LIGHTEN THE LOOK, WHICH MAKES IT EASIER TO READ (WHICH MEANS IT COMMUNICATES BETTER).

In large sizes, as in big headlines, the compact words in all caps emphasize the amount of space between the lines; it can look disproportionate. You will probably want to decrease the space between the lines so the entire headline looks like a compact package rather than separate lines.

THE DAYS ARE ENDLESSLY DULL
Eurostile Bold, 15/18

THE DAYS ARE ENDLESSLY DULL
Eurostile Bold, 15/16

If, for some reason, you need to set headlines or other large type in all caps, you will probably need to remove some of the linespace. Without the descenders, the space appears to be excessive.

· ·

Sans serif text

Sans serif typefaces tend to have large x-heights. These large x-heights fill the spaces between the lines, almost always necessitating extra linespacing. But look carefully at the face first! Do you think this paragraph could use a little extra leading? Yes? You're right. This paragraph is set with the standard extra 20 percent.

Special effects

Sometimes you want to increase or decrease the linespacing dramatically for a special effect. Do it! Just make sure you do it with gusto. Don't just add a tiny bit more linespace—add a lot! Don't just make the text very tight between the lines—make it extraordinarily tight! *If you are going for the effect, then go all the way.* Don't be a wimp or it will simply look like a mistake.

Watch for these features

Large x-height: Increase linespacing.

Small x-height: Decrease linespacing.

Tall ascenders: You can get away with less linespacing because the
                       x-heights are relatively small, but you might want to
                       actually add dramatic linespace to emphasize the tall
                       ascenders.

Reverse type: Along with increasing the point size by a point or two
                       and increasing the weight a bit, you should probably
                       also add a tiny bit more linespace.

Long lines: If you must use long lines of text, add a tiny bit more
                       linespace so the reader can find the beginning of the
                       next line easily.

Wide letter spacing: If the typeface is set with lots of letter spacing, add
                       more linespace for balance.

Paragraph Spacing

The space between paragraphs is an important issue. Well, in the grand scheme of things I suppose it doesn't rank very high, but in typography it's important. If you space or indent your paragraphs poorly, your work betrays you as an amateur.

First of all, let's clear up one thing: either indent your paragraphs *or* put extra space between them. Don't do both. The purpose of an indent is to tell the reader that this is a new paragraph. A small indent does that just fine. A small amount of space between the paragraphs does the same. But if you use *both* an indent and extra spacing, it's like hitting your reader over the head with a baseball bat because you think he is too stupid to read the clues for a new paragraph. He is not stupid. Choose one method.

Paragraph indents

So let's say you are going to indent your paragraphs. Are you going to indent them five spaces? One-half inch? No way. I know that's what your typing teacher taught you, and if you ever type across a page on a typewriter (if you can even find one) you usually need a five-space indent in proportion to the line length. But you are rarely setting lines that long on your computer, and besides, the standard typographic indent is one *em space*. An em space is a blank space as wide as the point size of the type; in 12-point type, an em space is 12 points; in 36-point type, it is 36 points. If you can set an indent with a measurement, set one em space. Otherwise fake it—an em space is more like two spaces than five.

Use your software to set the indent automatically. All word processors and page layout programs let you set a first-line indent; when you hit a Return, the text starts *at wherever you set the first-line indent.*

· ·

First paragraphs are not indented

The purpose of an indent is to warn the reader that a new paragraph is about to begin, right? Well, if it's the *first* paragraph on the page or the first paragraph after a subhead, the reader does not need that clue—it's redundant. This is another one of those details where it might not look correct at first, but once you know it *is* correct and you apply it, other work will look foolish to you when the first paragraphs are indented.

Space between the paragraphs

If you want space between the paragraphs, *don't hit double Returns!* That is, don't hit the Return or Enter key twice to make the space between the paragraphs. Learn to use your software to put an extra space after each paragraph, a space generally about half the amount of your linespace. If you hit two Returns you get a big gap, a gap that separates the very things that should be visually connected. The paragraphs on other pages in this book have a linespace (leading) value of 14 with 5.5 extra points of space after each paragraph.

But on this page I have hit double Returns. Aren't these huge spaces between paragraphs horrendous? It makes the work look so juvenile.

Again I must reinforce: learn to use your software. Every word processor and page layout application gives you control over the space between your paragraphs. Be smart. Look smart. Use it.

Alignment

The alignment of your text plays a vital part in the look and the readability of your work. It's not the only factor—typeface, line length, style, size, linespacing, and case (caps or lowercase) also contribute. Type that is easy and pleasant to read encourages people to read what is written. Type that is not so readable can discourage a significant portion of the audience.

In short text, as in an advertisement or a package design, you can often get away with using a design feature that detracts from the readability but adds to the attractiveness and impact of the piece (such as extreme letter spacing, all caps with a justified alignment, or fringe type)—but this only works when you can justify that the *look* of the piece is more important than the accompanying loss of readability.

Passion without
reason is blind;
Reason without
passion is dead.

Will Durant
paraphrasing Spinoza

*A centered alignment
is very stable and secure
and tends to have
a more formal appearance.
It can be dull
because of this formality.*

Passion
without reason
is blind;
Reason
without passion
is dead.

Will Durant
paraphrasing Spinoza

*A strong flush right
or left alignment
has a clean edge
with an almost visible
line running along it.
The strength of this edge
adds strength to the design.*

. . . .

Left aligned

Speaking just in terms of alignment, text aligned on the left is the most readable. Left-aligned text uses the optimum word spacing and letter spacing that the designer built into the font, and the spacing is very consistent so you don't have to struggle through the words at all. And as you read, your eye can quickly find the beginning of the next line.

When you align text left, strive to keep the right, "ragged" side as smooth as possible, or in a slightly concave shape. Sometimes this necessitates forcing line breaks to fill in holes or to prevent long text strings from hanging beyond the rest of the lines. Below, the word *of* is hanging off the right edge, while in the line just below it there is clearly plenty of room to accommodate the word. Bump *of* down to the next line (see Chapter 22 on Line Breaks for details).

If you bump words down, be sure you do it as the last touch in your final layout. Otherwise when you edit the text, change the type size or column width, or alter the layout in any way, you will end up with tab spaces, empty spaces, or line breaks in the middle of your sentences. Fortunately, in a flush left alignment you can easily make type corrections and adjust lines, often without affecting the rest of the text at all.

1. I declare! Sometimes it seems to me that every time a new piece of machinery comes in at the door some of our wits fly out at the window.

   Aunt Abigail in *Understood Betsy,* by Dorothy Canfield Fisher

The word "of" in #1 will bump down to the next line, as shown in #2, but we get an even better "rag" by narrowing the entire paragraph just a tiny bit so the lines break as shown in #3.

2. I declare! Sometimes it seems to me that every time a new piece of machinery comes in at the door some of our wits fly out at the window.

   Aunt Abigail in *Understood Betsy,* by Dorothy Canfield Fisher

3. I declare! Sometimes it seems to me that every time a new piece of machinery comes in at the door some of our wits fly out at the window.

   Aunt Abigail in *Understood Betsy,* by Dorothy Canfield Fisher

· ·

Right aligned

Text aligned on the right creates a definite *look,* as shown below, quite different from left-aligned. The letter and word spacing still retain their ideal built-in settings, and corrections can often be made without affecting the rest of the text. The biggest drop in readability comes from the fact that the left edge, where your eye returns to find the next line to read, is not consistent so your eye has to find the beginning of the line again every time it moves to the left. In small amounts of text, this isn't a major problem, and the sacrifice can be worth it in exchange for the distinctive layout.

When you use a right alignment for the look it creates, then emphasize the look—don't be a wimp. Instead of keeping the ragged edge as smooth as possible, try exaggerating it.

There is no excuse for widows or hyphenated words when you set a right alignment. Since you are determining the line endings and since this format is rarely used with an extended amount of text, you can help compensate for the lower readability by being thoughtful in the grouping of phrases. And while you're at it you can completely eliminate any hyphenation.

I'VE ALWAYS WANTED TO
BE SOMEBODY. BUT I CAN
SEE NOW I SHOULD HAVE
BEEN MORE SPECIFIC.
Lily Tomlin

I'VE ALWAYS WANTED
TO BE SOMEBODY.
BUT I CAN SEE NOW
I SHOULD HAVE BEEN
MORE SPECIFIC.
Lily Tomlin

If you're going to align text on the right, don't try to disguise it. It's difficult to tell if the text above is supposed to be right-aligned or not. Typeface is Las Bonitas.

If you make the right alignment strong, it adds another dimension to the type and takes it beyond merely words on the page.

· ·

Center aligned

A centered alignment also gives a particular look to text: a more formal, sedate, and potentially more boring sort of look. People who are just beginning to work with text tend to center everything because it's safe. It's symmetrical. It fills the space, everything balances automatically. However, a centered alignment can create a dreadfully dull piece, and it often creates an amateurish page.

A centered alignment has consistent letter and word spacing, but you have to keep finding the beginning of the lines as you read so it is not the most readable arrangement. But if you're going to do it, then do it. Make it clear that the text is centered, not just poorly justified. Varying line lengths make the page visually interesting. Also, a centered alignment gives you a chance to group the lines into logical thoughts. And remember, there's never an excuse for hyphenated words.

On with the dance! Let joy be unconfined;
No sleep til morn, when youth and pleasure meet
To chase the glowing hours with flying feet.

Lord Byron

This is nice, but it doesn't have much strength or passion;
it's hard to tell the poem is centered.

On with the dance!
Let joy be unconfined;
No sleep til morn, when youth and pleasure meet
To chase the glowing hours
with flying feet.

Lord Byron

This layout has a much more intriguing shape.
Take advantage of the flexibility
of centered lines.
Also read "Consider those phrases" on page 124.
Typeface is General Menou.

· ·

Justified

When you justify text, the computer forces the lines to extend to a certain length by adding or deleting space between the words, and sometimes between the letters. Some programs let you specify the minimum and maximum amounts the spacing can adjust, but the computer will override your specifications if necessary.

The greatest problem with justified text, both in terms of readability and aesthetics, is the uneven word spacing and letter spacing: some lines of text have extra spacing between the words and letters, some less. This irregularity is visually disturbing and interrupts reading. The shorter the line length in relation to the size of the type, the worse this problem becomes because there are fewer words between which to add or delete space (see below).

One simple rule for determining whether a line length is "long enough" to justify is this: The line length in picas should be at least twice the point size of the type: if you're using 12-point type, the minimum line length before you should try to justify is 24 picas (6 picas equal 1 inch). This line length you are reading is 28p6 (28 picas, 6 points), and the type size is 11/14.

For many years, justified type reigned supreme as the way to set most text. But the trend over the past couple of decades has been to allow the natural spacing of flush left text to dominate, losing the structured look of the "block" of text, but maximizing readability.

So sweet a kiss the golden sun gives not to those fresh morning drops upon the rose, as thy eye-beams, when their fresh rays have smote the night of dew that on my cheeks down flows: nor shines the silver moon one half so bright through the transparent bosom of the deep, as doth thy face through tears of mine give light; thou shinest in every tear that I do weep.

Love's Labor's Lost

So sweet a kiss the golden sun gives not to those fresh morning drops upon the rose, as thy eye-beams, when their fresh rays have smote the night of dew that on my cheeks down flows: nor shines the silver moon one half so bright through the transparent bosom of the deep, as doth thy face through tears of mine give light; thou shinest in every tear that I do weep.

Love's Labor's Lost

Even with a long-enough line length, you will still get uneven word spacing when you justify the text. But notice how terrible the word spacing is in the example to the left—hold the page at an angle, squint, and you can see all the holes, and even "rivers" of white space running through the type. At least with a longer line, the gaps aren't so obvious. Typeface is Bembo.

· ·

Consider those phrases

I want to elaborate a little on the concept I keep mentioning: grouping words into phrases. We read and hear words in context, not as isolated items each with its own meaning. That is another reason all caps are hard to read—we have to read each word of all caps, but we understand whole clusters. Our mind has to work to put the individual words into those clusters.

Typographic beauty is a function of visual aesthetics combined with an intellectual assimilation. A page can look good with "greek" text or nonsensical combinations of words, but the type really packs a punch when the content (which is visible) is integrated into the design.

In the Durant quote on page 119, the visual impression is enhanced by the strong right edge. But it is also strengthened because of the phrases that are emphasized. With the flush right alignment, "without reason" and "without passion" are forcefully isolated, juxtaposed, and begging to be considered as a unit. The meaning of the words in these lines give more power to the whole piece. Always consider the phrasing when you have the opportunity to adjust where the lines break, as you do when the alignment is not justified or when the line length is short.

It's your choice

Choose one alignment per page—don't mix centered with flush left, for instance. With any alignment you choose, be aware of its strengths and weaknesses. Each alignment presents an initial visual image to the reader, has a different level of readability, and has particular quirks in regard to setting it. Evaluate these strengths and weaknesses, and base your decision on the combination of factors that best communicates your message.

In this book, I am using justified type. The uneven word spacing bothers me, but because there are so many typefaces and type examples on these pages, I wanted the clean lines of a justified text block. It acts as a contrast to the extra stuff, and also as a solid, stable, repetitive background for the play of the other text. I was willing to make a conscious choice to justify the text and accept less-than-ideal word spacing in exchange for the clean lines of the edges of the paragraphs.

Details

In which we explore effective ways to set headlines and subheads, captions, and pull quotes. We also experiment with various ways to emphasize type, and discuss the importance of sensitive line breaks and hyphenation.

Logic only gives man what he needs.
Magic gives him what he wants.

Baba the Idiot

Headlines and Subheads

The headlines and subheads in a document do more than simply give clues as to the content of the stories. They provide an organization to the page; they provide a repetitive element that unifies the publication; they provide the visual contrast that attracts our eyes to the page. Here are a few guidelines for using heads and subheads to effectively take advantage of their presence.

- **Avoid using all caps or small caps.** They are difficult to read, which defeats their purposes as headlines or subheads. Plus all caps take up too much space. Using lowercase letters, you will have more room to use a larger and bolder font.

- **Watch the leading** on multiple-line heads. The larger the type size, the less leading you need. If there are few or no descenders, it is particularly important to remove the excess space. Your intent is to keep the two lines together as one visual unit.

- **If your text is flush left,** keep your heads and subheads flush left, *not centered.* This is particularly important if your page feels a little cluttered; keeping the heads flush left with the text will reduce some of the visual clutter. When a head is centered, our eyes connect its placement with the first line of the first paragraph. If the first line of text does not stretch all the way across the column, the centered headline won't have a good connection to the story.

- **Don't indent the first paragraph in the story.** This is to preserve the strength of the alignment and to be typographically correct. Any indent you do use should be only about two spaces wide, about one em space (as wide as the point size of your type; see page 117).

- **There should always be a little more space** *above* a subhead than below it to ensure that the subhead is visually connected with the text it refers to. If the subhead is too far away, or if it is the same distance between the text above and below it, the subhead appears to be an unconnected, separate element.

* **Create a clear distinction between heads and subheads.** If the only difference between your head and subhead is size, then make sure they are significantly different sizes. You might want to italicize the subheads, or if you have a rule (a drawn line) beneath the headline, remove the line from the subhead.

* **Avoid awkward line breaks.** Read your heads and subheads carefully. Check for line breaks that might cause confusion or ambiguity. Make sure there are no silly line endings. And of course don't hyphenate.

* **Choose a typeface** for your heads and subheads that provides a strong contrast to your body text. This creates a contrast on the page that not only is visually attractive, but also strengthens the organization and makes a clearer path for the reader to follow.

Generally, your body text is a serif face, since extended amounts of text are easier to read with serifs. If so, a strong, bold sans serif is a good choice for heads and subheads. If you don't have a strong, bold face in your font library, you'll find that an investment in one is your single best investment toward more effective design and communication.

If your body text is a lightweight sans serif, the strong bold in the same font would work well for headlines. Just make sure there is a solid difference between the light weight and the heavy weight. For instance, the Helvetica Bold or Arial Bold that comes on your computer is not bold enough to stand out effectively.

You might also want to consider a heavy slab serif face as a headline type, which is so different in structure and weight from any readable sans serif or serif that it works well as a headline type with almost any face.

. . . .

Now that you've read through the guidelines, circle the appropriate places in the story below where you see the principles being used. Not every single guideline has been used in this one example, of course. How many do you follow in your work?

Giacche Enne Binnestaucche

Uans appona taim uasse disse boi. Neimmese Giacche. Naise boi. Live uite ise mamma. Mainde di cao.

Uane dei, di spaghetti ise olle aute. Dei gonna feinte fromme no fudde. Mamma sci sai, "Orai, Giacche, teicche di cao enne treide erre forre bocchese spaghetti enne somme uaine."

Giacche commes

Bai enne bai commese Giacche. I garra no fudde, i garra no uaine. Meicchese mesteicche enne treidese di cao forre bonce binnese. Uate giacchesse!

Mamma, scise engri. Giompe appe enne daonne craine, "Uara iu, somme caine creisi?" Denne sci tro olle binnese aute di uindo. Necchese dei, Giacche lucchese aute enne uara iu tincche? Ise si disse binnestaucche uate ricce appe tru di claodese. Somme uide!

Giacche gose appe di binnestaucche. Ise disse ogghere! Ise menne nainti sicchese fit taulle uite tri grin aise! Enne i garra ghusse uate leise ghode egghese!

Giacche ielle "Ciao!" Denne ise grabbe di ghusse enne cuicche claime daonne fromme di binnestaucche. Ise go cioppe cioppe uite di acchese. Di nainti sicchese futte menne ise faulle enne breicche di necche. Auce!

Cucchede ghusse

Mamma sci giompesse fromme gioi. Meicchese naise ghusse cacciatore. Bai enne bai, dei garra no morre fudde. Dei gonna dai! Uatsa iuse? Uara iu gonna du uenne iorre ghusse ise cucchede?

Many thanks to Michael Howley for passing this delightful story along to me!

Typefaces are Eurostile in the heads and subheads, Bembo in the body copy.

Have fun with it!

If appropriate for your content, experiment with different ways of setting heads. Perhaps add a rule above and/or below the heads, or reverse them, set them extra large, or use an initial cap. If you have a special story, perhaps create a special headline. Keep in mind, though, that if every story has a special and different headline treatment, not one of them stands out as different or more important. Most stories should have typographically consistent headlines to retain the unity of the publication.

Always, always remember, your purpose is to communicate. No matter which technique you use, your heads and subheads should support that purpose.

Headline typeface is Mister Frisky.

Pull Quotes

Many times you must design or write a page that has no accompanying graphic to lighten the page and make it more enticing to read. That's where **pull quotes** come in so handy. A pull quote is when you take a quote from an article, story, or dull report and emphasize it on the page in some graphic way (as shown below). There are many ways to do this, and this chapter shows you several examples and provides some basic guidelines.

Pull quotes are often seen in the middle of the page, but there is no rule to force you to do this. Try some variations, such as a flush right or left quote in a wide outer margin (flush with the column of text); a quote in a background that cuts into one column of text; or a quote that runs

Evanescent wan think, itching udder.

horizontally across 1.5 or 2 columns. Use interesting punctuation marks, such as ampersands or questions marks, as graphic elements; perhaps set them large or colorful.

On the following two pages are samples of pull quotes. Have fun with them, make them attractive—that's their point! Be sure to read page 134 for guidelines on working with pull quotes.

· ·

Be creative!

More often than not, the purpose of a pull quote is to add some visual interest to the page. So do it. Make that pull quote beautiful, provocative, interesting, dynamic! This is not the place to be a wimp.

"Wail, wail, wail," set disk wicket woof. "Evanescent Ladle Rat Rotten Hut."

A simple rule above and below the quote sets it apart. Notice the punctuation is hung off the left edge so the text retains its strong left alignment.

Typeface is Antique Olive Bold.

You can't let the seeds stop you from enjoyin' the watermelon.

With a colored or black box, you can inset this quote so it tucks halfway into the adjacent column and hangs halfway out into the margin.

Typeface is Antique Olive Compact.

The
harder
you
work,
the
luckier
you
get.

Tall, narrow settings with lots of linespace work well in outer margins. Align the flush edge with the edge of the column. That is, the quote in the outer margin of the left-hand page should be flush right, aligned against the column of text. On the outer margin of a right-hand page, the quote should be flush left.

Typeface is Bernhard Modern.

· ·

Ιν Δεχεμβερ α γυψ δελιϖερεδ α βυνχη οφ ωοοδ τηατ ηε χηοππεδ ιν μψ δριϖεωαψ. Ηε χηοππεδ τηε πιεχεσ τοο βιγ το τ ιν μψ στοϖε. Ηε σα ιδ ηε ωουλδ ρε τυρν ανδ χ ηο π τηεμ σμρ αλ λερ. Ηε νϖερ διδ. Ι παιδ ηιμ ρεπ εϖεν τηουγη ηε ασκεδ φορ Συ βεχαυσε ιτ ωασ α λοτ οφ ωοοδ ανδ Ι διδντ ρεαλιζε ηοω μανψ πιεχεσ ωερε υνυσαβλε

φορ με. Σο ηε σαιδ ηε ωουλδ βρινγ με α λοαδ οφ κινδλινγ. Ηε βρουγητ οϖερ ειγητ ρεδειγητ ρ ε δ ω ο ο δ ρουνδσ, εαχη αβουτ φερ 18 ινχηεσ λονγ ανδ φδτηρεε φεετ αχροσσ. Ι κεπτ ωαιτινγ φορ τηε κινδλινγ ανδ ωηεν ϑιμμψ ναλλψ τολδ ηιμ Ι ωασ ωονδερινγ ωηερε τηε κινδλινγ ωασ, ηε σα ιδ τηε ρεδωοοδ ωασ τηε κινδλινγ.

She claims the secret to success is understanding that **your attitude is your life.**

Try a horizontal quote extending across several columns. As with all pull quotes, leave plenty of white space surrounding it. Typefaces are Antique Olive Light, Antique Olive Compact, and Symbol for the Greek text.

To ensure success, learn to maximize your options.

Apply a gray shade or a pale color to large drop caps. This adds visual interest without overpowering the short quote.

Typeface is Belwe Medium for the body copy and Antique Olive Nord for the cap T.

full of **sound** & **fury** *signifying nothing*

Whenever possible and appropriate, take advantage of provocative punctuation and symbols.

Typeface is Antique Olive Nord with a Goudy Oldstyle Italic ampersand and text.

· ·

Guidelines for pull quotes

Here are a few guidelines for setting pull quotes in your documents:

- ❦ Always hang the punctuation (see Chapter 5).

- ❦ Reduce the size of punctuation in large type.

- ❦ Use only one alignment; for instance, don't set part of the
  text flush right and part of it centered.

- ❦ Make centered type obviously centered; break the lines
  at logical endings to create an interesting visual arrangement.

- ❦ Position initial caps on one of the baselines.

- ❦ Create a style for your pull quotes and use it consistently
  throughout your publication.

Captions

Captions are an important little feature of printed material. Every photo or illustrative figure should have an explanatory sentence or two accompanying it. People expect captions, so a photo without one confuses the reader momentarily. Often this explanatory text is the only thing people read. Take advantage of this fact, and don't let your captions be dull or useless—make them an integral part of the story and of the page design.

Choosing a typeface

The typeface for captions should either be a member of the same font family as your body text, or a font that is very different. Don't choose a font that is different but similar to the body text!

For instance, if you are using Garamond for your body text, feel free to use Garamond Italic or Semibold for your captions. Keep in mind that many OpenType Pro fonts, especially the oldstyle serif faces, include a specially designed caption font, as explained in Chapter 8.

If you want to use another face altogether, choose something that is obviously different from your serif face, such as a sans serif—don't choose another serif. If you are using a sans serif typeface for your headlines, use a light weight of the same sans serif for the captions.

In my book, *The Non-Designer's Design Book,* the entire second half deals specifically with the problem of using more than one typeface on a page.

· ·

Choosing a type size
and leading value

Captions are traditionally a bit smaller than the point size of the body copy, but keep in mind that many people read only the captions, so you don't want them to be difficult to read! Generally, use a size that is one to two points below the size of the body text (unless your body text is already tiny). If your body copy is 10 or 11 point, you can easily use 9- or 9.5-point caption type.

Alternatively, use the same size as your body text, but use the italic or semibold version of the font. You want it to be clear to the reader that these few lines are not meant to be in the flow of the story.

Your choice of leading value (linespace) depends on whether or not you are trying to align all your elements to a **grid:** Are you consciously aligning your baselines across columns? If so, your headlines must be set in a leading value, or linespace, that is a multiple of your body copy linespace.

> For instance, say your body copy is 10-point type with 12-point leading. If your heads have a *leading value* of 24 or 36 (two or three times the 12-point leading), all your text will always line up across columns. Your captions should follow the same guidelines— maintain that 12-point leading value.

> This assumes, of course, that you are indenting paragraphs instead of adding paragraph space between them.

If you are not forcing all elements into a grid format, then you have more flexibility with the leading value. Smaller type can usually get away with less leading. For instance, most faces at 9-point can get away with adding only a half a point or one point of linespace. Remember that sans serif faces need a little more linespace because their x-heights are usually larger than serif faces.

Alignment

Whether or not you are using a grid, the baseline of your caption should be on the same baseline as the text in the nearest column. The bottom of your photograph or illustration should also be aligned with a baseline in the next column. *This arrangement must be consistent throughout your publication!*

An even more important alignment is the relationship between the text and the photo or illustration. If your body copy is flush left or justified, then your captions should be flush left with the edge of the photo! Don't center captions unless everything else on the page is centered! You see, most photos have a strong, hard edge along both sides, yes? Your body text also has a strong hard edge along its side, yes? So don't weaken those clean lines by centering your captions—follow and increase the strength of those edges by aligning the caption with them.

Ms. Isabella Melanzana
will be speaking
at our next meeting.

▶ A strange figure was discovered
in the office late last night.

See the nice straight edge along the left side of this column? Follow that alignment with your caption! Don't weaken the entire page by centering your captions and losing the strength of that alignment.

Typeface is Memphis Light.

If you have some sort of detail you are using as a repetitive element throughout your publication, perhaps use it also in your captions. For instance, in the document from which the above graphic was taken, there are lists that use triangles as bullets. The triangle has been pulled into the caption as a unifying element.

Typeface is Formata.

· ·

Be consistent

Whatever you're doing with your captions, be consistent. Don't confuse your reader; be thoughtful. Use the same alignment, typeface and style, size and leading. Be consistent about the placement—such as how far below the bottom edge of the photograph you place it, or aligning it with a baseline. Use a style sheet for the captions. (If you don't know how to use the style sheets in your application, you must learn! Style sheets are one of the most important features you can master.)

There are little tricks in every application for ensuring that the placement of captions is consistent—ask other people who use the same page layout application what tricks they use.

Emphasizing Type

Every page of type contains at least a few words or headlines that need to stand out, either because they are important to the content, or perhaps the words need to be emphasized to add enough visual interest to the page so a reader is attracted to it. No matter what the reason, there are appropriate and inappropriate ways to call attention to particular words.

DON'T DO THIS

The inappropriate ways of emphasizing certain words or phrases are generally holdovers from using the typewriter, when our only options were to type words in ALL CAPS or <u>underline them.</u> Rarely should you use all caps, and never should you underline words in print. Never. That's a law.

When words are set in all caps, we lose the recognition of the shape of the word and are forced to read the word letter by letter (how many times have you read that now?). For instance, the word "cat" in lowercase has a different shape from the word "dog," and that shape helps us identify it. When the words CAT or DOG are set in all caps, their rectangular shapes are identical.

Italic, not underline

Typewriters, obviously, could not type in italic, so an underline on a typewriter was meant to fake an italic; that's why you were taught to type book titles with underlines, and why you underlined words in mid-paragraph when you wanted to emphasize them. But on your computer you have true typesetting choices—you don't have to fake it anymore, you can actually type in italic. Besides, the underline is usually too close to the bottoms of the letters and actually cuts into the descenders. And <u>*underlining*</u> an italic word is simply redundant.

. . . .

But you *can* do this

You have other options for emphasizing type that will create a more sophisticated or exciting typographic look, as well as help in the organization of information.

Using *italic* instead of an underline, where appropriate, is one way you can emphasize text in a subtle way, of course. For a stronger emphasis, use the boldest version of the typeface, or perhaps the ***bold italic.***

For a more dramatic emphasis, use a different typeface altogether, one that has a strong contrast to the rest of the text. For instance, if your text is a classic oldstyle face (like what you're reading right now), use a very bold sans serif for **emphasis.**

But don't use a weight that is *similar* to the other text, especially for headlines — notice how much more effective the **emphasis** is when the sans serif is a strong black, as above.

If you have the opportunity to use another color, take advantage of that color in your text or headlines when you need an emphasis. Just remember that the less that second color appears, the more dramatic the emphasis will be. Warm colors (reds, oranges) are the strongest, and very little goes a long way (and it's very easy to have too much). Cool colors (blues, greens) recede, and you can use more of them without overwhelming the page.

• •

Add space

If your design allows, add empty space around the text to immediately draw more attention to it. I know, your boss doesn't like empty space—she says that she paid for it and she wants to use it. But think of those ads in magazines or newspapers where there is nothing at all except a few words in the middle of the page. Ask your boss if she noticed that ad. Ask her if she read that ad. Ask her if it is possible for anyone to open to that page and *not* read that ad.

No it is not.

The boss who had the courage to pay for all that space and let it be empty had the highest readership of any page in that entire publication. When there is clutter, our eyes are attracted to the resting places of the blankness. Have courage. Let the white space be there. Do you notice how much attention is called to that one line above, "No it is not"? It appears very important because of all the empty, white space surrounding it. In fact, you probably read *that* line before you read the paragraphs on this page.

Rules and size can be effective

You don't ever want to use the underline feature in your software, but you can often apply a rule, or line, for emphasis, as shown in the headline above (in most programs you can add the rule to your style sheet so it shows up automatically). The advantage to the rule is that you can make it as thick or thin as you like, and you can make it a different color, dotted, or dashed. You can position the rule so it doesn't bump into the descenders, or, as you see in the running heads on each page, you can let it run through the descenders in exactly the position you choose.

Or:

Of course you know you can emphasize type by making it bigger. But don't be a wimp—try making it *really* big, making the letterforms themselves into a design element, or perhaps enlarging just the interesting punctuation such as the question mark or ampersand or quotation marks. Or try setting the text very small, surrounded by lots of space. Either choice, large or small, will call a great deal of attention to itself.

So stretch yourself—go beyond the basic italic or bold word.

Be emphatic!

Line Breaks and Hyphenation

Your design project is complete. Graphics are in place, colors have been chosen, paper has been selected, your client has signed off on the project, it's ready to go to press. But you need to check one last thing—your line breaks, or how each line of type ends. Yes, that means every line in your entire project, every headline, every caption, every line in every paragraph! Certain elements are inappropriate at the ends of lines, such as too many hyphens, small words that hang over an empty space in the next line, awkward phrases, the last half of a hyphenated word as the last line of a paragraph, among others. These are details that might not seem important at first, but these details are what give your document or your publication a professional, polished, and precise appearance.

See, isn't that line break tacky?!

Yes, checking every line break can be time-consuming, but it will give your publications that added touch of professionalism.

· ·

How to fix line breaks

Sometimes the easiest and best way to fix bad line breaks, especially if they involve long words that are hard to manage, is to have editing privileges: change a long word to a short word, or a short word to a long one; rephrase the sentence; eliminate superfluous words. But since that is not always possible, here are a few other tricks for adjusting the ends of your lines:

- ✸ Most software packages that work with text have a *line break* feature, sometimes called a "soft return." Instead of hitting the Return or Enter key, you hit Shift Return/Enter or perhaps Option Return or Alt Enter. This creates a hard line break, but it does not pick up any of the paragraph formatting you would get with a Return, such as extra space before or after, or a first-line indent or a style change.

- ✸ Most packages also have a *discretionary hyphen,* affectionately called a "dischy." You've probably noticed hyphens that occasionally appear in the middle of words in the middle of sentences (where someone manually hyphen-ated the word at the end of a sentence, later edited the sentence, and the hyphen stuck). Well, if you use a discretionary hyphen, usually by typing Command or Control Hyphen instead of the plain ol' hyphen, that hyphen will disappear when the word moves to another location. Check the manual for your software.

    Also (and this is the point), if you *type a discretionary hyphen in front of a hyphenated word,* it will not hyphenate at all, ever. Use this to make sure you never end up with a hyphen in the middle of the text, as shown above. Also use it so names of people or places don't hyphenate.

- ✸ You can often use subtle kerning or tracking in a line or in a few words, just enough to bring up the end of a hyphenated word.

- ✸ Try widening or narrowing the column just a tiny bit. Especially if it is set rag right, the difference won't be noticeable.

- ✸ For one-liners that are a bit too long, such as headlines or index entries or parts lists, try justifying the line. This will often squeeze ornery text onto one line.

. . . .

What are bad line breaks?

Look for bad line breaks throughout every line of body copy. Of course, *do this only on final copy,* after all editing has been done! Here are several examples of the sorts of things to look for:

Casing Adder Bat ❶

Heresy borsch-boil starry a ❷
boarder borsch boil gam
plate lung, lung a gore in- ❸
ner ladle wan-hearse torn
coiled Mutt-fill.

   Mutt-fill worsen mush of- ❹
fer torn, butted hatter putty
gut borsch-boil tame, an off
oiler pliers honor tame, door
moist cerebrated worse Cas- ❺
ing. Casing worsted sickened
basement, any hatter betting
orphanage off .526 (fife toe
sex). ❻

   Casing worse gut lurking
an furry poplar—spatially
wetter gull coiled Any-bally.
Any-bally worse Casing's
sweat-hard, any harpy cobble
wandered toe gat merit, ❼
bought Casing worse toe pore
toe becalm Any-bally's ❽
horsebarn. (Boil pliers honor
Mutt-fill tame dint gat mush
offer celery; infect, day gut
nosing atoll.)

   Butt less gat earn wetter star- ❾
ry.

Casing Adder Bat

Heresy borsch-boil starry
a boarder borsch boil gam
plate lung, lung a gore inner
ladle wan-hearse torn coiled
Mutt-fill.

   Mutt-fill worsen mush
offer torn, butted hatter putty
gut borsch-boil tame, an
off oiler pliers honor tame,
door moist cerebrated worse
Casing. Casing worsted
sickened basement, any hatter
betting orphanage off .526
(fife toe sex).

   Casing worse gut lurking
an furry poplar—spatially
wetter gull coiled Any-bally.
Any-bally worse Casing's
sweat-hard, any harpy cobble
wandered toe gat merit, bought
Casing worse toe pore toe
becalm Any-bally's horsebarn.
(Boil pliers honor Mutt-fill
tame dint gat mush offer celery;
infect, day gut nosing atoll.)

   Bought less gat earn wetter
darn starry.

❶*Justify the headline so it stays on one line.* ❷*Use a line break (Shift Return/Enter) to bump "a" down to the next line, where it fits very nicely.* ❸*Kern the line a tiny bit to bring the rest of the word up.* ❹*Type a dischy in front of the word to bump it down.* ❺*Never hyphenate a person's name. I had to go up a few lines, bump "off" down, which bumped the other line endings down. This also took care of the inappropriate widow in* ❻*.* ❼*There is plenty of room to squeeze "bought" on this line, perhaps by kerning the line a tiny bit.* ❽*"Horsebarn" is a good long word that could be hyphenated; type a dischy. Better yet, when "bought" moved up, it gave enough room to move "horsebarn" up. If that doesn't work, try opening the text block or text box a wee bit.* ❾*Edit: to get rid of that terrible widow, exchange a short word for a long word.*   Story is by Howard L. Chace.

· ·

Headlines

Don't hyphenate headlines. That's a law.

**Don Quixote de la Man-
cha**

*Don't laugh—I have actually
seen this as a printed headline.*

Also, watch where the first line of a two-line headline ends—does it create a
silly or misleading phrase? Fix it.

**Professor and The-
rapist to Lecture**

**Don't Lose Your Self
Respect**

Don't leave widows (very short last lines) in headlines, especially when they
leave a misleading phrase behind.

**Man Walks Barefoot Across Bay
Bridge**

Fix it either way, or rewrite!

Man Walks Barefoot across Bay Bridge

**Man Walks Barefoot
across Bay Bridge**

· ·

Captions

Generally captions don't need to stretch all the way across a column width. This flexibility gives you the freedom to break lines at appropriate places to create sensible phrasing. This is especially true if you center captions—you don't want all the lines the same length anyway.

Breaking sentences into complete phrases creates a more readable caption, and since many people read only the captions, it behooves you to make them as readable as possible.

> Will Rogers said, "We can't all be heroes because some-
> one has to sit on the curb and clap as they go by."

Why hyphenate in a caption?

> Will Rogers said, "We can't all be heroes because
> someone has to sit on the curb and clap as they go
> by."

There is no excuse to leave a widow in a caption!

> Will Rogers said, "We can't all be heroes because someone
> has to sit on the curb and clap as they go by."

> Will Rogers said, "We can't all be heroes because
> someone has to sit on the curb and clap as they go by."

These last two would not look good as paragraphs, but
would work fine aligned under a photograph or illustration.

Hyphenation

If your text is flush left, right, or centered, hyphenation isn't a big problem. The only rule is to watch out for too many hyphens in a row and word breaks that are too short. Personally, my preference is never to allow more than one hyphenation in a row, and preferably no more than one in a paragraph. Other people whose opinions I respect are comfortable with, say, no more than three in a row. Also personally, I abhor those hyphenations that leave one or two letters at either end of the line. Others don't mind. No one, however, finds a hyphenated word as the last word in a paragraph to be acceptable.

If you are going to *justify* your text, you have other considerations to weigh because the computer hyphenates words in an attempt to maintain the most even word spacing possible. It's impossible to have totally even word spacing in justified text—the computer has to unnaturally force words to the beginnings and ends of the lines.

There are two schools of thought on justification with hyphenation: Some people are willing to put up with lots of hyphenated words, including two-letter ones, to ensure that the word spacing is as even as possible. Others are willing to accept uneven word spacing in exchange for fewer obnoxious hyphens at the ends of the lines—hyphens that interrupt the flow and color of the text much more than does a subtle change in or less-than-ideal word spacing. Guess to which school I belong? Guess which paragraph on this page makes me twitch with horror?

You can set your page layout application to get the effect you want. I have Adobe InDesign set to not allow hyphenations that would occur within three picas of the end of the line (depending on the length of my line), thereby eliminating two-letter breaks, and to not allow more than one hyphen in a row. You can usually add the hyphenation controls to your style sheets.

Special Effects

In which we experiment
with ornaments
and dingbats,
swash characters,
initial caps, and
black-and-white "color"
in type, as well as
effective ways to use
distressed typefaces.

In mAtters
of grave importance,
"STYLE"
not sincerity,
is the
Vital thing.

Oscar Wilde

The Importance of Being Earnest

Swash Characters

Have you ever wanted to give an extra-special look to some type without being too bold? Perhaps you want a strong yet elegant look? A judicious use of swash characters can add a touch of sophistication to headlines, titles, quotations, etc.

Swash characters are specially designed letterforms that have "tails" or elaborate shapes, usually swooping away from or under the rest of the letters. Swash characters are like cheesecake—use them sparingly for a delectable (not disgusting) effect. In the three examples below, the first one is the regular face, the second is the italic version, and the third is a combination of the italic and its matching swash font.

Kissing Potion   *Kissing Potion*
Kissing ❦ Potion

Swash characters are not included in most regular font character sets—you must buy a specially designed swash font in conjunction with your text font. Some OpenType families, especially the Pro versions, include swash characters in the italic font. The example above is a PostScript family called Zapf Renaissance Light and Light Italic, with a special swash face designed to complement them called Zapf Renaissance Light Italic Swash. You need to use the faces in combination with each other. It's common to use the italic swash with the regular face as well as with the italic face.

Many swash faces also contain a set of ornaments that can be used to complement the type. Their proportions and style are designed to work smoothly with the text. Several of them are used in this chapter, but also see Chapter 26 for details on ornaments and dingbats.

The Character Palette in Mac OS X and Character Map on the pc show the characters available in OpenType and swash fonts and allow you to insert them in applications that are programmed to accept them. See Chapter 8.

Guidelines for using swashes

There are a few guidelines to follow when working with swash characters:

◆ Please, don't *ever* set text in all capital swash characters.

OH MY GRACIOUS THIS LOOKS SO STUPID!

Besides looking stupid, it is also dreadfully difficult to read.

◆ Swashes are designed to add elegant curves *to otherwise empty spaces,* such as under or over letters or at the beginnings or ends of sentences. So don't insert the kind of swash in the middle of a word that creates an unsightly gap, or even at the end of a word in mid-sentence if it disturbs the word spacing.

He͜r spe͜cia͜lty ͡was an͜alyzin͜g goblins.

◆ In a typeface that imitates handwriting, swash characters can add to the effect of a personalized note, making it look handlettered. Below, the typeface General Menou includes many alternate and swash characters (notice the alternate characters for d, s, e, and g, among others). But don't limit a handlettered face such as this to only personal notes! General Menou is so beautiful it could easily be used for any elegant occasion.

Dear John,
I miss you. Wish you could have dinner with
me tonight at Rancho de Chimayó, with dessert
in front of the fire and the snow falling outside.
Love, R.

• •

❧ If you are going to use another typeface on the same page as the swash face, be careful. Avoid faces with similar characteristics, such as any other italic or script. Either stay in the same family, such as the Zapf Renaissance family, or choose a font that has strong contrasts (such as thicker strokes or a roman or sans serif or monoweight font).

❧ Don't overdo the number of swashes. As you've seen, swash characters add elegance only if they are used with discretion.

❧ The Character Palette in Mac OS X (see page 87) shows all the characters available in a font. On a PC, use the Character Map (see page 228). The Glyphs palette in InDesign offers easy access to all the alternate characters in a font; see Chapter 8.

❧ OpenType fonts can include a wide variety of swash characters and contextual and stylistic alternate characters. InDesign can automatically insert these characters for you, but you'll prefer to use more discretion.

What a Time to Be Me!

What a Time to Be Me!

What a Time to Be Me!

What a Time to Be Me!

Above is Ministry Script, a gorgeous OpenType font from Veer.com.

In the first example, I turned off InDesign's "Discretionary Ligatures" and "Swash" options for OpenType.

In the second example, I turned on the OpenType option of automatic insertion of "Discretionary Ligatures" and "Swashes."

The third example has automatic insertion of "Discretionary Ligatures" and "Contextual Alternates," but not "Swashes."

In the last example I used InDesign's Glyphs palette and was selective about which alternate characters to use.

. . . .

Don't be a wimp

Don't be shy! If you find a swash or two that is exceptionally beautiful, set it extraordinarily large and use it as a graphic element on your page—show it off! Set it in a pale color or a shade of grey and let it swoop under your body text or behind a photograph. Use a huge swash character as an initial cap or as a lead-in to an article or chapter. Combine one large italic swash character with heavy, bold, black sans serif characters for a striking contrast in a title or quote. Look through this book and take note of where and how I've used swash characters. Oh, the possibilities are endless and exciting!

Lord, what fools these Mortals be!

Puck in A Midsummer Night's Dream

Typeface is General Menou.

Initial Caps

LARGE OR ORNATE LETTERS at the beginning of first paragraphs, also called initial caps or drop caps, not only add interest to a page, but help guide the reader's eyes and pull the reader into the text. There are many ways to create an initial cap, as shown in the examples following. Be brave, be strong, be big where appropriate. Here are just a couple of simple guidelines to remember.

- The baseline of most initial caps or the bottom of the graphic image belonging to the initial cap should align with one of the baselines of the text.

- Don't overdo it. One initial cap is beautiful; an initial cap beginning every paragraph on the page is redundant and destroys the effect. Sometimes on a text-heavy page you can use two or three initial caps in lieu of graphics or pullquotes, but be aware of their impact and don't overdose the reader.

For only the very young
saw Life ahead, and only
the very old saw Life behind;
the others between were
so busy with Life
they saw nothing.

Ray Bradbury

Typeface is Isadora.

. . . .

Examples of initial caps

There is a wonderful variety of ways to use initial caps. Here are several examples, which I hope will inspire you to play and create even greater and more interesting ways to use them.

Sometimes the seas are calm, and that's wonderful. Sometimes the seas are not calm, and that's the way it is.
Rabbi Nathan Seagull

Typeface is Bodoni Poster Compressed.

In InDesign, I set the letter "O" in a text block of its own so I could custom text wrap it. Typeface is Schmelvetica.

O time, strength, cash, and patience! Small erections may be finished by their first architects; grand ones, true ones, ever leave the copestone to posterity. God keep me from ever completing anything.   Herman Melville, *Moby Dick*

I set the "W" separately from the text. I used the Direct Selection Tool (the white pointer) in InDesign to reshape the text block with an angle on the left to match the angle of the W. Typefaces are Belwe Condensed and Light.

When I'm in a good space, I see obstructions as instructions. When I am in a bad space, even instructions look like obstructions.
Norm Howe

Typefaces are Printers Ornaments M for the decorative block, Dear Sarah for the cap "I" and byline, and DeconStruct Medium for the body copy.

In the midst of all the doubts which we have discussed for four thousand years in four thousand ways, the safest course is still to do nothing against one's conscience.
Voltaire

• •

Letters sometimes give ear to a disturbing tremor which seismically runs the gamut of the entire alphabet. They are plagued by the lascivious laughter of the old satyrs of the woods and the painful cries of the dying. In the valleys of rich abundance and in their dwelling house, the atmosphere seems to them suffocatingly oppressive.

One unforgettable night they quit with light abandon the heavy encumbrance of words to seek the wordless heights where the air is purer and the horizon infinite. They have been freed by the whim of a capricious god. The great silence of the heights feels like a soothing caress across the feverish brow . . .

they have reached the top of the mountain and fulfilled the longing of a lifetime.

But, should they remain there until the dawn streaks the sky, they will be torn to pieces by the wolf of abstractions. In a frightened, concerted mass, they rush down the slopes, bleating miserably. Only when they reach the sanctuary of the pen do they feel happy and secure.

One of them, however, stands with its nose pressed between the bars of the closed gate; it is the O, longing to return to the mountain heights.

Olof Lagercrantz

If the text is rather playful, experiment with lots of initial caps. Experiment with pale colors or tints, and don't let them overwhelm the body copy. Try letting the pale initial caps slide under the text above them, as on page 155. Typefaces are Eurostile Bold Condensed and Caslon Pro Regular.

Notice I kerned the cap "T" out to the left a little so its stem aligned with the cap "T" in the next line. Typeface is Bernhard Bold Condensed.

Take it as it comes.
If it doesn't come, go get it.
If you can't get it, create it.

The ditches were rushing rivers; the ponds were full, the earth was already turning green, the swish of the rain upon the trees was terrific; but deafening, drowning all other noises was the ecstatic chorus of millions of frogs from every ditch and pond and field and compound, a wild, mad, maddening, corybantic, croaking and creaking orgasm of sound of wet, wallowing frogs.

Leonard Woolf

Typefaces are Fantasia Initial Caps for the cap "T" (which is actually an EPS file) and Dirty One for the body copy.

. . . .

Automatic drop caps

AGE layout applications can apply drop caps (one form of initial caps) automatically. You can determine how many characters drop down and how many lines they drop. The drop cap in this paragraph is from Massele, a set of EPS initial caps from Aridi.com. They have a wonderful variety of sets. I inserted the graphic as the first character of the paragraph, and InDesign just accepts it and applies the drop cap specs to it.

> **InDesign:** Use the two "Drop Cap" fields in the Paragraph palette. Set the number of lines the cap is to drop into the text, and the number of characters you want to act as drop caps.
>
> **PageMaker:** Use the "Drop Cap" plug-in from the Utilities menu.
>
> **QuarkXPress:** Look in the Formats dialog box under the Style menu.

Also take a look at the initial letters offered by many font vendors. Many come as graphics in EPS format (as the one shown in the first paragraph, above, and on the previous page), which means you can text wrap them, color them, or resize them endlessly. There are some incredibly beautiful caps to choose from—get a set and see what they inspire.

Everything must end. Meanwhile, we must amuse ourselves.

Voltaire

This is a drop cap created instantly in InDesign using the Drop Cap feature. Typeface is Jim Casual.

Typographic Color

Typographers have always referred to black-and-white type on a page as having "color." It's easy to create contrast with paintbox colors; it takes a more sophisticated eye to see and take advantage of the color contrasts in black-and-white. Often, black and white are the only "colors" available, but don't let that limit you—this chapter will give you some ideas to use to ferment your own.

A gray, text-only page can be very dull to look at and uninviting to read. I'm sure you've opened up newsletters or technical documents and found these dull pages, or perhaps you've had to create them. It's not always possible to have graphics on a page to break up the text, but something needs to be done. A gray page can also create confusion by not giving the reader any clue as to the importance of a story or whether two separate stories on the page are related to each other. An effective typographic technique to aid in the organization of a page is to add "color."

Just as the voice adds emphasis
to important words,
so can type:
it shouts or whispers by variation of size.

Just as the pitch of the voice
adds interest to the words,
so can type:
it modulates by lightness or darkness.

Just as the voice adds color
to the words by inflection,
so can type:
**it defines elegance, dignity, toughness
by choice of face.**

Jan White

It's pretty easy to see what is creating the different colors in the typefaces above. Not only is it the weight of the stroke, but also the structure of the letterforms: tall and condensed vs. long and squatty. Also notice the color of the lightweight text in the example compared to the body copy in the paragraphs above. Typefaces are Eurostile Condensed and Eurostile Bold Extended Two.

What makes "color"?

The color of a typeface is determined by a combination of details: the space between the letters and between the lines, the space built into each character, the x-height, the thickness of the strokes, the serifs or lack of serifs, etc. A light, airy typeface with lots of letter spacing and linespacing creates a very light color (and texture). A bold sans serif, tightly packed, creates a dark color (with a different texture). You can clearly see the contrast of colors in the samples below.

In the time of your life, live . . . so that in that wondrous time you shall not add to the misery and sorrow of the world, but smile to the infinite delight and mystery of it.
William Saroyan

Caslon Regular 8.5/10.5

In the time of your life, live . . . so that in that wondrous time you shall not add to the misery and sorrow of the world, but smile to the infinite delight and mystery of it.
William Saroyan

DeconStruct Bold 8.5/9.5

In the time of your life, live . . . so that in that wondrous time you shall not add to the misery and sorrow of the world, but smile to the infinite delight and mystery of it.
William Saroyan

Dear Sarah 10/10.5

In the time of your life, live . . . so that in that wondrous time you shall not add to the misery and sorrow of the world, but smile to the infinite delight and mystery of it.
William Saroyan

Memphis Medium 8.5/9

In the time of your life, live . . . so that in that wondrous time you shall not add to the misery and sorrow of the world, but smile to the infinite delight and mystery of it.
William Saroyan

Bernhard Regular 8.5/12

In the time of your life, live . . . so that in that wondrous time you shall not add to the misery and sorrow of the world, but smile to the infinite delight and mystery of it.
William Saroyan

Jimbo Condensed 8.5/10.5

In the time of your life, live . . . so that in that wondrous time you shall not add to the misery and sorrow of the world, but smile to the infinite delight and mystery of it.
William Saroyan

Regular Joe 8.5/10.5

In the time of your life, live . . . so that in that wondrous time you shall not add to the misery and sorrow of the world, but smile to the infinite delight and mystery of it.
William Saroyan

Times Roman 8.5/10.5

In the time of your life, live . . . so that in that wondrous time you shall not add to the misery and sorrow of the world, but smile to the infinite delight and mystery of it.
William Saroyan

Flyer ExtraBlack Condensed 8.5/10.5

Why use black-and-white color?

If you add color to your heads and subheads by using a typeface with a heavier weight, or if you perhaps set a quote or a passage or a short story in a different "color" (as in a pull quote), the page becomes more visually appealing. If it's visually appealing, readers are more likely to stop on a page and actually read it. And that's the point, right?

Besides making the page more inviting to read, this change in color also helps organize the information. Below, which of the two arrangements gives you an instant visual impression of what's going on, as opposed to having to read the actual text to see what the organization is?

Center Alley

Center Alley worse jester pore ladle gull hoe lift wetter stop-murder an toe heft-cisterns. Daze worming war furry wicket an shellfish parsons, spatially dole stop-murder, hoe dint lack Center Alley an, infect, word orphan traitor pore gull mar lichen ammonol dinner hormone bang.

Oily inner moaning disk wicket oiled worming shorted, "Center Alley, gad otter bet an goiter wark! Suture lacy ladle bomb! Shaker lake!" An firm moaning tell gnat disk ratchet gull word heifer wark lacquer hearse toe kipper horsing ardor, washer heft-cistern's closing, maker bets, gore tutor star fur perversions, cooker males, washer dashes, an doe oily udder hoard wark. Nor wander pore Center Alley worse tarred an disgorged!

Hormone Derange

O gummier hum warder buffer-lore rum Enter dar enter envelopes ply, Ware soiled'em assured adage cur-itching ward An disguise earn it clotty oil die. Harm, hormone derange, Warder dare enter envelopes ply, Ware soiled'em assured adage cur-itching ward An disguise earn it clotty oil die.

With this page being so dull and gray, it is not instantly clear whether there are two separate stories, or perhaps they are both part of the same one. And the page has no contrast to attract your eyes.

Typefaces are Caslon Pro Regular and Bold.

Center Alley

Center Alley worse jester pore ladle gull hoe lift wetter stop-murder an toe heft-cisterns. Daze worming war furry wicket an shellfish parsons, spatially dole stop-murder, hoe dint lack Center Alley an, infect, word orphan traitor pore gull mar lichen ammonol dinner hormone bang.

Oily inner moaning disk wicket oiled worming shorted, "Center Alley, gad otter bet an goiter wark! Suture lacy ladle bomb! Shaker lake!" An firm moaning tell gnat disk ratchet gull word heifer wark lacquer hearse toe kipper horsing ardor, washer heft-cistern's closing, maker bets, gore tutor star fur perversions, cooker males, washer dashes, an doe oily udder hoard wark. Nor wander pore Center Alley worse tarred an disgorged!

Hormone Derange

O gummier hum warder buffer-lore rum Enter dar enter envelopes ply, Ware soiled'em assured adage cur-itching ward An disguise earn it clotty oil die. Harm, hormone derange, Warder dare enter envelopes ply, Ware soiled'em assured adage cur-itching ward An disguise earn it clotty oil die.

The "color" now does two things: It attracts your eyes to the page, and makes it clear that there are two separate stories. Can you see what is creating the different "colors" of type?

Typefaces added are variations of Eurostile.

Stories are by Howard L Chace.

Please keep in mind that there are certainly times when you want a lovely, elegant, subdued page with no strong contrast. Using many of the techniques in this book, you can also create that look. Whether you include contrast or not, creating an elegant page takes time and thought.

Color as in crayons

"Color" is a term with various interpretations, one of them, obviously, being color. When you are using actual colors, like those in a crayon box, an important thing to keep in mind is that warm colors (reds, oranges) come forward and command our attention. Our eyes are very attracted to warm colors, so it takes very little red to create a contrast, to catch your eye, to lead you around the page. It is easy to overdose on warm colors by applying too much in too many places. I know you paid for that second color, but I guarantee it will be more effective if you use it in small doses. I also know it is hard to convince your boss of that. Find examples of where color has been used sparingly to great effect and keep those examples in a file. Also find samples of color being used obnoxiously. I have a newsletter in my file that uses a second color of an ugly red—this ugly red covers more than half the newsletter, defeating the purpose of using color to make important items stand out.

Cool colors (blues, greens), on the other hand, recede from our eyes. You can get away with larger areas of a cool color; in fact, sometimes you *need* more of a cool color to create an effective contrast on the page. But even with cool colors, if the point of the color is to emphasize a point or to add a sophisticated splash, less is usually more.

Scribble some red color in this little shape. Hold the page up and glance at it. Where does your eye land first? Tiny spots of color are powerful.

Ornaments & Dingbats

❧ Ornaments and dingbats are delightful and easy ways to add visual interest to your pages. They are simply little decorative elements you can set along with your type because they are characters in the font. ❧ OpenType fonts and expert sets often have ornaments as extra characters. You can also buy entire sets of them as typefaces. ❧ What's the difference between ornaments and dingbats? It's a fuzzy line, but you might say that dingbats are the sorts of little elements you would use as bullets, whereas ornaments are more sophisticated decorations for more elegant type. But then again you might also say the two are the same. ❧ One use for ornaments or dingbats is as you see here—markers that indicate new paragraphs without actually making a paragraph space or indent. This can be an interesting effect for a short amount of copy, but more than one page of it would be difficult to plow through. ❧ Notice I added more linespace to this page, in addition to the ornaments; this was to lighten the color (see the previous chapter) and give a more inviting, open look to this solid block of text that really should be several short paragraphs. ❧

Oh for a Muse of fire, that would ascend
the brightest heaven of invention.

Chorus in Henry V

· ·

Other uses for ornaments and dingbats

Here are several other ideas for using ornaments. Once you own a font or two of dingbats and ornaments, you will discover all sorts of places to throw them in. Don't be a wimp.

- It is very common to see an ornament at the end of a magazine story indicating the end of that article. If you decide to use this technique, be consistent with the ornament so readers know what to expect when they see the mark. ❀

- Use ornaments in pull quotes to set the text apart, as on the previous page. This can be a beautiful and interesting alternative to a simple rule (line).

- Also experiment with using special dingbats as bullets in a list of items, or in a row as a border.

- Try throwing playful dingbats into your memos, letters, faxes, and other correspondence. There is no excuse for being dull. ☞

- Use a repetitive pattern of dingbats as a background texture, as shown below. Because the dingbats are a font, you can easily resize them, space them, and adjust their linespacing to make the pattern as light or dense as you like.

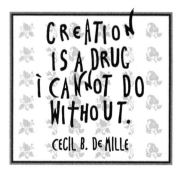

Typeface is Pierre Bonnard.

Pi & Picture Fonts

Pi (pronounced "pie"), pictograph, and picture fonts are similar to ornaments and dingbats (see the previous chapter) except that they tend to be more specific. Many smaller vendors provide these specialty fonts that don't enjoy a large market, and they are often just what you need for a particular project. There is a font for just about everything. If you need a specialty font, order the catalogs of the smaller vendors (check Appendix B at the back of this book for vendor addresses).

Pi fonts

A pi font is a special typeface with mathematical and scientific characters, indispensable for use in technical manuals or scientific treatises. What a blessing these fonts can be! And beyond the obvious practical use, many of these characters are interesting symbols that can be used in other ways. If you have one, print up all the characters and keep your eyes open for creative new ways to use them.

What would you do if you needed these characters and didn't have this font! Typefaces are Mathematical Pi 5 and Mathematical Pi 6.

These can come in handy when writing technical manuals. There is also a companion font to this set that displays all the other keys, such as Shift, Control, Command, and the rest. Typefaces are PIXymbols Stylekey and PIXymbols Function.

Pictograph fonts

Similar to pi fonts are pictograph fonts, which provide international symbols. Many of these symbols are so interesting that they beg to be used in ways you might not immediately think of: in logos, perhaps, or as identifying organizational symbols in a brochure or annual report, or as decorative elements on their own.

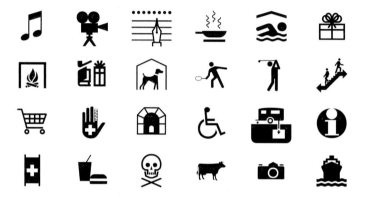

If you ever need symbols like these, check out the fonts. You can even open the font in a font-editing program like Fontographer and customize it. Typefaces are PIXymbols Hotel and PIXymbols Travel.

Instant logos!
Typefaces are Jimbo Standard Black Expanded, Isadora (script), PIXymbols Travel (pictograph).

Picture fonts

Picture fonts, where each character is a little picture, can be used in oh so many ways. Similar to dingbats, you can use them as bullets. Or instead of a dotted or dashed line, try a line made of a picture font character or a combination of characters. Use them as borders, as clip art, as custom art. You can make them very small, add space between them, or even change their color easily.

Picture fonts are great for quick, easy, and inexpensive logos. You can enlarge a picture character to the maximum size in your program, sometimes as large as 18 inches. You can change their color, condense or expand them, kern them, and build them right into the text of the logo. If you know how to use a program like Fontographer from FontLab, you can customize the character and still use it as easily as you would the letter A.

The character shown on the left, from the picture font Printers Ornaments M, had the right feel but slightly the wrong look for the intended logo. I opened the font in Fontographer and just moved a few points to give the character more female lines, as shown on the right. The other face is Eurostile.

These fonts are so much fun to collect and use everywhere. Drop pictures into memos to your boss, love letters, signs, business cards, t-shirts— have fun! Typefaces are MiniPics Lil Ancients, Birds, and MiniPics Doohickies Too.

You can create interesting borders out of many picture fonts. Typeface is MiniPics Doohickies Too.

Rebus stories

And when you run out of things to do, gather your kids, a couple of picture and pi fonts, and create a rebus story. Although the stories are generally pretty silly, I guarantee the process will make you laugh, and that's a valuable thing.

ONCE upon a time there was a little 🧍 who had a 🐕 named Fido. One ☀ day the 🐕 chased a 🐈. This 🐈 had just caught a 🐁. The cat's friend was having a birthday party with a 🎂 and the 🐈 was bringing this dead 🐁 as a birthday present. Before the 🐈 could get to the 🏠 for the party, the 🐕 started chasing him. A little 🐭 saw the predicament and jumped in his new red 🚗 and sped off to get his friend the ✈ who really couldnt do anything to help and so the 🐕 ate the 🐈 who had killed the 🐁 on this ☀ day and that was that.

Typeface is Hansel, which includes the letters and the pictures.

Note!

When you print picture and pi fonts, check your Print dialog box and see if you have a button that says, "Use Symbol font for special characters." If you do, *un*check this button or you will print the wrong symbols!

Don't be a Wimp!

ype has just recently become a household item. The media tells us that people are reading less and less, yet type is becoming more and more important. How many typefaces could you name ten years ago? How many do you now have on your computer? How many billboards, book covers, t-shirts, and ice cream containers do you now look at and wonder what the typeface is?

A result of this increased awareness of typography is increased power and strength of printed words. Everyone is more conscious of the words—not just what they say, but how they are presented. Type is art, but art with a clear purpose. The next chapter talks about evocative typography, and about choosing typefaces that reinforce your message. But in this short chapter I simply want to exhort you to take full advantage of this new typographic consciousness. It is so easy to make your pages alive, exciting, provocative—but never forget that your purpose is to communicate.

Extremes

Don't be afraid to go to extremes. Find ways to use type extremely large or extremely small, at least in proportion to the piece. I recently received a letter with the name and address of the sender in some really funky type at least two inches tall. It had an incredible impact—full of chutzpah and creativity. In phone book advertising, newspaper ads, brochures, flyers, in many, many places, try using extraordinarily large type. A good contrast would be to have the body of the piece in a decently small size, say 10 point. Don't think that because the heading is so large that the rest of the type has to be larger than average also—no no! It is specifically that strong contrast between the large and the small that makes the piece so effective.

· ·

White space

It's okay to have white space, empty space on your page that is not filled with text or graphics or anything but clean empty space. It's okay. You can do it. Your type will love it. When you find type treatments that appeal to you, take a moment to see where that designer let the white space be. Chances are there is a fair amount of it. Look through this book at all the white space. Look through other books and see how much white space they have, and be conscious of your reaction to the ones that have very little. Be brave enough to let the empty space just sit there. It's okay.

Odd typefAces

There are so many wonderfully offbeat typefaces available—oh my my my! Once you get up the nerve to use them, you'll find they are appropriate in many more ways that you might have first thought. If you're a little shy, start off using them on projects for which you don't have clients, such as postcards to friends, invitations to your daughter's birthday party, flyers for your lost dog, the family chore list, your Christmas letter, or as graphic text on your web page. Once the odd typefaces become part of your repertoire, sneak them into a memo to your boss—just one word for now:

Memo   MEMO   Memo   MEMO

She'll hardly notice. Start infiltrating it around the office—notices in the lunchroom, minutes to the meetings, instructions in the restrooms. It is a sad fact of human existence that we tend to fear what we don't know, so make your favorite wild font a local, familiar face. Everyone will become friends and then you can introduce it to your stationery and business cards. Ha!

Typographic Choices

In which we explore typefaces that evoke a response from the reader, tips on choosing a typeface, trends in type, and desktop publishing pitfalls.

Watzlawick's First Axiom of Communication:

You cannot *not* communicate. Paul Watzlawick

Evocative Typography

Evocative typography refers to a choice of typeface that reinforces the message of the words, type that evokes a desired response. Designers have always been very careful about their choice of type, and I know you have been through that process many times. You have a definite idea of which faces would be appropriate for different projects. You wouldn't make a Garage Sale sign in German blackletter. You wouldn't do a brochure for fire safety in a grungy, deconstructive font that's hard to read (or set the directions in all caps).

What I want to accomplish with this chapter, though, is to encourage you to push the concept of evocative typography even further than you have been, and also to take a closer look at what you are evoking. If the first thing that comes to mind for a Japanese tea garden festival is a typeface made out of little pagodas, toss it. Corny and overused. Consider what symbolizes the festival—grace, beauty, tradition? Perhaps try a lovely oldstyle with graceful curves, set large so you can enjoy its beauty. Do some research, discover that the most popular typeface in Japan for many years was Baskerville, a transitional oldstyle—try that. Maybe you need to do a flyer for the children's museum. Your first thought is to use a hand-scrawled typeface with backwards characters. If the flyer is for kids, try using real letters instead of cute lettering that reinforces backwards letters. Try New Century Schoolbook, which was designed for children's books, or a clean sans serif that emulates the way children write their alphabet. You can always use picture fonts to add playful illustrations all over the page.

Next time you need to decide on a typeface that reinforces the text, think it through carefully. Don't always go with your first idea. Since we are on computers, it is so easy to play with all of our options, to change faces with the click of a button. Typefaces are cheap now—invest in a variety! Remember, you can never have too much money, too much RAM, or too many fonts.

Easy choices

Some choices will be very easy, some you will have to think about. The ones below are easy—circle the typeface that would probably communicate the message best for each of these examples:

Lost Shih-Tzu Puppy!   *Fette Fraktur*

Lost Shih-Tzu Puppy   *Carpenter*

Lost Shih-Tzu Puppy!   *Myriad Pro Black*

TOULOUSE-LAUTREC SHOW OPENS FRIDAY   *Pierre Bonnard*

TOULOUSE-LAUTREC SHOW OPENS FRIDAY   *Karton*

Toulouse-Lautrec Show Opens   *Prestige Elite*

   *Gladys*

'62 Willys Pickup For Sale   *Franklin Gothic Roman*

'62 Willys Pickup For Sale   *Emily Austin*

More difficult choices

Many of the choices you will have to make are not so easy (unless you only have six fonts on your computer). Push your creative process, think about what you really mean, play with visual puns, make people think about what they read.

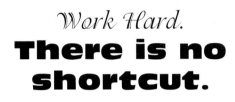

I'll bet these type choices bother you. I'll bet you think "Work Hard" should be the phrase in big, solid, bold type. Well, y'see, it all depends on your point of view and what you want to express.

*In my life, this is how I see it: Ya work hard. **THERE IS NO SHORTCUT** (please excuse the all caps). That's the way it is—it's a fact of life that you work hard. What was difficult to get through my teenagers' heads is that **there is no shortcut**.*

Typefaces are Isadora and Antique Olive Nord.

So how would you quit? It might depend on the job and the circumstances, of course. Maybe one day you would quit in ❶ Marie Luise and another day you would quit in ❷ Clarendon. Maybe your boss drives you to quit in ❸ Chicken. I can tell you that most any day I would quit in ❹ Shelley Volante, with a sassy smile on my face and my fingers toodle-ooing goodbye. See ya later, alligator!

· ·

Think it through

If you have something important to say and you want to reinforce the message with typography, think it through very carefully. There is a place for platitudes. Sometimes the most obvious solution is the best, just as the trite phrase, "like looking for a needle in a haystack" is very clear—a reader can make no mistake about what you mean. All of our tired phrases have a reason for being true—we get it. We get the point. We see the connection. We understand the analogy. So there is also a place in typography for the old saws.

But don't neglect the beauty of a new turn of phrase, a new way of expressing an old thought, a new twist on a tired idea. Sometimes it will behoove you to probe a little deeper, think about the project, and write down the various ideas you are trying to project. Look at your type choices carefully—the more you work with type, the more you will become conscious of the details that project an image.

It is not just the details of the typeface that create a response, it is how you use it. Say you choose a tall, narrow modern to project a sophisticated, highbrow appearance to the ad for your small store. Emphasize that tall and narrow with a strong flush right or left with narrow line lengths, perhaps lots of linespace, maybe a trendy ornament or two.

Keep a file of graphic design pieces that created a strong response in you—good or bad. Take a few moments to put into words how an appropriate response from the reader was created: note the details, the alignments, the white space, and the combination of typefaces. In pieces that evoked an inappropriate response (different from what you think they wanted), figure out where the contradictions are—the typeface, the linespace, the angles, or other details? *The more you are able to see and put these things into words, the more control and power you have in designing your own work.*

Keep your eyes open, and be conscious!

Choose a Typeface

WHAT TYPEFACE SHALL I USE?
THE GODS REFUSE TO ANSWER.
THEY REFUSE BECAUSE THEY DO NOT KNOW.
W. A. Dwiggins

Dwiggins' cry to the gods is one with which we are all familiar. Even though there are more than 50,000 typefaces available to us, finding the perfect font for a particular job can be a stressful task. Or more likely it is *because* we have 50,000 fonts to choose from that the task often appears monumental. There are steps you can take, though, to narrow the selection down to a handful of appropriate choices.

Remember those categories of type?

First of all, remember those general categories of type you read about in the beginning of this book? And remember the sections on readability and legibility? Understanding those categories and concepts is important in helping narrow your choices, so let's review them.

Oldstyle faces have slanted serifs, gradual thick-to-thin strokes, and a slanted stress (the O appears tilted). The original oldstyle faces were created for books, so they are eminently readable.

Modern faces have thin, horizontal serifs, radical thick-to-thin strokes, and a vertical stress (the O does not appear to tilt). If there is more than a paragraph or two of a modern face, the strong thick/thin contrast in the letterforms creates a "dazzling" effect that makes modern typefaces less than perfectly readable. The more pronounced the contrast in the stroke, the less readable in extended text.

Slab serif faces have thick, horizontal serifs, little or no thick/thin transition in the strokes, and a vertical stress (the O does not appear to tilt). If the slab serif is not too heavy, it can make a very sturdy and solid readable face.

• •

Sans serif faces have no serifs, and almost all sans serifs have monoweight strokes (no thick/thin contrast at all). The absence of serifs and the monoweight strokes make sans serifs slightly *less readable* than oldstyles, but because they have such clearly defined letterforms without the addition of little diddlies like serifs, this style is actually *more legible* than serif faces in short bursts of text.

Remember, on a computer monitor, sans serif can be easier to read because there are fewer fine details, like serifs, that get lost or clunky on the screen. Just be sure to make the line lengths shorter and stay away from heavy weights when setting lots of text.

You probably need no review on what defines a typeface as **script, decorative,** or **fringe**—they're pretty self-explanatory.

And do you also remember reading about **readability** and **legibility?** The more distinctive features, the *less* readable it is, the less suitable for long blocks of text. The oldstyle category and the light weights of slab serifs are the *most* "invisible" and subsequently the most *readable.* Sans serifs tend to be more *legible* because they have clean, straightforward letterforms.

Questions about your project

To narrow the choices of faces for a printed project, here are questions to ask yourself. The questions are not ranked in order of importance—each one is a critical consideration.

What is your output printer resolution:
Low (72–144 dots per inch; this would have to be a very old printer),
Medium (300–600 dpi), or
High-resolution imagesetter (1270–2540 dpi)?
Are you going straight through a fax machine
(consider it low resolution)?

What will be the final reproduction method:
Copy machine, quick press, high-quality press?

On what kind of paper will you be reproducing the project:
Newsprint, cheap bond, textured stock, glossy stock, fax paper?

. . . .

Quality

The common thread between these questions is *quality*—the quality of type onscreen, the quality of the type itself that comes out of the printer, the quality of the reproduction method, and the quality of the paper. If each of these variables is on the high end, then you can use any typeface you choose as far as technical reproduction is concerned. If any of these variables is on the low end (or on textured paper, even though it's high quality), you need to be more selective to make sure your type will reproduce well.

Less than very high quality

- ❧ Type from a lower resolution printer or some cheap color printers cannot retain subtle design characteristics, such as very fine lines or delicate serifs.

- ❧ A copy machine or a fax machine also loses some of the fine details in the reproduction process.

- ❧ Inexpensive paper, especially newsprint, absorbs ink and loses even more, sometimes to the point of filling in the counters (those spaces inside letters like **e** or **d**).

For any of the poorer conditions, choose a typeface that has sturdy serifs, no fine lines, and a larger x-height with open counters, such as those shown below. Most sans serifs will hold up very well under any conditions, and are the easiest to read onscreen due to their simplicity of form. Also look through font catalogs for typefaces with these characteristics.

Clarendon Plain or Clarendon Light
New Century Schoolbook
Bookman
Memphis

*All of these faces have solid strokes and serifs that
will not fall apart under difficult printing conditions.*

· ·

Is there an extensive amount of text to read?

If you have an extended amount of text, as in a lengthy newsletter, an annual report, or a book, you need a body typeface with maximum readability (see Chapter 2). Under the best printing conditions (high-resolution output, smooth paper, and a good printing press), try a classic oldstyle for best readability. You are reading Adobe Caslon Pro Regular right now, which is a classic oldstyle.

Under the worst printing conditions, try a typeface in the slab serif category. It will be extremely readable but will not fall apart in the reproduction process.

This typeface (in the modern category) would give you a headache in a long body of text. It's too extreme in many ways. In fact, don't you find it difficult to read even in this short bit? Great for headlines:

Hats off to you!

This typeface will hold up well even under the worst conditions, is clean and orderly, has a business-like presentation, and would be readable in extensive text (not quite as readable as an oldstyle face). This is Clarendon Light, a slab serif. **It also comes in this Clarendon Plain which is a little heavier, and this Clarendon Bold for a great and sturdy impression.**

Compare reading these two samples, plus the two paragraphs above the samples. Do you get a feeling for which are easiest to read? Once you are conscious of it, the details that make a typeface readable become obvious. Typefaces are Bodoni Poster Compressed on the left, Clarendon family on the right.

Are you cramped for space, or do you need to fill space?

You've probably noticed that different typefaces take up different amounts of space, even at the same point size (see page 16 on the anatomy of type). The most critical factor for this difference is the width of the characters. The type family Times has an average x-height, but the characters are slightly condensed to fit more on the page. Other faces, such as Garamond, are more round and open and fill a page easily. Plus, if a typeface is open, it also likes to have extra line spacing and wider margins to complement its spaciousness, which you can take advantage of to further fill the space.

You'll find differences even between typefaces that have the same family name but have been created by different font vendors, as in the example below!

There are entire books of type which display paragraphs of text set in a wide variety of fonts. By comparing the paragraphs you can see which fonts can fit more text in a given space at a given size. Check your local public library or college library for type books.

13-pica line

The loss of the state of innocence in which Baskerville looks like Bembo, and Helvetica is indistinguishable from Univers, has the compensating advantage that we become more aware of the tiny details and the 'subtle allure' which go to make up the best faces.

Sebastian Carter

Adobe Garamond Pro Regular 10.5/13

13-pica line

The loss of the state of innocence in which Baskerville looks like Bembo, and Helvetica is indistinguishable from Univers, has the compensating advantage that we become more aware of the tiny details and the 'subtle allure' which go to make up the best faces.

Sebastian Carter

ITC Garamond Book 10.5/13

Even though the two paragraphs above are both set in Garamond at the same point size, the Adobe Pro version takes up less space than the ITC version. You can imagine how this could change your entire newsletter or novel!

Is the purpose of the piece rather sedate, or can the text be a little playful?

Sometimes even when there is a fair amount of text, as in a brochure, you don't want or really need an invisible typeface. There are many typefaces that are certainly readable enough for short text, but also distinctive enough to create a look that emphasizes your message. Realize you are making a choice between ideal readability and an impression, and get as playful as you like as long as you can justify your choice.

A casual look versus a serious look

❶ I'm sure you already have a sense of which typefaces appear more casual and informal than others, but noticing exactly what kinds of features create that look gives you more strength behind your choices.

❷ Casual faces tend to be more distinctive; their features often have quirks. Rounded, soft edges make it more comfortable; serifs that curve or branch off at odd angles give it a friendly twitch. Faces that resemble handlettering or handwriting of course have a casual feel. These quirky or softened features are comparable to wearing red cowboy boots or sneakers—they create a distinctly casual impression no matter what the words themselves say.

❸ The typefaces with a more professional or serious and stable look are the "invisible" faces I mentioned in the readability chapter, the ones that simply communicate clearly with no quirks. These are the gray suits of typography, the bastions of respectability, the guys in the mold.

So which of the three paragraphs above is the gray suit, which is the evening gown, and which is the t-shirt?

Typefaces are Bernhard Modern, Improv, and Caslon Pro Regular.

Is the project to be skimmed or really read?

In a job like a catalog or parts list where the reader will primarily be skimming headlines to find the text they want to read, keep in mind that sans serif faces are more legible, meaning the separate character forms are more easily distinguished at a quick glance (as long as they are not set in all caps!). You are also more likely to find condensed versions of sans serif faces, which are often necessary in the kind of piece where you're trying to get a lot of information onto the pages. And a sans serif will hold up well under the often less-than-ideal printing conditions of many catalogs or parts lists.

If the sans serif catalog headlines are meant to lead readers into *paragraphs* of text, consider using a serif face for the paragraphs, both for maximum readability and for visual contrast.

HEADS
Storage for the mind. Available in many sizes and preferences.

SHOULDERS
Come in broad, narrow, strong enough to carry the worries of the world.

KNEES
Choose from knobby, knock, bad, or weak.

TOES
Order ten at a time for the most comfortable fit.

EYES
Wide range of colors. Can choose an attitude to go along with.

EARS
Everything from small and sweet to large and winglike.

WAISTLINES
Whatever you order, keep an eye on it as it tends to disappear as you get older.

Heads
Storage for the mind.
Available in many sizes
and preferences.

Shoulders
Come in broad, narrow,
strong enough to carry
the worries of the world.

Knees
Choose from knobby,
knock, bad, or weak.

Toes
Order ten at a time for
the most comfortable fit.

Eyes
Wide range of colors.
Can choose an attitude
to go along with.

Ears
Everything from small and
sweet to large and winglike.

Waistlines
Whatever you order,
keep an eye on it as
it tends to disappear
as you get older.

So what makes the second list easier to read, and makes the heads easier to scan?

- *Upper- and lowercase instead of all caps.*

- *Extra space above each head.*

- *Contrast with the body copy.*

- *Sans serif for heads (Formata Bold), serif for body copy (Garamond).*

· ·

Evocative typography

Notice these questions don't even address the subject of whether a particular typeface suits your job emotionally; that is, whether the look-and-feel of the face itself reinforces your message. I do hope you read Chapter 29 on "Evocative Typography" for some suggestions on this most interesting of typographic questions.

Within the limits of your reproduction process, push your creativity here. Experiment with new and different faces, faces you might not have considered at first. Don't analyze them—get your gut reaction. Keep your eyes open for what others have done, consciously clip examples of unusual type choices and file them for later inspiration. You'll be surprised at what can work!

DECORATIVE AND FRINGE FONTS

There are so many wonderful and wild typefaces now, with more being created every day. Obviously, these intriguing fonts are for special occasions, but what occasions! Just be careful not to overdose your reader with too much of a special face—its strong impact will be diluted. Rather than use a uniquely creative face for all the headlines in your newsletter, save it for one very special article. The contrast between the stable headlines and the wild one will give your special article more impact.

Headline typeface is Erosive.

An exercise and method

I recommend you go to the web sites of the font vendors listed in Appendix B of this book. If they provide a printed catalog, request it. Spend a few minutes looking carefully at many faces on the web site or in the catalog and try to place each one into one of the general categories of type. Once you have found its basic place (many will not fit neatly into a category—that's okay, just get as close as possible), then make some judgments. Does it have distinctive features or is it invisible? Does it wear red cowboy boots or a gray suit? Does the face have fine, delicate features that might not hold up through a fax machine, a copier, or on textured or cheap paper? Or does it have sturdy features that can go through the wash?

Analyze your project

❨ Know your output method and final reproduction process, and narrow your choices down to appropriate faces that will retain their design qualities. (Reread, if necessary, Chapters 2 and 3 on readability and legibility.)

❨ Decide on the look you want to convey, then narrow your choices to the distinctive or the invisible (or a combination that is exciting and still readable).

❨ If you use more than one face, make sure the fonts are decidedly different from each other. If you have chosen a beautiful oldstyle for the body text, try a bold sans serif for headlines. (If you haven't yet, you might want to read another book of mine, *The Non-Designer's Design Book*. The second half of the book focuses on the specific issue of combining typefaces.)

❨ Don't be afraid to use wild fonts where they are appropriate, and remember they are most effective (as is any rich item) when used sparingly—the richer, the more powerful. But don't be a wimp!

THE GOOD THING IS THAT
WE HAVE SO MANY FONTS.
THE BAD THING IS THAT
WE HAVE SO MANY FONTS.

Telltale Signs of
Desktop Publishing

Desktop publishing has matured from the classic ransom notes we were inundated with in the mid-1980s. People have become much more visually aware and informed about the professional way to set their own type and design their own pages. But telltale signs of do-it-yourself desktop publishing still creep into even the most professional work. Some of these signs are a result of not knowing the software well enough to control certain features, and some are simply evidence of using convenient features that really shouldn't even be options—or, in some cases, defaults—on the computer.

Give yourself three penalty points for each of the following telltale signs that you perpetrate. If you score three or above, you lose.

. . . .

1. Helvetica

Type has trends, just like hair styles and clothing and eyeglasses and architecture. **Helvetica** was the most popular typeface in the world in the 1960s, and in the '70s it was a way of life. By the '80s Helvetica was becoming as passé as beehive hairdos and then it appeared in the Macintosh font menu and then in the PC font menu under the name **Arial.** Just as a beehive hairdo creates a certain look, Helvetica creates a certain look. A dated look. A '70s look. Just because it's on your computer doesn't mean you have to use it. The greatest thing you could do for your publications is to invest in another sans serif face, one with a strong, bold black version in its family. As with all trends, Helvetica will someday be back in style—in about two hundred years.

This is Helvetica—groovy, man.

Try anything else: Trade Gothic, **Formata, Antique Olive,** Eurostile!

2. Straight quotes

It is amazing that after all these years people are still typing straight quotes. Learn the keystrokes to type real quotes, and in every application you use, take advantage of the feature that types them for you automatically (read your manual!). But don't type curly quotes when you need inch and foot marks (in fact, use prime marks; remember Chapter 4)! And don't type an opening quote at the beginning of a word that really needs an apostrophe! And put the quotation marks and apostrophes in the right places!

"Can you believe that dog stands 7'3" tall? Its huge!"

"Can you believe that dog stands 7'3" tall? It's huge!"

Notice the prime marks for the numbers, and the quotation marks are hanging!

. . . .

3. Double returns

Hitting the Return or Enter key twice between paragraphs or after headlines separates the text with big, awkward gaps. Double Returns also make it possible to end up with a blank line at the top of a column.

Learn to use the feature to set "Paragraph space after" and "Paragraph space before." It's in every word processor and page layout application. With that feature you can determine exactly the amount of space you want between paragraphs, after headlines, above subheads—an elegant space that tells the reader a new paragraph has begun without physically separating the text so much.

Notice the difference between these three paragraphs and the rest of the paragraphs in the book—wouldn't you agree that the gap appears unnecessarily large?

4. Two spaces after punctuation

I know, I know—if you are still typing two spaces after periods it is probably because you firmly believe it looks better that way. If all the work you create is for yourself, go ahead and continue to type two spaces. But you would be doing your clients a disservice to set *their* type with two spaces after periods because by now most people have become visually astute enough to notice the unsightly gaps created by that double space. Publications typed with two spaces have an unprofessional appearance, whether you agree with it or not, and your work will be ridiculed. Open any novel on your shelf—see any double spaces? Did you read that novel and complain to yourself that you couldn't tell where the sentences ended? The high-quality type you are using, with its proportional widths and kerning pairs that tuck the letters so close together, does not need two spaces to separate sentences. Squint at this paragraph—notice any holes?

. . . .

5. Gray boxes behind text

Just because you *can* make gray boxes doesn't mean that you have to. Beginners often use gray boxes to make important parts of the text stand out because they don't have other ideas about how to make type a focal point, or at least make it a little more important than average. Besides screaming "amateur," type on that dotted, gray background is difficult to read. (Even worse are gray boxes with rounded corners. I know you have a tool for making rounded corner boxes. So.)

If you want to make a portion of the text stand out, try something else: a dramatic headline font, reverse bold heads, heavy rules (lines) above and below the article, extra space around the type. Keep your eyes open and see what others do—copy those ideas!

> *Warning:*
> Do not touch the red knob while cleaning this machine or you will detonate the blasting cap and the machine will explode.

Besides looking plain ol' dumb, the lack of contrast between the gray background and the words also makes the text difficult to read.

Warning!

Do not touch the red knob while cleaning this machine or you will detonate the blasting cap and the machine will explode.

White space, heavy and thin rules, bold typeface—oh, so many ways to call attention to text without using gray boxes.

6. Centered layouts

Centered type creates a stable, sedate, formal look because it is so symmetrical and balanced. It can also create a deadly dull look. New designers center type because it is a very safe thing to do. If you center the page because you *want* a more formal look, that's one thing. But if you center the page because you simply haven't thought about it, or because you are afraid of uncentering it, that's another thing. As you flip through any magazine, stop at the layouts that interest you. Most of the pages and ads that have a strong, dynamic feeling are not centered. An invisible line connects the elements in a flush left or flush right alignment, and the strength of that line gives strength to the entire page.

If you are going to center, then do it with gusto. Don't try to make all the lines similar lengths; instead, show off the fact that it's centered. And if you're going to center, center *everything*—don't stick something in the left-hand corner just to fill the corner. Corners don't mind being empty.

I think and think for
months and years. Ninety-
nine times, the conclusion
is false. The hundredth
time I am right.

Albert Einstein

I think and think
for months
and years.
Ninety-nine times,
the conclusion is false.
**The hundredth time
I am right.**

Albert Einstein

*Mmm, nice and boring. And the
typography in no way reinforces
the message of the text.*

*What did I do
to this centered arrangement
to make it a bit more
dynamic?
Name five things.*

*Typeface is Obelisk Light, Bold,
and Italic.*

7. Borders around everything

One border around a page often indicates a beginner who feels unsafe with type that is uncontained. The more boxes of type with borders around them, the more insecure the designer. I know, it feels safer to box it in; it gives the type a place to *be*, without just floating in the space. But y'know what? It's okay to let it be. Really. That white space (the "empty" space) is itself a border—it encloses the type, yet lets it breathe; it defines the edges, yet maintains a freedom.

8. Half-inch indents

Yes, I know your typing teacher taught you to indent five spaces or one-half inch, but that's a very old habit left over from typewriters. Typically on a typewriter a person was typing all the way across the page, and the type was relatively large.

A standard typographic indent is one em space, which is a space as wide as the point size of the type. In 10-point type, an em space is 10 points wide; in 36-point type, an em space is 36 points wide. This is roughly equivalent to *two* spaces, not five. Especially when your type is in columns, a half-inch indent is way out of proportion.

9. Hyphens or asterisks for bullets

- Using hyphens or asterisks as bullets is a typewriter habit, and it looks dumb in professional type.
* The round dot bullet (•, type Option 8) is a little better, but experiment with more interesting bullets.
- You can get strong little squares or triangles out of Zapf Dingbats, or play with other picture fonts. Make them smaller and use the baseline shift feature to raise them off the baseline (read the manual!).
* It's amazing how this little touch can add more sophistication to a piece. See Chapter 26.

10. Outlined shadowed type

Type that has been outlined and shadowed automatically by the computer still shows up, and in the most surprising places (like book covers, billboards, and annual reports). Don't do it. If you're just starting to use your computer, I know the temptation is great because with the click of a button you can make your type fancy. And that's the impression it gives—someone trying to make their type look fancy because they don't know what else to do with it. When you let the computer add a shadow with the click of a button, you have no control over where the shadow goes or how thick it is, and most often it just looks cluttered and junky because of all the different parts of the letters in various layers. It creates an especially bad effect if the type is a script face.

Again, look around, try to put into words what other people have done to make their type stand out without resorting to using outlines and shadows.

Meet the host!

11. Twelve-point type and auto leading

Just because the default is 12-point type with auto leading doesn't mean you have to use it. For most typefaces, 12-point is a tiny bit too large for body copy. Take a paragraph of 12-point text and set the same paragraph in 10, 11, or perhaps 10.5 point. Compare the two printed pieces; notice which one gives you a more professional, sophisticated impression. Add an extra 1 or 1.5 points of linespace (leading). Compare them again. What do you think?

. . . .

12. Underlines in print

This is a law: **never use the underline feature.** An underline in print means one thing: *italicize* this word. I know you were taught to underline titles of books, but that's because the typewriter (or your teacher) couldn't set italics. And <u>*underlining italic text*</u> is one of the most redundant things you can do in life. I know you sometimes underlined to emphasize a headline or a word, but that's because you didn't know how to make the type bolder or bigger or a different face. Now you know. Now you have no excuse.

Drawing a rule ("rule" means line) under text is very different from hitting the underline keystroke. When you draw a rule you have control over how thick it is, how long it is, and how far below the type it sits. But when you tell your computer to underline, the line bumps into the letters, obscures the descenders, is a clunky thickness, and looks dumb.

Some layout applications, such as Adobe InDesign, let you determine how thick a computer underline is, how far away from the text it is, what kind of line it is (dotted, double, etc.), what color the line should be, and if there is a gap in the line, what color the gap should be. Essentially, this feature lets you create a rule *under selected characters,* as opposed to the paragraph rule feature, which sets a line of your choice under or above the first or last line of a paragraph.

13. All caps

All caps are more difficult to read. That's just a fact: we recognize a word not only by its letters, but by the shape of the whole word. When text is in all caps, every word has the same shape so we have to go back to reading letter by letter.

All caps are fine sometimes, when you *consciously* choose to accept their lower readability because you need the look of all caps. But when you're setting headlines, subheads, lists in a parts directory, catalog entries, or other items that need to be skimmed and absorbed quickly, all are read more easily and quickly if they are in lowercase. If you use all caps because you want the words to stand out, or because it makes them appear larger and you think it's easier to read, THINK AGAIN. Find an alternate solution, such as **bold lowercase,** more space surrounding the text, **a different typeface,** a rule beneath, behind, or above the text.

And of course no one reading this book would ever put a font like Zapfino or Zapf Chancery in all caps. And outlined and shadowed. Score fifty-one points for yourself if you do. The capital letters in script faces are always more elaborate because they are meant as swash characters to introduce a word. When you set these froufrou letters in all caps, they bump into each other, overlap where they shouldn't, fit poorly together, and generally look stupid. Add the outline and shadow and you have the worst possible typography on earth, worse than any grunge type you may cringe at.

THE BLUES IS HARD TO LOSE.

Your score?

If you scored above three points, don't worry. Creating professional-level type is mainly a matter of becoming more aware of details. It usually doesn't take any more time to do it "right," and it is certainly not difficult to gain control over these details. If you scored less than three, then congratulations, and consider it your obligation to gently teach others the things you know.

I base my fashion taste on what doesn't itch.

the late great Gilda Radner

Trends in Type
by John Tollett

Fifteen years ago, how many typesetters and typographic designers did you know on a first-name basis? And how many do you know today? I'm willing to bet my last, crumpled, 1980s vintage sheet of press type that *most* of the people you know have a better type selection at their fingertips than many professional typographers used to have in their shops. I'll do better than that. I'll bet my treasured, white-handled, tooth-marked x-acto knife that within the past hour or so, you've made a life-or-Helvetica decision.

Back when I was using that x-acto knife's handle to burnish down that sheet of press type, if someone had asked me to bring them up to date on current type trends, I would have noted the revival of some dated faces like Cheltenham, or the popularity of extra-tight letter spacing in headlines. They would have looked at me and smirked, "Golly, I'm *so* impressed! Tell me [yawn] more."

But that was then and this is now. The technology of desktop and web publishing has transformed the old graphics neighborhood into a much more exciting, innovative, and creative world. And that's why identifying trends is difficult… there's so much happening on such a steep curve of change that current trends don't have the opportunities that our ancestor trends had. But, hey, this is the digital era and if you want to make it as a trend, you're going to have to really wow us with your stuff.

For the sake of this discussion, let's say that *trends in type* refers to both *font design* (the look and feel of the individual characters of a font) and to *typographic design* (using type as the major visual element in layout and design). This makes a huge category, but I nominate the following six entries as the most obvious candidates for trendom.

. . . .

1. MOST CONTROVERSIAL

TREND:

This one really rocked the boat. If you haven't seen it, you've been spending too much time at the Helvetica User Group meetings. Some people think these ugly fonts are a fad that has started to fade. But if you look around, you'll realize that grunge type and lawless design is not only everywhere, it's so common that it doesn't shock us like it used to. Ugly fonts are not only outrageous by traditional standards, sometimes they range between barely legible and you-gotta-be-kidding-if-you-think-I-can-read-this. But
g   u   e   s   s
what else they are? They're interesting.

Designers who are trying to get your at-

tention, who are trying to convey a feel-

ing with type, are using ugly fonts and ugly design. Ugly design abandons most things that are familiar to us, such as consistent leading, symmetrical columns, reasonable contrast between words and Background, in favor of lines of type crashing into each other, columns of type crashing into each other, columns of type on top of each other, words bleeding off

the page and anything else that would terminate your employment in most places. There are some traditionalists who are getting close to marching through the streets with torches and pitchforks to round up grunge design before it destroys our typographic village. Some aren't worried at all because it's laughable that such a ridiculous thing could have much influence. Uh oh. Look around you. mtv. espn. National magazines, national advertisers... everyone is feeling the graphic influence of grunge. Like trends in fashion, designers take elements of what's happening in the most extreme cases and use them in more conservative ways. You'll

. . . .

see ugly fonts used in traditional layouts. I've used

some very stranGe fonts for some very conservative clients
(a community college, a banK, and a magazine
for CAD engineers). Some designers
prefer using traditional, classical typefaces in a grun-
ge-inspired layout. Some do both. You Don't have to plunge into
grunge, but it's really fun to
get your feet wet.

2. Most Amazing Trend: Special Effects Type

The first time I saw a designer stretching and squeezing type on a computer monitor, I knew my graphic life was going to change, but little did I know how magical changes those changes would be.

Some of the things you can do with type today aren't new. Dazzling effects were being created before desktop publishing, but mainly by those lucky enough to have giant budgets and lengthy production schedules. Most of us flipped through the design annuals of yesteryear and wondered how this was done or what genius did that? Who has that much time or budget? Fortunately, there was a digital daybreak on the horizon emblazoned with the motto: New Ballgame, Amigo!

Tired of flat type just lying there, staring at you? With software and software plug-ins available today you can transform your headline into a piece of

art, or at least an eye-stopping dynamic graphic. You can render a word or a sentence in 3D, rotate it, render it in color, and specify what direction the light is coming from and what color the light is. Change the color of the ambient light and map a texture to the surface of the type. Bevel the edge of the type. Create a soft drop shadow that blends into the background color. Twirl, zig, zag, ripple, shatter, or vector warp your type. Shade the inside of the type with blends of color. You can do all this at your desktop in less time than it used to take you to find the phone number of some master handlettering expert.

The software tools for creating special effects are getting more powerful, more affordable, and easier to use, so this is a trend that is just becoming a way of life. The only designers jumping off this bandwagon are ones who are looking for the next big whatever. The next time one of these techniques jumps off the page at you, say hello to a trend.

3. Most Beautiful Trend: Rendered Type

I've separated this category from the previous one because this is really a combination of illustration, animation, and typography. These typographic examples *really* used to be out of reach. Before desktop graphics, how often were you going to hire photographers, illustrators, retouch specialists, or animators just so you could have a snazzy print headline or a dazzling video title? But now it's *everywhere*. It's everywhere because the software that enables such effects is available and affordable for the designer middle-class (designers who don't have international clients and unlimited budgets)!

The typographic possibilities would have been unthinkable a relatively short time ago: Type that's partially blended into a photograph or embossed with a texture; photomontages rendered on top of headlines; textures and effects that look photographic but were created from scratch on a computer; patterns that have never even been created before; animated, editable fonts for video that explode, burn, wiggle, or do anything you can imagine. If you really want to dazzle 'em, this one's for you.

4. Most Obvious Trend: Abundance of Font Choices

For many years I felt that I was familiar with every typeface available. Even if some got past me, it was very seldom that I saw a typeface and didn't know its name or at least recognize it. And it was *guaranteed* that I knew every font available in my local area. Plus every style of press type available at the local art supply store. Here's another "that was then" pause. Now I can't even remember all the fonts on my own computer, much less have a comprehensive idea of all the available fonts from the outside world.

I was looking at a friend's type catalog recently and I didn't know a single font in the entire catalog. Everyone's on the font bandwagon. It's not just the large, professional typesetting houses buying fonts out there anymore—it's millions of desktop publishers expressing their individual and eclectic tastes. Traditional type designers are generating new designs, both classical and grungy. New type design companies are springing up and making quite an impact. Freelance designers are designing fonts. Fonts are being designed specifically for web pages and low-resolution monitors. Robin's daughter Scarlett designed a font (named Scarlett) when she was seven years old—and I've seen it used in full color brochures both here in the USA and in Europe.

Fonts used to be very expensive. Now vendors practically give them away. As a matter of fact, sometimes they do give them away. In addition to commercial font prices dropping tremendously, there's a large and growing collection of shareware and freeware fonts available. Don't plan on collecting them all unless you have a hard drive with several terabytes of space.

You may argue that you'll never use or even see half of these fonts. That may be true, but until the government limits type usage to Times and Helvetica, font creation is a huge trend.

5. Most Fun Trend: Breaking the Rules

Breaking the rules of design. Big deal. "I do it everyday," you say. That's partly because the rules are fairly subjective and trying to agree on exactly what the rules are could cause a Holy Graphics War. Going out on a graphic limb or out on a design ledge is pretty common, even encouraged. The rules I'm talking about are the untouchable sacred cows of legibility and readability. If there's one rule that I made sure I *never* broke, it was this one: no matter how wild and unorthodox the design, you *had* to be able *at least* to read the copy. Ah, those were the good old days. Fortunately, not many designers are feeling compelled to carry their desktop creations this far. But on the other hand, there are enough people pushing the conventional legibility envelope (even normal, well-adjusted designers) that I'm proclaiming this an official recognizable trend. I know, I know . . . you're probably saying, "I'll believe it's a trend when *Robin Williams* designs a grungy type book." Start believing. Robin wrote that one already—several years ago.*

*See A Blip in the continuum by Robin Williams, illustrated by John Tollett

. . . .

6. Most Important Trend: Typographic Independence

In the past, our design choices were limited. First, our font choices were limited to whatever our typesetter had decided to include in her library. Her choices were usually the most mainstream, commercially acceptable, and popular font designs. Now, with the large commercial libraries, freeware, and shareware (and all of them available online), our choices are almost unlimited. If you think you're going to run out of choices, you can create your own font design.

Next, we were limited by time and budgets. Okay, those limitations are still there, but they've been minimized by our ability to experiment, create, and produce typographic design on our computers for a fraction of the time and money it used to take. The argument you still hear from the disappearing contingent of desk op critics is that computers just can't deliver the finesse that a type master can give you. I always wondered who those type masters were and why they never worked the midnight shift while my job was being set. My beloved x-acto knife saved a lot of typesetting jobs, but it can't compete anymore. So to the typesetter who once kicked me out of her office because I wanted her to reset some type: Game over, man.

Typographic Independence is here!

Future Trends

This is the exciting part. Some of our documents are no longer flat images of type and photographs fixed to a static page. With the advent of the web, many documents are interactive and dynamic. A headline can animate while it moves around on the page; a logo can change into a headline with the click of the mouse; type can change colors or size; and 3D type can rotate or spin. While all this sounded futuristic not long ago, it's commonplace on the web and in video. Certainly a future trend is more interactive type.

Even when designing print material, type can be interactive. OpenType is a "smart" font format—in the right application, you will see characters automatically change their letterforms based on the characters to the left and right. Hyphens and dashes raise and lower themselves depending on whether the text is in caps or not; letterspacing adjusts itself depending on how large or small the type is. Amazing.

Another future trend is the design and use of more fonts created specifically for display on computer monitors. The driving force for font technology up to this point has always been to optimize the output quality for publishing in the print media, but fonts designed for web publishing and video are making a splash and will likely influence print design as well.

As web technology, programming languages, and the speed of Internet access improves, designers will have more freedom in typography, and the creative possibilities of typographic design will be more versatile and more powerful than ever before.

So, in the future, when a student intern in the cubicle down the hall is trying a new holographic feature on a cutting-edge multimedia document, I'll just have one thing to say: "Go get your own x-acto knife, dude. This one's got sentimental value."

BE NOT

too tame neither,

but let your own discretion be your tutor;

suit the font to the word,

the word to the font...

paraphrased (forgive me) from HAMLET

Glossary of Type Terms

In which to discern
an apex from an
ascender and an
orphan from a widow.

Type Terms

A

alignment: Refers to whether text is aligned on the left (flush left), the right (flush right), on both edges (justified), or centered.

all caps: When you set type in all capital letters.

ampersand: Name of the "&" symbol that stands for the word "and." The symbol is derived from the Latin word "et," which means "and."

apertures: Partially open spaces within letters such as C, G, S, a, c. Fully enclosed spaces, as in the letter O, are called *counters*.

apex: The top point of a capital letter, such as the peak of a capital A.

arrangement: See *alignment*.

arm: Horizontal stroke of a letter that is unattached at one end. A capital E has three arms.

ascender: The part of a lowercase letter that rises above the height of the lowercase x.

asterisk: The * symbol, often called a star.

asymmetrical: Not even or equal on both sides.

ATM: Adobe Type Manager. A utility that smooths the edges of font characters onscreen. ATM is no longer needed in Mac OS X or Windows XP.

auto kerning: When a software program accesses the *kern pairs* built into a typeface.

axis: A line through the thinnest parts of a letter O in a typeface that has a *thick/thin* stroke contrast.

The picture font on these pages is Renfield's Lunch, by Mary-Anne King, available at GarageFonts.com.

B

ball terminal: The round ball at the end of the arm in letters such as a, c, and r. It's most common in modern typefaces.

bar: Horizontal crossbar connecting two sides of a letter, as in A or H.

baseline: The invisible line on which type sits (excluding *descenders*).

beak: The *serif* at the end of an *arm*, such as in E and L.

bitmapped font: The part of a font that is created with and displayed on the screen with pixels, as opposed to *outlines*.

blackletter: A style of type, also called German Blackletter, Gothic and mistakenly Old English. 𝕿𝖍𝖎𝖘 𝖎𝖘 𝖇𝖑𝖆𝖈𝖐𝖑𝖊𝖙𝖙𝖊𝖗.

bleed: Any element on a page that is printed over the trimmed edge of the paper.

body: Sometimes the *x-height* is called the body of a typeface.

body clearance: Horizontal space designed into the typeface above the ascenders and below the descenders so the lines of type don't touch each other.

body copy: Text type set in paragraphs. Point sizes range from about 8 to 12 point.

bold face: A font variation that has thicker strokes in the letterforms.

bounding box: The invisible rectangle that surrounds blocks of text or graphics in software programs.

bowl: The curved stroke that makes an enclosed space within a letter, such as the stroke that encloses the *counter* on the letter b.

bracket: The curve that connects some serifs and the stems of letters.

bracketed serif: Serif that is connected to the main stroke of a letter by a small curved stroke (the *bracket*).

bullet: A dot (•), box (■), or other tiny element used as a graphic in text, often to indicate an item in a list.

· ·

C

cap height: The height of the capital letters within a typeface. The cap height may be greater than or less than ascender height.

capitals: The uppercase letters of the alphabet, affectionately called "caps."

caption: Text accompanying a photo or illustration.

center alignment/centered: The text on each line is centered within the line length.

character: One single letter, number, punctuation mark, etc.

character set: The entire set of all the letters, numbers, symbols, punctuation, dingbats, etc., within a font.

characters per pica (cpp): A measurement of how many characters in a particular face and size could fit in a pica. Before *desktop publishing*, knowing the cpp of a font was necessary for calculating the fit of type.

cicero: A unit of measure slightly larger than the pica. One cicero equals 0.178 inch, 12 didot points, or 12.75 PostScript points.

Clarendon: The name of a type family in the slab serif category. Sometimes the entire category is called Clarendon because the face is a perfect example of a slab serif.

color: The overall tone, density, and texture of a page of type in black and white.

column: Type set in vertical sections separated by a blank space (gutter). This glossary is set in two columns of type per page.

condensed type: Type that has a narrower character width than regular text type, useful for fitting a lot of copy in a small space.

contrast: The difference between the thin and thick strokes of a letterform. Or the overall difference between the looks of different typefaces.

copy: All the text on a page or in a document.

copyfitting: Calculating how much space is needed to fit a certain amount of type.

counter: Fully or partially enclosed white space within a letter.

crop marks: Thin lines at each of the four corners of a page that define the outer edges of the document.

curly quotes: A descriptive name for true *quotation marks*.

cursive: Type that flows, such as script or italic fonts.

D

decorative face: A typeface designed for a distinctive, ornate, or otherwise graphic look.

descender: The part of a letter that extends below the *baseline*.

desktop publishing (dtp): The use of the personal computer to create (publish) pages that contain text and graphics.

didot: A unit of measure similar to a *point*. Twelve didot points make one *cicero*, similar to a *pica*.

dingbats: Decorative elements such as symbols, icons, or ornaments. These may be entire fonts or individual *glyphs* contained within a font. Zapf Dingbats and Wingdings are well-known examples.

discretionary hyphen (dischy): A hyphen you can type in your software that disappears when it's not needed.

display type: Type over the size of 14 point, as in headlines or advertising titles.

dotless i: A lowercase i with no dot. This is useful when the dot bumps into another letter or when you want an accent over the letter instead of the dot. To type a dotless i on a Mac, press Shift Option B.

dpi: Dots per inch, a measure of the *resolution* of a printer and of the text and images on a printed page. Also see *ppi*.

drop cap: A large or ornate letter at the beginning of a paragraph, also called an initial cap.

drop out type: When you put text on top of an image and "drop out" the text so the white of the paper shows through where the type is.

dumb quotes: Fake quotation marks like those made on the typewriter ("). A painfully obvious sign of unprofessional type.

· ·

E

ear: Small stroke projecting from the top of the lowercase g.

Egyptian: A category of type that has slab serifs and little contrast in the strokes. The category is also known as slab serifs.

elite: A monospaced typewriter typeface that sets 12 characters per inch.

ellipsis: Three dots (…) used to indicate an omission of text or a thought that trails off.

em: A horizontal unit of measure equal to the point size of the type in use. It's about the width of the capital letter M.

em dash: A long dash used to indicate a shift in thought—it sets off emphatic material that is too important to put in parentheses.

em space: A non-breaking space as wide as the point size of the type in use.

en: A horizontal unit of measure equal to half the point size of the type in use. It's about the width of the capital letter N.

en dash: A dash used to indicate a range, as in 9–5. Use as a substitute for the word "to."

en space: A non-breaking space half as wide as the point size of the type in use.

expert set: Additions to basic font sets that contain alternate and special characters such as *small caps, swash characters,* and *oldstyle numerals.*

extended type: Type that has a wider character width than regular text type.

extenders: *Ascenders* and *descenders.*

eye: The *counter* (enclosed space) of the lowercase "e."

F

family: A font family contains all the related fonts with the same design characteristics and the same name.

figure space: A space that is the same width as a *lining figure* (number).

finial: The tapered, curved end of a stroke not ending in a serif (c, e). Also a variation of a letter for use as the last letter in a line.

first-line indent: The indent of the first line after you hit Return or Enter.

fleuron: A typographical ornament, often leaf or flower shaped.

flush left: Text *aligned* on the left.

flush right: Text *aligned* on the right.

folio: A page number.

font: One weight, width, and style of a typeface.

font family: See *family.*

font ID conflict: Some operating systems and programs identify a font by its number, some by its name. It is possible to have fonts installed with the same number or the same name and this can cause conflicts.

font ID number: Every font on the Mac is identified by a particular number.

font management: Using a program that allows you to open and close fonts as needed, create font sets, and handle font ID conflicts and corrupt fonts.

font metrics: The detailed design specifications of the font, such as the thickness of the underline, how tall the capital letters are, the kerning pairs, etc.

footer: The repeating text that appears at the bottoms of document pages. Also known as the "running foot." It might include a page number, date, etc.

format: To apply certain characteristics (font, size, style) to the words on the page.

fraction bar: A non-breaking slash used in fractions. It's slightly different from a regular slash in that it's a bit thinner and tilts more.

fringe type: Distorted or deliberately trashed type, often difficult to read, but fun to use.

G

glyph: A symbol that represents a character. For instance, in an OpenType font you might have eight different glyphs that all represent the letter A.

gothic: A name sometimes used for sans serif or blackletter fonts.

gutter: The vertical blank space that separates columns or pages.

H

hairline: Thinnest stroke in a character, specifically in the modern category.

hairline rule: One-quarter point *stroke* or line.

hairline serif: A flat, thin serif as on a letter in a modern typeface.

hanging indent: When the first line of a paragraph hangs out to the left of the rest of the paragraph. Also known as an *outdent.*

hanging punctuation: Punctuation that is moved beyond the edge of the text to avoid the appearance of an indent.

hard copy: A printed copy. "Hard" means you can touch it.

hard line break: When you press Shift Return or Shift Enter to force a line to break, but it does not create a new paragraph.

hard Return: When you press the Return/Enter key to manually start a new paragraph.

hard space: A non-breaking space between two words. A hard space prevents those words from being separated at the ends of lines.

header: Text that is repeated at the top of each document page. Also called a *running head.*

headline: The title of a body of text.

hints: Extra information included in some fonts that ensures optimal appearance and output.

hyphenation zone: A designated width at the right margin whose measurement determines if words will hyphenate or not.

I

I-beam: The text cursor that you use to select text or move the *insertion point.*

icon: A little picture that represents a file on your computer.

imagesetter: A large, high-end PostScript printer used for high-resolution output on paper or film.

indent: The amount of space between the *margins* of a page and the actual text.

inferior: See *subscript.*

initial cap: See *drop cap.*

insertion point: When you click the *I-beam* in text, it sets a flashing bar known as the insertion point. The insertion point indicates where text will appear when you start to type and where a graphic will appear when you insert it.

italic: A style of type where the letters slant to the right. True-drawn italics do not simply slant—they have been completely redesigned.

J

jump line: A brief line at the end of a column or page telling the reader where the text continues.

justified: Text that is aligned on both the left and right sides of the text block.

K

kern, kerning: The process of adjusting the space between letters so the spacing appears to be visually consistent.

kern pairs: Pairs of letters that have tighter spacing built into them so they tuck into each other nicely.

L

leaders: A series of repeated periods, dots, or other little symbols that lead your eye from one column to the next, as in a table of contents.

leading: (pronounced "ledding") The amount of space between the *baseline* of one line of text and the next baseline.

legibility: How easy it is to tell one letter from another in any given typeface, which determines how easy it is to read short bursts of type like headlines or signage.

· ·

letterspacing: The space from one character to the next.

Also, if you "letterspace" a line or block of text, it implies that you aded extra space, sometimes lots of space, between all the characters to create a certain graphic effect.

ligature: A special character combining two or more characters into one.

line break: The point at which any line ends. This is different from a *hard line break.*

line spacing: See *leading.*

lining figures/numbers: Numerals that are the same height as the capital letters in a typeface. "Tabular lining figures" will align in columns.

link: The stroke connecting the top and bottom parts of a letter, as in the lowercase g.

loop: The lower portion of a lowercase g.

lowercase: The small letters of an alphabet.

M

margin: The white space between the copy on the page and the trimmed edge of the paper.

mark-up: To take a pen and write typesetting specifications all over the page.

measure: The width of a column or the length of a line of type.

metrics: See *font metrics.*

modern type: A category of type that has a strong thick-thin contrast in the stroke weights and thin horizontal serifs.

monospaced: A font whose characters each take up the same amount of space. That is, a period uses the same width space as a capital W.

monoweight: The strokes of a letterform have very little difference in thickness all the way around.

N

negative leading: A *leading* measurement in which the leading value is smaller than the *point size* of the type. For example, 24/20 would be negative leading.

nonbreaking characters: Special characters (such as hyphens or slashes) that force words or fractions to stay together even at the ends of lines.

nonbreaking space: A word space that keeps two words together, preventing them from breaking onto two separate lines.

O

oblique: Slanted type, typical of most sans serif "italic" faces (but not all).

offset printing: A process of printing in which the image goes from a special printing plate, onto an intermediary roller and then is printed onto the paper.

oldstyle figures/numbers: Numerals with ascender and descenders that blend well with lowercase letters. They might be *proportional* or *lining.*

oldstyle type: A category of serif type with moderate *stroke* contrast and diagonal *stress.* Easy on the eyes and easy to read.

OpenType: A cross-platform file format that can contain over 65,000 characters. Not all operating systems or software programs can handle OpenType fonts.

optical kerning: Automatic kerning based on the shapes of the letters.

optical size: A font optimized for specific point sizes. For instance, you might have a display font specifically for type larger than 14 to 18 point, or a caption font specifically for small type sizes.

orphan: The last line of a paragraph alone at the top of a column or page, or the first line of a paragraph alone at the bottom of a column or page.

outdent: The first line or first several lines of a paragraph start to the left of the rest of the text. Also called a *hanging indent.*

• •

outline font: A font in which each character is stored as a mathematical "outline" of the character shape. Also known as a *scalable font* and a *printer font.*

output: Whatever comes out of your computer, such as hard copy from the printer.

P

pagination: The process of putting pages into consecutive order.

pair kerning: Using the pairs of kerned characters that a designer has built into a font. See also *pair kerns.*

pi font: A typeface with mathematical and scientific characters.

pica: A typographic measurement of twelve *points.* Six picas equal one inch.

pica: On a typewriter, a pica is a generic, *monospaced* font that has ten characters per inch (as opposed to *elite,* which has twelve).

picture font: A font that has little pictures instead of characters. Useful for logos, bullets, decorative borders. The small images on these glossary pages are all picture fonts.

point: The smallest typographic measurement. In digital typography, there are 72 points per inch, 12 points per pica. Traditionally (in hot metal), there were 72.27 points per inch.

point size: The measurement of type at a particular size. You are reading 9-point type. Also see *point.*

PostScript: A programming language designed specifically for printing electronic documents.

PostScript font: A font designed for use with the PostScript printing process.

ppi: Pixels per inch, a measure of the digital resolution of an image on the screen.

prime marks: Symbols used to indicate inches and feet and hours and minutes.

printer font: The component of a *PostScript* font that enables the font to print to a PostScript printer. Also called an *outline font.*

proof: Final printed draft. If the proof is perfect, then you can proceed to printing your final version, ready for reproduction

proportional spacing: The characters each take up a relative, or proportional, amount of space according to how wide they are. That is, a cap W takes up more space than a lowercase i.

pull quote: A passage of text emphasized on the page in a graphic way.

punctuation: All the characters in a font that are used to define our grammar, such as commas, questions marks, periods, etc.

Q

queue: An orderly line, such as jobs waiting to print.

quotation marks: Punctuation marks used to mark the beginning and end of quoted material.

R

range kerning: Adjusting the letterspacing over a range (group) of characters.

readability: How easy it is to read a large amount of text.

recto: The right-hand page in a book, always odd-numbered.

resolution: How clearly "resolved" an image or typeface looks on the screen (measured in *ppi*) or when printed (measured in *dpi*).

reverse: The opposite of the standard of black text on a white background—white text on a black (or dark) background. As opposed to *drop out.*

river: Poor wordspacing in justified copy creates a "river" of white space that flows vertically through the text.

roman: Any typeface, serif or sans serif, that does not slant. This font is roman.

rule: Typesetter jargon for a drawn line. A rule's thickness is measured in points, as in a "3-point rule."

run-around: When text flows around the edges of a graphic or shape. Also known as a *text wrap.*

running head: Repetitive text that appears at the tops of document pages.

• •

S

sans serif: A category of type that does not have *serifs*. The bold type in these definitions is a sans serif font.

scalable font: A font that can be resized to any point size without becoming distorted, either on the screen or the printed page.

screen font: The bitmapped part of some fonts used to display the type on the screen. Also known as a *bitmapped font.* It is one component of a PostScript Type 1 font.

script: Typefaces that emulate handwriting.

serif: A very short line that extends from upper and lower ends of main strokes. There are many variations—cupped, rounded, square, slab, bracketed etc.

service bureau: A business that produces high-resolution output of digital files. They use an *imagesetter* and print to a variety of color devices or to film.

set solid: A leading measurement in which the *leading* value is the same as the *point size* of the type, such as 20/20.

set width: The horizontal width that is built into a character when it is designed.

shoulder: Curved stroke of a letter with a convex shape, as in h, m, and n.

slab serif type: A category of type that is *monoweight* with thick, flat serifs. Also known as *Egyptian* type.

small caps: Capital letters that are approximately the size of lowercase letters.

smart apostrophe: Refers to a true apostrophe, not a straight one. ' not '.

smart quote: Refers to true quote marks, not straight ones, such as " and ", not " and ".

soft Return: A soft Return is sometimes mistakenly thought of as a *hard line break,* where you press Shift Return/Enter to force a new line without starting a new paragraph. But a soft Return is really when the text bumps into the right indent and automatically returns to the left indent. This is sometimes also known as "word wrap."

solid: See *set solid.*

spine: Central curved stroke of the letter S.

spur: Small projection off a main stroke, found on many capital Gs.

standoff: In a *text wrap,* the distance between text and the graphic around which the text is wrapping.

stem: Main vertical or diagonal stroke of a letter.

stress: Direction of thickening on the curved stroke of a letter.

stroke: Any straight or curved line of a character.

style sheet: A collection of formatting options that can be applied easily and consistently to text. Style sheets are the most important and time-saving feature in page layout and word processing software.

subscript: A small character written beneath another one, such as the lower number in a fraction or the 2 in H_2O.

superior/superscript: A small character written above and/or to the side of another character. The top half of a fraction or the letters following an ordinal number (1st, 3d, 5th) are common examples.

swash characters: Specially designed letterforms that have *tails* or elaborate shapes, such as $\mathcal{Q}$ or $\mathcal{R}$.

T

tabular figures: Numerals designed to be *monospaced* so they will line up in columns of numbers.

tail: The descender of Q or the diagonal stroke at the bottom of R or j.

terminal: The end of a stroke of a letter that doesn't end with a serif, as in e or r.

text wrap: When the edge of a text block wraps around the edge of a graphic.

thick/thin: Refers to the change of stroke weight in a letterform as it moves from the thin point to the thicker part.

thin space: A non-breaking space one-quarter width of the point size in use.

tracking: Adjusting the space between *glyphs* in a range of text. Often this is called range *kerning.*

true-drawn: Refers to typeface variations that have been drawn by the type designer rather than modified by the computer.

TrueType: An *outline* font developed by Apple and Microsoft.

type family: A group of fonts that includes all the members of a single typeface *family.*

Type 1 font: A high-quality *PostScript outline* font.

typeface: A collection of letters, numbers, symbols, etc that share a specific design.

type size: The size of the type measured in *points.*

type style: A variation within a type family, such as a weight or width variations. For instance, italic is a type style.

typo: Short for "typographical error."

typographic color: See *color.* Letter- and word-spacing, leading, ink, and paper colors affect the "color" of the type, even if the type is all black.

typography: The art or process of designing with type and letterforms.

U

unbracketed serif: A serif without a small curved stroke (a *bracket*) connecting it to the stem of the letter.

underline: A line directly under the type, put there by using a menu command or keyboard shortcut (as opposed to a *rule*). Never use an underline in professional-level type.

Unicode: A coding system that creates fonts that can contain more than 65,000 glyphs, as opposed to the ascii format that can only contain 256 glyphs. Not all operating systems and software applications use Unicode.

uppercase: Capital letters of the alphabet.

U/lc, upper and lowercase: Capital and lowercase letters used together, as opposed to *all caps.*

V

verso: The left-hand page of a book or newsletter, always even-numbered.

weight: The thickness of the strokes that form the characters in the font.

white space: The space in and around the type and graphic elements on a page.

widow: A very short (proportionally) last line of a paragraph.

width: One of the variations possible in a type family describing the horizontal width of characters. Ranges from ultra-condensed to ultra-expanded.

word spacing: The space between words created by pressing the Spacebar.

WYSIWYG: What You See Is What You Get. This refers to whether the text and images you *see* on your screen match what you actually *get* when it's printed.

X

x-height: Height of the body of lowercase letters, excluding ascenders and descenders.

Your attitude is your life.

Robin Williams *(not the actor)*

Other Info

In which there is
important information
regarding the
fonts in this book,
setting special
characters,
and several font
utilities.

Appendix A
Listen to your eyes

Kerning, Tracking, and Letterspacing in InDesign: Why It's Important and When to Use It

Excellent letterspacing isn't the sexiest thing InDesign can do, but it makes the difference between good type and great type, and it displays the difference between a good designer and a great designer. Inappropriate or unconscious letterspacing can make type difficult to read, difficult to comprehend, and difficult to respect.

There is no formulaic method for adjusting the spaces between letters—it is entirely dependent on the typeface, the type size, the paper, the color of ink, the purpose of the piece. The final judge is your eyes. Your eyes know if the spacing is uneven, too tight, or too loose. Listen to your eyes. Listen to your eyes and know how to control your software.

Watermelon
Watermelon

InDesign has controls for kerning, tracking, letterspacing, and word spacing, and all of these individual controls are affected by the justification, hyphenation, and composition settings. So we'll start at the most intimate level and move up to the most global. But first let's look at the preference that controls your kerning values. You should change this preference when you have no document open on your screen—this will set the value as the default for all *new* documents.

· ·

From the InDesign menu, choose "Preferences…," then "Units & Increments…." You see that the default kerning value is "20" thousandths of an em. This means if you take the point size of the type (which is called an em), say 24 point, and divide it into 1000 parts, each default kerning space is 20/1000, which is much too much. Change this to 5 units and click OK.

Change the kerning value to 5.

Auto kern pairs, the lowest common denominator

Now, a well-designed typeface includes a number of auto kern pairs. Certain pairs of letters always need kerning, such as "To" or "Va." A well-designed face has the kerning built into the font metrics so when you type certain combinations of characters, they tuck into each other nicely. A font might have anywhere from fifty to several thousand auto kern pairs. InDesign, by default, applies these auto kern pairs, as you can tell by the kerning field: it typically says "Metrics."

This means it's using the font metrics and applying the kerning value built into the font. That's why when you click the insertion point between two characters, this same kerning field displays a number in parentheses—that's the kerning value of the auto pair. (That's also why type automatically looks better in InDesign than it does in most word processors because most word processors don't apply the auto kern pairs.)

· ·

If you use a typeface that does not have built-in kern pairs, or if you use a combination of fonts, styles, or sizes, that's when you want to use the "Optical" option in the kerning field. Optical looks at the shapes of the letters and tries to adjust them as well as it can—without eyes.

This is a typeface designed by my daughter when she was seven years old; it has very few kerning pairs so I turned on the Optical kerning.

Manual kerning

Manual kerning means to adjust the space between two characters, and it's the most important letterspacing feature because it is the only one dependent on your eyes. This is what you'll use to fine-tune your text after all the other options have been adjusted.

When you use the keyboard shortcut to kern, InDesign applies the amount you have set in the preferences pane you changed earlier. That is, if you put the insertion point between two characters and use the keyboard shortcut Option LeftArrow, each tap of the left arrow removes 5/1000 of an em. Option RightArrow increases the space 5/1000 of an em.

Hold down the Command key in addition to the Option and arrow keys and you decrease or increase the amount by five. That is, Command Option LeftArrow removes 25/1000 of an em instead of 5.

Any manual kerning you apply is added to the auto pair kern that might be built into the two characters. The kerning field displays the total amount of the auto pair kern and any manual kerning you apply.

Note: The kerning value is applied to the character *on the left.* You can copy and paste that character and the kerning value goes with it. Delete the character and the kerning is deleted.

• •

Tracking

Tracking means to adjust the space between a selected range of characters. Instead of applying an individual amount between a pair of letters, tracking applies the same amount to all the characters that are selected. Because tracking does not take into account the shapes of the letters, it's really only useful to get a start on adjusting the space—you'll still need to fine tune with manual kerning.

Any tracking you apply is added to the manual kerning and to the auto pair kerns. That's why you might select an entire word and apply one value of tracking, but when you click between two characters in that same word, the kerning field displays a different value. But the tracking value does not affect the kerning value! You can manually kern between individual characters until they are visually consistent, then apply tracking and everything will tighten or loosen proportionally.

Use the same keyboard shortcuts for tracking as for kerning. To track, select a range of text first.

Tips: To remove all kerning and tracking (but not the auto pair kerns), select the text and hit Command Option Q.

To remove the auto kern pairs, select the text and choose "0" in the kerning field menu.

Paragraph-specific letterspacing

The kerning and tracking values are "character-specific," meaning you can apply them to selected characters. But sometimes you want to open up the letterspacing in an entire paragraph of text, a story, or an entire document.

Because letterspacing does not take into consideration any tracking or kerning or pair kern values, it is the fastest and most processor-efficient way for InDesign to adjust the space between lots of characters. This is the feature you want to use if you have a lot of text to open up or tighten. You won't see the paragraph letterspacing value reflected in the tracking or kerning fields.

To adjust the paragraph letterspacing, use the "Justification" dialog box in either your style sheet options or from the "Paragraph" palette menu; see the following page.

. . . .

Justification				
	Minimum	Desired	Maximum	
Word Spacing:	80%	100%	133%	OK
Letter Spacing:	0%	20%	25%	Cancel
Glyph Scaling:	100%	100%	100%	☐ Preview
Auto Leading:	120%			
Single Word Justification:	Full Justify			
Composer:	Adobe Paragraph Composer			

We're only going to use the first two rows of specs in this dialog box. Now, there are two things to remember about these specs:

One, the "Minimum" and "Maximum" amounts only apply if you justify the text. That is, text that is set flush right or flush left will ignore whatever is in those fields.

Two, the "Desired" amount must be between the "Minimum" and "Maximum." So if you want to change the "Desired" letterspacing to 25 percent, first you must change the "Maximum" to 25 percent or more.

Just as with kern pairs, the typeface designer has built into the font the amount of space on the sides of each character, particularly the right side, or the "pen advance." The percentages that you enter in the "Justification" dialog box are how much you want to *deviate* from the amount that is built into the font metrics.

You probably know that the smaller the type size, the more letterspacing it needs, proportionally, and the larger the type, the less letterspacing it needs. So let's say you have a large block of small type and you want to open up the space a little. You could do it with tracking, but it will be faster and more efficient to use the paragraph letterspacing.

So select the text. In the "Justification" dialog box, first enter an amount in the Letter Spacing "Maximum" field. If your text is justified, enter the percentage that you want to increase the spacing by, and enter that same amount in the "Desired" field. If your text is not justified, enter any amount in the "Maximum" field, then enter your desired increase in the "Desired" field.

If you're working with large type that needs less letterspacing, you can enter negative numbers in the "Minimum" and "Desired" fields.

• •

Paragraph-specific wordspacing

The Word Spacing in the "Justification" dialog box works the same as Letter Spacing: The designer has built into the font metrics the "spaceband," or the amount of space that appears on the page when you hit the Spacebar. You can *deviate* from this amount by a desired percentage. In a number of fonts I open up the word spacing just a wee bit for clarity.

There's a great keyboard shortcut for manually kerning just the spacebands (the word spacing) in selected text; see the chart on the following page.

But wait—there's more!

Now, after all the work you put into adjusting the letterspacing, tracking, and kerning of your type, your carefully chosen specs are further influenced by the hyphenation controls you set and the composing method you choose. And InDesign can't always do what you want, especially if you justify the text. But that's another story.

For now, become familiar with the manual kerning, manual tracking, and automatic letterspacing features. Know when and why to use each one and how to have complete control over them. **And listen to your eyes.**

. . . .

Letterspacing chart for InDesign

KERNING applies when the insertion point is flashing between two characters. The kerning value is actually applied to the glyph on the left.

> **Auto pair-kerns** and **Metrical kerning:** Default
>
> **Optical kerning:** Use when a font has minimal pair kerns or when mixing typefaces.
>
> Click between two characters after applying Optical kerning to see the exact value in parentheses.
>
> **Manual kerning:** Insertion point is between two characters.
>
> | | | |
> |---|---|---|
> | **Add space:** | *Option RightArrow* | *Alt RightArrow* |
> | **Delete space:** | *Option LeftArrow* | *Alt LeftArrow* |
> | **x5 increment:** | *Add the Command key (Mac) or Control key (PC) to the above* | |

TRACKING applies when more than one character is selected.

> **Tracking:** Adds to the manual kerning (if any) and auto pair-kerns.
>
> *Same shortcuts as above*

REMOVE all kerning and tracking from selected text.

> | | | |
> |---|---|---|
> | **Remove:** | *Command Option Q* | *Control Alt Q* |

PARAGRAPH-SPECIFIC letterspacing

> This applies the same value between all letters in the entire paragraph; does *not* take into account the auto pair-kerns as tracking does.
>
> Use the "Justification" dialog box. *(Command Option Shift J)*
>
> "Minimum" and "Maximum" only affect text when justified.
>
> "Desired" must be between Minimum and Maximum.

WORD SPACING

> **Manual word kerning**
>
> | | | |
> |---|---|---|
> | **Add space:** | *Command Option * | *Control Alt * |
> | **Delete space:** | *Command Option Delete* | *Control Alt Backspace* |
> | **x5 increment:** | *add the Shift key to above* | |
>
> **Paragraph-specific word spacing:** Use the "Justification" dialog box, as explained above.

VISUALLY DISPLAY custom kerning or tracking

> Use the Composition preferences; check "Custom Tracking/Kerning."

Appendix B
Font & Product Vendors

Font Vendors

Altemus Collection
An artistic collection of dingbat fonts.
www.Altemus.com

Luc Devroye
Links to fonts in different languages, history, articles.
http://jeff.cs.mcgill.ca/~luc/fonts.html

Atomic Media
Bitmap fonts that are perfect for Flash, web, and WAP design.
www.AtomicMedia.net

Font Bureau
Custom typefaces and retail fonts.
www.FontBureau.com

FontFreak
Thousands of free and shareware fonts, plus links to font software.
www.FontFreak.com

FontGeek
A valuable collection of advice, information, fixes, and news about using fonts in Mac OS X and professional graphic design applications.
www.FontGeek.net

FontHaus Inc.
Fonts, clip art, illustrations, and stock photos.
www.FontHaus.com

FontShop
Over 30,000 fonts by many designers.
www.FontShop.com

The FontSite
Fonts, articles, and more.
www.FontSite.com

GarageFonts
Over 750 typefaces from designers around the globe.
www.GarageFonts.com

Hoefler & Frere-Jones
A library of original and licensed fonts.
www.Typography.com

International Typeface Corporation (ITC)
Over 1500 fonts and an informative web site.
www.ITCfonts.com

LetterPerfect
Original display fonts and custom lettering.
www.Letterspace.com

Linotype
More than 6,000 fonts, plus lots of articles and info.
www.Linotype.com

Monotype Corporation
Not only fonts, but articles, news, technology, and more. Monotype is forming a non-profit organization dedicated to the advancement of the typographic arts.
www.Fonts.com

My Fonts
Find, try, and buy fonts. They will also help you identify fonts.
www.MyFonts.com

P22
Fonts inspired by art and history.
www.p22.com

Phil's Fonts
More than 35,000 fonts from 75 foundries.
www.PhilsFonts.com

Plazm Media Cooperative
Experimental type foundry specializing in custom fonts.
www.Plazm.com

T26
Fonts, EPS illustrations, merchandise.
www.T26.com

Three Islands Press
Links to OldFonts.com, TypeQuarry.com, and others. Specializes in exquisite, old letterwriting scripts.
www.ThreeIslandsPress.com

Veer
Fonts and more! See what your headline looks like in any font.
www.Veer.com

• •

Font Products

You Control: Fonts (Mac only)
Organize your font menu, display fonts in their styles in the menu, choose fonts with a keyboard hotkey, and much much more. $19.95; download a free trial.
www.YouSoftware.com/fonts

PopChar Pro, PopChar X, PopChar Win
PopChar X is a utility for easy access to all the characters within a font.
www.Macility.com

FontLab
A great resource for all sorts of type tools including Fontographer, a program for font manipulation and creation.
www.FontLab.com

Font Management Utilities

Extensis Suitcase   **$99.95**
Font Reserve   **$99.95**
www.Extensis.com

FontAgent Pro $99.95 (Mac only)
www.InsiderSoftware.com

Page Layout Applications

Adobe InDesign
Adobe PageMaker
www.Adobe.com

Adobe Studio
Adobe software tips and tutorials.
www.Adobe.com/studio

QuarkXPress
www.Quark.com

Type Sites

Chris MacGregor's Internet Type Foundry Index
This is an incredibly useful site for typophiles. Chris keeps up on who is doing what in the type world and works very hard to maintain this site so it benefits you. He provides a link to every type vendor in the world, plus information on many other aspects of type and a variety of resources. Tell Chris I said hello.
www.TypeIndex.com

Will-Harris House
Daniel Will-Harris provides another labor of love, the Will-Harris House, directed to people who care about type. You'll find articles, opinions, humor, and history here. You'll also find an interactive method for determining the most appropriate typeface for a job. Daniel is an expert on working with and using fonts on PCs. Tell Daniel and Toni I said hello.
www.Will-Harris.com

Typophile
A member-supported type community with forums, blogs, articles, downloads, merchandise, and more.
www.Typophile.com

Counterspace
Type info presented in an interactive format. Get out your reading glasses, however.
Counterspace.Motivo.com

About.com
Judy Litt runs a great site on About.com for graphic design and typography. Unfortunately, About.com has added so much advertising and other junk that every site on About has become very difficult to use.
GraphicDesign.About.com

TypePhases Design
Illustration fonts, text fonts, and more, plus articles on typography. Includes a great tutorial for managing fonts in Windows, including a number of utilities.
http://inicia.es/de/jmas/

Appendix C

Special Characters

This section contains information about the special characters available in most typefaces. If you're using an OpenType font that includes thousands of glyphs in a program that can take advantage of them (like Adobe InDesign), use the Glyphs palette as explained in Chapter 8.

ANSI chart ▪ Windows

The following characters can usually be added into most word processing and page layout documents by using the ANSI code. To type these codes, hold down the Alt key and type the four numbers (always a zero first) **on the numeric keypad,** then let go of the Alt key. Do not use the numbers across the top of your keyboard! You must use the numeric keypad on the right side of your keyboard.

If you use InDesign, PageMaker, Word, or QuarkXPress on a PC, check your manual—there are regular keyboard shortcuts you can use to insert these characters instead of using the ANSI code. Also check the Character Map, as described on the next page.

Character	Type this code	What is it?
'	Alt 0145	opening single quote
'	Alt 0146	closing single quote
"	Alt 0147	opening double quote
"	Alt 0148	closing double quote
•	Alt 0149	bullet
–	Alt 0150	en dash
—	Alt 0151	em dash
…	Alt 0133	ellipsis
™	Alt 0153	trademark symbol
©	Alt 0169	copyright symbol
®	Alt 0174	registration mark
¢	Alt 0162	cents symbol
£	Alt 0163	British pound sterling
¥	Alt 0165	Japanese yen
é	Alt 0233	e with acute accent
ñ	Alt 0241	n with tilde
€	Alt 0128	euro symbol in fonts that include it

. . . .

Character Map ▪ Windows

The font utility Character Map is installed with Windows. Go to the "Start" menu, go to "Programs," then "Accessories," then "System Tools."

When "Advanced view" is checked, the dialog box offers additional options, including a Search feature.

Choose a font from the menu. Every one of its characters will appear. Hold your left mouse button down and slide your pointer over the characters— each one will show up enlarged, as shown above.

Double-click on any character and it gets added to the "Characters to copy" field. You can then click the "Copy" button, return to your document, and paste that character (or as many characters as were in the "Characters to copy" edit box) into your document. Remember, they will paste in wherever the insertion point is flashing.

An alternative to double-clicking the character as mentioned above: Single click on the character and click the "Select" button to add it to the "Characters to copy" field.

Also note the bottom-right corner: Character Map tells you the code to insert that character directly into your document. Remember, you have to hold the Alt key down while you type those four numbers, using the numeric keypad (not the numbers across the top of your keyboard). Not all characters have a code you can type.

. . . .

Special Characters ▪ Mac

You can type all of these characters in any application on the Mac—word processing, page layout, spreadsheets, paint or draw programs, etc. To type: *Hold down* the modifier key (Option, Command, and/or Shift), then *tap* the character key *once*.

Character	Type it this way	What is it?
'	Option]	opening single quote
'	Option Shift]	apostrophe, closing single quote
"	Option [	opening double quote
"	Option Shift [	closing double quote
‹	Option Shift 3	opening single French quote (guillemets)
›	Option Shift 4	closing single French quote (guillemets)
«	Option \ (backslash)	opening double French quote (guillemets)
»	Option Shift \	closing double French quote (guillemets)
–	Option - (hyphen)	en dash
—	Option Shift - (hyphen)	em dash
…	Option ;	ellipsis
®	Option r	registration symbol
©	Option g	copyright symbol
™	Option 2	trademark symbol
•	Option 8	bullet
·	Option Shift 9	raised period
˙	Option h	really raised period, or a dot
°	Option Shift 8	degree symbol
/	Option Shift 1	fraction bar (slash: /; fraction bar:/)
fi	Option Shift 5	ligature for the f-and-i combination
fl	Option Shift 6	ligature for the f-and-l combination
œ	Option q	lowercase oe diphthong, or ligature
Œ	Option Shift Q	uppercase OE diphthong, or ligature
æ	Option '	lowercase ae diphthong, or ligature
Æ	Option Shift '	uppercase AE diphthong, or ligature
¶	Option 7	paragraph symbol
§	Option 6	section symbol
†	Option t	dagger
‡	Option Shift 7	double dagger
◊	Option Shift V	diamond, lozenge
¢	Option 4 (the dollar sign)	U.S. cent
£	Option 3 (pound sign: #)	British pound sterling
¥	Option y (y for yen)	Japanese yen
€	Option Shift 2	euro symbol

—continued

¿	Option Shift ?	inverted question mark
¡	Option !	inverted exclamation point
ß	Option s	Beta, or German double s (ss)
ø	Option o	lowercase letter o with slash
Ø	Option Shift O	uppercase letter O with slash
≠	Option =	does-not-equal sign
≈	Option x	approximately-equals sign
≤	Option < *(above the comma)*	less-than-or-equal-to sign
≥	Option > *(above the period)*	greater-than-or-equal-to sign
±	Option Shift +	plus-or-minus sign
÷	Option /	division sign
√	Option v	radical sign; square root symbol
ƒ	Option f	function symbol or freeze
∫	Option b	integral symbol
∞	Option 5	infinity symbol
¬	Option l *(the letter el)*	logical NOT, negation symbol
‰	Option Shift R	salinity symbol
ı	Option Shift B	dotless i
ª	Option 9	feminine ordinal indicator
º	Option 0 *(zero)*	masculine ordinal indicator
∂	Option d	lowercase delta
Δ	Option j	uppercase delta
π	Option p	lowercase pi
Π	Option Shift P	uppercase pi
μ	Option m	lowercase mu
Σ	Option w	uppercase sigma; summation
Ω	Option z	uppercase omega
ˆ	Option Shift i	circumflex
˘	Option Shift . *(period)*	breve*
¯	Option Shift , *(comma)*	macron*
˙	Option h	dot*
˚	Option k	ring*

* In regular fonts, these diacritical marks cannot be placed above letters, as can the ones below. But if you have an OpenType font, you'll find individual glyphs for all characters that use these marks.

Accent marks directly over the letters

~	Option n	as in ñ in piñata	tilde
´	Option e	as in é in résumé	acute
`	Option ` *(to left of number 1)*	as in à in voilà	grave
¨	Option u	as in ï in naïve	diaeresis
^	Option i		circumflex

To type the letter with the accent mark above it, do this:
Hold down the Option key and type the key noted in this chart (such as Option n). Nothing will appear to happen!
Let go of the Option key, then type the character you want (n).
The character will appear with the accent mark directly over it.

Index

About the Author

I live and work in Santa Fe, New Mexico, on
2.5 acres of high desert. I can see every sunrise
and sunset, and every moonrise and moonset.
The Milky Way is in my front yard. The kids
are gone, the dogs are old, and life is great.

About this Book

I created the first edition of this book on a
Mac in Adobe PageMaker 6.5, which I loved.
I designed the pages, wrote the text, did the
production, and produced the index and table
of contents in PageMaker. For this second
edition, I opened the original, eight-year old
PageMaker files in InDesign cs2; the layout,
typographic features, even the index were
intact. Amazing.

The cover was designed, illustrated, and
produced by John Tollett, an incredibly
talented and nice man. He used Photoshop
and InDesign.

Main fonts in the book: Ministry Script, an
OpenType font, for the chapter headings;
Bailey Sans for the headings and subheads;
Adobe Caslon Pro, an OpenType font, for the
body copy. The section openers use Dorchester
Script for the giant initial, Jimbo Standard
Condensed for the large head, and Canterbury
for the small type.